Royal Air Force Swinderby Recruits

by

Glenn Johnson

Chapter 1

Clem Harrison watched with an avid interest, as a Royal Air Force Careers Advisor presided over a talk at his school about the modern Royal Air Force, with great enthusiasm, and Clem was immediately thinking about signing up. It wasn't just the shiny brochure that Clem was holding in his hand, or the smart blue uniform that he would be issued with, or the trade training that would be a great foundation for his future career. But it was something else, which he couldn't for the life of him, put his finger on. It was the lure of adventure, that he felt he had to pursue, like it was his destiny or something. That was it! thought Clem, I was fated to join the Royal Air Force.
He took the glossy brochure home, and read through the pages with even keener interest than earlier. He knew there and then that his mind was made up. He was going to leave the 6th Form at school, half way through his A level

studies, and join the RAF, and at 17 years of age, he knew that the time was right to venture into the wild blue yonder, leave home and do something with his life.

Next day, after school, Clem travelled to the city centre of Hull by bus, and visited the Royal Air Force Careers Office, to talk to a careers advisor there, with the intention of signing on the dotted line immediately. He was determined more than ever to join up, and nothing was going to stop him.

"Good afternoon," greeted the Royal Air Force sergeant, as Clem entered the premises.

"Good afternoon, I would like to join up!" exclaimed Clem, without hesitation.

"Okay, is there any trade you prefer?" asked the RAF sergeant.

"Nope, anything will do, I'm not bothered, I just want to sign up," replied Clem.

"That's fine, right, so before we do anything else, may I ask you to take a competency test, to see where we are with your skills and attributes," stated the RAF sergeant.

Clem nodded and agreed to complete the test, which was a mixture of mathematics and english, to the best of his abilities, and it didn't take him long to finish.

"This will give us a clear indication of what trade you are suited for," explained the RAF sergeant Careers Advisor.

"Okay, that's fine," replied Clem.

"If you could fill out this application form, while I mark your answers, then we will know where we are at," informed the RAF sergeant.

"Alright, I will do," replied Clem.

When Clem had completed the application form, the sergeant returned with the results for his test.

"I'm delighted to inform you that you have passed, and we can offer you three positions within the Royal Air Force, which you can go home and think about," stated the RAF sergeant.

"Okay, and what are the positions?" asked Clem.

"Admin, Supply or Steward," replied the RAF sergeant.

"Supply!" answered Clem quickly.

"Okay, but I've just noticed on your application form, that you are only seventeen years of age, so with all due respect to you, as you are under eighteen, I shall need your parents countersignature," stated the RAF sergeant.

"That's alright, I can arrange that," replied Clem nodding.

"Okay, so when you return the signed papers from your parents, I shall arrange for the RAF doctor that's based here, to carry out a full medical, including the cough and drop, and if everything goes to plan, you're in," explained the RAF sergeant.

"Just one question," said Clem.

"Yes, and what's that?" replied the RAF sergeant.

"What happens if my parents won't sign the forms?" asked Clem.

"A professional person, such as your family doctor's signature will be fine," replied the RAF sergeant.

"Okay, thank you, I shall return these forms as soon as possible," answered Clem, and he was away out of the Careers Office and heading towards the Pickadish cafe on the fifth floor of the Hammonds department store, that was a five minute walk, for a cup of tea and a slice of cake, to celebrate his big achievement in making the first moves in joining the Royal Air Force.

Clem ordered a pot of tea for one, and a slice of fruit cake, and sat on a stool near to the window and looked outside at the street, five floors below. The view from the window always relaxed him, as he watched the people moving about, with the buses coming and going from beyond the bus station opposite, that was next to the Paragon railway station, as the trains flowed in and out, and with the taxi's picking up the people getting off the trains to take them to their destinations. It was a hive of activity, which Clem found so fascinating. He poured out his tea into a small cup, added sugar and milk, and looked at the RAF documents that needed signing by his mother and father. The next big hurdle was having these forms signed. He hoped his parents understood his reasons for joining up. He knew they would oppose his plans, but he just hoped they would agree to countersign the declaration. He tucked into his cake and swigged back the tea, before getting up and leaving the building. He made his way outside and went to catch his bus, the number 55, from the bus station that he had just been observing.

When he got home, he was still famished, and was pleased to see his tea was waiting for him on the table as normal. It was a routine for his mother to have everybody back home for six o'clock and the meals were served on or around that time, with good old fashioned home cooking. This evening it was meat pie, mashed potato, peas and sprouts with gravy. It looked great, and it tasted greater. Clem was joined by his dad and two brothers.

"Thanks mam!" exclaimed Clem, with enthusiasm.

"You're home late Clem, where have you been?" asked his mother.

"I've been to sign up for the Royal Air Force," replied Clem.

"You're not joining up, are you? I wouldn't if I was you son," advised his dad.

"Yes, I am dad," insisted Clem, defiantly.

"Why do you want to join up for?" asked his dad.

"I think it will be a good career in the RAF," stated Clem, in no uncertain terms.

"It's not something you'll enjoy son, I'm sorry to say. I think you'll find it tough," stressed his dad, trying to put Clem off.

"Anyway enough about that, will you sign these forms please, as I'm not old enough to join up without your counter signatures," snapped Clem.

"No, I shalln't be signing them, as I think you should stay on in the Sixth Form at school, pass your A Levels, and get a good job, in Hull!" replied Clem's dad, shaking his head stubbornly.

"Will you sign them mam, please?" pleaded Clem.

"I'm sorry son, if your father says he doesn't want to sign them, then I fully support him. I think you should forget about it," replied Clem's mam.

"Okay, fair enough, I'll ask Dr Deighton to sign them. I'm sure he'll agree!" exclaimed Clem, and he finished his tea, and didn't say another word about the subject all night.

Next day, after school, Clem caught the bus that took him to the doctor's surgery and he approached the receptionist on the front desk.

"Would it be okay to have Dr Deighton sign this forms for me, please?" requested Clem politely.

"I shall see if the doctor is free, just a minute," replied the doctor's receptionist.

She returned a few minutes later.

"Yes, that will be fine, if you would like to see the doctor now in the room opposite, and he will fully oblige in getting your forms signed," the receptionist informed Clem.

Clem entered through the open doorway and into the doctor's office, and was greeted by a short stocky man, with light brown hair, that was slightly greying at the temples, and wearing a pair of thick black glasses, that were perched on the tip of his nose. He was humming a tune to himself, which Clem didn't recognise.

"Ah Clem, come in and sit down, I understand you want me to sign some papers for you," began Dr Deighton in a welcoming tone.

"Yes, that's right doctor, if you don't mind, as I'm interested in joining the RAF, but unfortunately my mam and dad are refusing to sign the forms for me, and because I'm only seventeen and too young to join up on my own accord, I wondered if you would sign them, as the RAF Careers sergeant said that would be okay," explained Clem, slowly and clearly.

"Ah, the RAF! I remember joining the RAF many years ago, it was a great life, and I managed to visit many different countries, including Cyprus, Germany, South America and Africa," replied Dr Deighton.

"Yes, that's what I would like to do, and it's one of the reasons I want to join up. I just feel it's fated for me to be in the RAF!" agreed Clem with honesty.

"Let me see those papers, where do I sign?" asked Dr Deighton.

"Just here," pointed out Clem, showing the doctor the dotted line.

"There we go, and good luck with your career in the Royal Air Force, I'm sure you'll make a great succes of your time in there. What trade is it you're doing?" asked Doctor Deighton, as he happily scribbled down his signature to authorise Clem's application.

"Supply," answered Clem.

"That's a key appointment, which is integral to the whole organisation. I wish you well!" stated Dr Deighton, and he handed the forms back to Clem fully signed, and then he showed him the door.

"Thank you doctor, I'm very grateful for this," replied Clem, and he quickly left the room, thanked the receptionist, and headed for home.

He got back just before 6 pm, and his tea once more was there for him on the table, and everyone was waiting for him to arrive back.

"You're late again," said Clem's mam.

"Yes, I had an errand to do," replied Clem.

"Oh, what was it?" asked his mam with intrigue.

"Nothing important, really," replied Clem, keeping things to himself.

"You haven't forged our signatures have you, and joined up for the RAF!" joked his mam.

"No mam, don't be ridiculous!" replied Clem.

"You won't have home made meat pie in the RAF!" exclaimed Clem's dad.

"That's true, I shall miss the home cooking," agreed Clem.

"You won't have your tea on the table every night," stated Clem's dad.

"That's also true, I shall miss that as well," replied Clem.

"So, when do you join up?" asked Clem's mam.

"I don't know yet, I have to pass a medical, and a cough and drop, whatever that is," replied Clem.

"It's a test to make sure you haven't got a rupture," replied Clem's mam.

"How do you know that?" asked Clem.

"I read about it somewhere," replied Clem's mam.

"Okay, well, I've got to pass that and then we'll go from there," explained Clem.

"So, do you still want to join up?" asked Clem's mam.

"Yes, I do, I've made up my mind. There's no going back now!" said Clem with a steely determination.

"Okay, if you insist, but I do hope you know what you are doing," replied Clem's mam.

Next day after school, Clem caught a bus into the city centre and was on his way to the Royal Air Force Careers Office to deliver the documents signed by Dr Deighton, and have the routine medical before recruitment. He was a little nervous, but excited at the prospect and hoped he would pass with flying colours. He had been thinking about this visit all day and had been wishing the hours away until the school bell rang at 3.55 pm.

At long last he had arrived at his destination to put the finishing touches to the recruitment stage, and hoped by the time he had left the Careers Office, he was a fully fledged RAF recruit and on the way to basic training at RAF Swinderby in Lincolnshire. Clem strolled through the doorway of the careers office and approached the corporal on duty.

"Hello, I was in here the other day and was informed by the sergeant that I had to bring in a countersigned document, signed by my parents or the family doctor, when I came for my medical," said Clem.

"What's your name please?" replied the corporal.

"Clem Harrison," came the reply.

"Ah, Clem Harrison, Yes indeed, I've got your name down here in the diary for a medical," instructed the corporal.

"Yes, that's correct, and because I'm not yet eighteen, I've brought in the form from my doctor, who has countersigned the document," repeated Clem.

"Right, let me take that off you and have it processed. Now I shall just go and see if the the doctor is ready to see you," said the corporal.

"Okay," replied Clem.

The corporal came back a few minutes later and nodded his head.

"Yes, we have lift off. The doctor is ready to see you now. So whilst you're having your medical, I shall prepare this document for posting to the Ministry Of Defence. Now, if you would like to follow me, I shall show you the way to the doctor's cubby hole," enthused the corporal positively.

"Many thanks," replied Clem following the corporal gingerly, as the nerves began to kick in.

They arrived at a door that was painted light blue, which was an apt colour for the Royal Air Force Careers Office, and it had the name Dr Deighton written in white, and when Clem followed the corporal inside the room, he was amazed to find that his own family doctor Dr Deighton, was also the RAF doctor. It helped to ease his nerves.

"Hello Clem, again!" exclaimed Dr Deighton.

"Wow, hello Dr Deighton!" replied Clem in disbelief.

"I told you I was involved with the RAF, and now I'm working part-time for them to assist in medicals and the such like," explained Dr Deighton.

"Okay, that's fine," replied Clem in amazement.

"Now, I shall start by taking your blood pressure, then checking your reflexes, height and weight, followed by the dreaded cough and drop, and that's about it," stated Dr Deighton.

"Very good, and wow, it's a small world!" exclaimed Clem.

"Yes it is, I should have mentioned it the other day, but it totally escaped my mind, and to be honest I hadn't realised you were having your medical today, because I assumed you had already seen the other locum doctor, Doctor Gloster," informed Dr Deighton.

"That's alright, no worries!" exclaimed Clem.

Dr Deighton carried out the necessary medical procedure, and was pleased to pass Clem as fully fit for RAF service, and he signed the appropriate documents.

"That's you all done Clem, I'm delighted to say. You can now return to the corporal, and find out when your joining up day is, for when you report to RAF Swinderby," stated Dr Deighton.

"Thank you doctor, I can't wait," replied Clem.

Clem reported immediately to the corporal, and felt he was already in the RAF as he was being passed from pillar to post, just like he would be in the RAF, for the duration of his career.

"How did it go Clem?" asked the corporal.

"'I've passed, and I'm ready to report to RAF Swinderby for the basic training," replied Clem.

"Well done, I have the next available slot at hand here, and it's 5th October," stated the corporal.

"That's only a week away, wow, yes that's fine, I'll be ready to start on that day!" exclaimed Clem.

"Great, you shall receive written confirmation in the post in the next few days, with all the precise details, including days, times, training duration, things to take, things not to take and also a rail travel warrant for transportation by train from Hull to Newark, where you shall be met by a corporal from RAF Swinderby, who will transport you by

RAF bus to the RAF Swinderby base," explained the corporal.

"Very good!" exclaimed Clem, with excitement.

"So that's it Clem, you're now a fully fledged new recruit! All I can say is good luck with your career in the Royal Air Force!" exclaimed the corporal.

Clem thanked the corporal, shook his hand, and went on his way to catch the bus home.

Clem left school for good the next day, and got himself a temporary position working for the city council in the leisure department, to earn some extra money and find out what it was like in the world of work. He didn't like the job much, as he was only the office junior, and the highlight of the day was when he had to make tea for the senior staff. He was stuck in a cupboard sized office for the rest of the time, and looked out of the window, day dreaming, and as he was three floors up, he had a good view of the people scurrying here, there and everywhere in their daily lives. He couldn't wait to join the RAF, and he told everybody in the office block what his plans were, and everyone wished him well.

5th October soon arrived, and Clem was at home and ready to catch the train to Newark. He had received his rail travel warrant as promised through the post, and all the details for his six weeks training at RAF Swinderby, and it couldn't come quickly enough for him. The taxi pipped its horn to signal it had arrived, and Clem travelled in style to the Paragon railway station in Hull. He was accompanied by his mam, who had failed in her attempt to make him change his mind, as Clem was adamant about this, and felt it was his destiny to join up.

"Will you be needing these?" asked Clem's mam as she held up a box of tissues.

"No, I don't think so mam, I'll be fine," replied Clem.

The taxi arrived at the Paragon railway station in Hull, and Clem retrieved his suitcase from the boot of the car, and his mam paid the fare. They walked towards the platform of the railway station and Clem could see his train was standing there waiting on Platform 1, and he quickly climbed aboard.

"Well this is it mam, no turning back now!" exclaimed Clem.

"Good luck son, and don't forget to ring and let us know you got there safely," replied his mam.

"Don't worry mam, I'll phone tonight, and let you know," stated Clem.

The short sharp blast of the rail guard's whistle sounded to inform the train driver that everyone was on board and that it was safe to set off, and slowly but surely the 10.56 am Hull to Newark train left platform 1, with Clem hanging out of the window and waving to his tearful mam, who grabbed a tissue from the box and wiped her tear stained face.

The journey was comfortable, Clem didn't feel any emotions and was more excited than anything. He was looking forward to a new adventure and a new way of life, with new scope, new friends, new opportunities and new commitments. He spent most of his time looking out of the window, watching the world go by, as the train sped towards the Newark railway station. And before Clem knew it, the train was arriving at his destination. Clem grabbed his suitcase and stepped off the train.

The next hurdle to overcome, was to find the RAF corporal that was driving the bus, that was going to take him on another journey, to RAF Swinderby, where he was to begin his new career as a raw Royal Air Force recruit.

Chapter 2

Clem used his initiative and decided to take a look in the car park. It wasn't a tough decision to make, as that was probably where the vehicle was parked. He handed his one way ticket to the official at the gate to prove he had not skipped paying, although he hadn't actually coughed up the money himself, the ticket had been paid for by the Royal Air Force, in the form of a railway warrant, but the ticket collector was not to know that, and Clem moved forward gingerly, with his heavy suitcase, towards the exit.

He arrived at the roadside and looked eagerly for any sign of an RAF bus, but at first glance, he couldn't see one. He decided to take a hike around the block to see if it had been parked somewhere else, and he marched like a Royal Air Force recruit towards the rear of the building. Clem didn't know the Newark railway station very well, as he had never been there before, but when his sixth sense locked in, he somehow managed to locate the blue Royal Air Force bus, that was parked in the coach car park. Ah, thought Clem, this place has three vehicle parks, one for cars, one for lorries and one for coaches, how appropriate, and he marched quickly towards the large blue RAF vehicle, with a spring in his step.

"Good afternoon!" bellowed the RAF corporal, dressed in a smart Royal Air Force uniform, consisting of blue trousers, blue shirt, shiny black shoes and a blue jacket that sported two chevrons, indicating his corporal rank.

"Good afternoon! Is this the bus for RAF Swinderby?" asked Clem.

"Yes it is, and welcome! Find yourself a seat on board and make yourself comfortable," replied the RAF corporal.

"Okay, thank you very much," replied Clem.

"What's your name please?" called the RAF corporal politely.

"Clem Harrison," was the reply.

"Ah, that's fine, you're on my list of names," shouted the RAF corporal looking down at the paper on his clipboard.

"Great, that's a good start then!" replied Clem jokingly.

The bus began to fill up with sheepishly nervous new recruits, that sat on their own, and didn't say boo to a goose, as the realisation of their decision to leave the comfort of their home's for pastures new in the Royal Air Force began to hit them straight between the eyes. But it didn't affect Clem Harrison one iota. He was lapping it up. He didn't feel homesick, nor regret his decision in making the big move to join the regular Royal Air Force. In fact he was super keen to get to RAF Swinderby and see what it had to offer. It didn't take too long for the bus to fill up to its capacity, with 50 airmen on board, and the RAF corporal that had greeted everyone on to the vehicle climbed into the driver's seat and started the engine. It rumbled with a loud roar and while the nerves kicked in even harder for some, Clem still didn't feel anxious or worried. He knew that this was his destiny.

The journey from Newark to RAF Swinderby didn't take long at all, along the A46, and a quarter of an hour after departing from the Newark railway station coach park, the RAF bus was parking at the rear of the RAF Swinderby station, beside a large hangar.

"Okay, if you can grab your suitcases, and disembark please, we are here!" shouted the RAF corporal that had been driving the bus.

The new recruits formed a queue and Clem got in line, as the bus quickly emptied. The RAF corporal led them all into the hangar and they congregated in a huddle, looking blankly at each other and waiting for the next step.

"If you can wait here, your drill instructors will be out shortly to organise you all into different groups. There are five intakes of ten, each with a sergeant and a corporal, so listen out for your name when it's read out, or else face the consequences, and the wrath of your drill instructors!" warned the RAF corporal.

The fifty new recruits nodded with understanding, and kept their eyes peeled and their ears opened for the next few minutes, as none of them wanted to be singled out for subordination embarrassment on their first day.

The five drill sergeants and corporals streamed out of the office in the corner of the hangar and Clem and the rest of the new recruits watched them as they were approaching. The NCO's showed a distinct sternness in their expressions, and they walked with a confident swagger, that demonstrated their cockiness and arrogance in abundance, which was required in an RAF Swinderby School of Recruit drill instructor.

"Good afternoon chaps!" called out one of the sergeants, as he addressed the recruits.

"Good afternoon sergeant!" replied the fifty new recruits in unison.

"Welcome to RAF Swinderby! My name's Sergeant Winner and I shall be calling out ten names for Flight A, which myself and Corporal Cherry will be overseeing, so listen carefully. If you miss your name, then you shall be sent home and put back a couple of weeks. Is that clear?" called out Sergeant Winner.

The new recruits nodded again with understanding and cooperation.

"Jacob Adams, David Ephraim, Stephen Gabriel, Clem Harrison, Joseph Job, Mark Lucas, Timothy Moses, Joshua Peters, John Rufus and Daniel Thomas, step forward!" shouted out Sergeant Winner.

Those ten recruits immediately reported to the front, and they waited for the drill sergeant to issue them with further instructions.

"Right, are we all here?" asked Sergeant Winner, looking at the ten recruits, that he had called out. "If so, then follow me, we're going for a walk to your accommodation block," added the drill sergeant, who was accompanied by Corporal Cherry.

Sergeant Winner handed over the reigns to the next sergeant in line, that was ready to announce Flight B, and he left him to it, and led the newly formed Flight A out of the hangar, along with his sidekick, Corporal Cherry.

They walked for a few minutes, and everybody was silent. Nobody dared to talk, as they were not sure if they were allowed to, and if they were, the new recruits wanted to make certain that they were fully focused on what was being said by Sergeant Winner, as after the threat of being back-flighted for not listening earlier, none of the new recruits wanted the embarrassment of that to disgrace them, at this early stage of their Royal Air Force careers. The group reached the accommodation block, or billet, which it was fondly known as, in the RAF, and Sergeant Winner and Corporal Cherry led the ten recruits inside the building. The first thing that Clem noticed was the smell of the polish on the extremely shiny floor, which was very strong and it filled the whole place. He had never seen a floor shine so much, and he couldn't take his eyes off it. He was only used to carpets at home. But he did recall that both his junior and primary schools had shiny parquet floors, but not as shiny as this floor.

"Okay, we're here. This is your home for the next six weeks. Get used to it, as you're not going anywhere else, unless you decide to quit the training. I shall go through a few basic things with you, and the first one is, who is good at kung fu or karate, and can contort their hands and arms into all sorts of different shapes, positions and movements, like in those wonderful Chinese and Japanese martial arts movies?" asked Sergeant Winner, weaving his hands in and out, like a black belt martial arts expert.

"Me!" shouted John Rufus, quickly putting his hand up into the air.

"And me, too!" called Joshua Peters, also volunteering keenly.

"That's good, you two can clean the toilets out, and get your hands and arms up and around the U bend, with all the contortions that you know!" replied Sergeant Winner, with a chuckle, as he weaved his arms around and around again, to show them what he meant.

All the new recruits laughed, and the ice had been broken. Clem thought that if it was going to be as funny and as lighthearted as this, it was going to be even better than he had expected.

"Now, do we have any good drivers here?" asked Sergeant Winner.

"Yes, me!" yelled Joseph Job immediately.

"And me too!" called out Timothy Moses, raising his hand.

"Good, you two can drive the floor polishers around the billet floor, and make it shine even better than this!" replied Sergeant Winner.

The new recruits laughed again at that quip from the drill sergeant, as the fun continued, and it helped steady their nerves.

"Any more good drivers here?" asked Sergeant Winner, looking around.

"Yes, I'm pretty good," piped up Mark Lucas.

"And so am I," shouted Jacob Adams keenly.

"You two can drive the irons and press the uniforms immaculately. I need to be able to cut my finger on the creases of your trousers and shirts, after they've been ironed," bellowed Sergeant Winner facetiously.

The recruits laughed again once more at this remark, as the chores roster continued to be entertaining.

"Have we any builders here?" asked Sergeant Winner.

"Yes, I'm a trained builder," replied David Ephraim.

"And so am I," piped up Stephen Gabriel.

"That's good, you can build the bedpacks, with different layers of blankets and sheets that are shaped like a brick wall," replied Sergeant Winner. "So, that leaves just two more; Clem Harrison and Daniel Thomas, who shall be in charge of the polishing of all the brass door handles, in the billet," explained Sergeant Winner. "Now, before you go for a haircut, and collect your uniform, I shall demonstrate how a perfect bedpack is made, that you will display for inspection, at seven fifteen every morning," stated Sergeant Winner.

The recruits looked on, as Sergeant Winner expertly made an immaculately shaped bedpack, created with three blankets and two sheets, in a way that the new recruits could hardly believe. They were astounded by it. It was neat and tidy and it would have passed inspection.

"You will make yours better than this one!" stated Sergeant Winner, after he had completed the finishing touches. "Tuck in the counterpane on the bed, in a precise manner, like this, known as the hospital corner," added the drill sergeant, as he tucked the flaps of the bedspread at an angle, under the mattress, to complete the job.

"We shall inspect the insides of your lockers too, so please make sure they are neat and tidy," piped up Corporal Cherry, in the middle of the huddle of recruits.

"Yes, and when the bedpack is completed, display your belt, boots and shoes at the foot of the bed, with your number one cap on top of the bedpack, all ready for inspection," stated Sergeant Winner.

"Has anyone been in the Air Training Corps?" asked Corporal Cherry.

There were blank faces in reply to that question, from all of the new recruits, with shrugs of the shoulders and the shaking of the heads.

"I'll take that as a no, then, but it's a shame, as it would have helped you," said Corporal Cherry.

"Here's a tip for you, when you're bulling your shoes. Buy Kiwi shoe polish, as it has a greater effect, and set the polish on fire with a match, to provide a mirror shine," advised Sergeant Winner. "You only have to do that fire shine once in a while, as it lasts quite some time," he added.

"We need to see those shoes gleaming!" piped up Corporal Cherry.

"Yes, we do, indeed, and that's an understatement! Has anyone brought an iron with them?" asked Sergeant Winner.

The question received more blank stares from the new recruits.

"Irons are available at the NAAFI shop for a reasonable price, but if you can't afford one, because you're skint, there are half a dozen available from the stores, for you to share," stated Sergeant Winner.

The new recruits nodded in acknowledgement, and took on board everything that had been said to them throughout the afternoon.

"Okay, now is the time you've been waiting for; the visit to the barber, so without any further ado, we shall go there immediately. Follow me and Corporal Cherry please," instructed Sergeant Winner.

The ten recruits followed Sergeant Winner and Corporal Cherry to a small room within the accommodation block, where an old man was waiting patiently, with a pair of shears in his hand.

"There's no need to form a queue, we shall call your name in alphabetical order, so Jacob Adams is first in line, followed by David Ephraim, Stephen Gabriel, Clem Harrison, Joseph Job, Mark Lucas, Timothy Moses, Joshua Peters, John Rufus, and last but not least Daniel Thomas," called out Sergeant Winner, clearly and fairly.

One by one, the recruits filed into the small room in the billet block, the door was closed, and the sound of shearing was heard for a few minutes, before the door was opened, and a recruit appeared with shorn hair and was hardly recognisable. When it was Clem's turn, he didn't have time to blink before he watched his hair fall from his head, on to his shoulders, and down to the ground, in a matter of seconds, and he had quite long hair beforehand, but was now as bald as a newborn baby.

Within twenty minutes, all the recruits hair had been cut off to meet the standard requirements of the RAF Swinderby School of Recruit training, and whether they liked it or not, this is how short it would be for the duration of their six weeks training.

"Good, now on to the Clothing Store, to pick up your uniforms!" exclaimed Sergeant Winner.

They arrived at the Clothing Store, which was situated in an hangar nearby, and one by one the recruits received their items of uniform, ranging from a pair of steel toe capped boots, to a pair of number one shoes, and they were supplied with two blue RAF long sleeved shirts, two pairs of blue RAF trousers, a number two RAF tunic jacket, two blue RAF woollen jumpers, two black ties, an RAF beret, a number one RAF cap, an RAF raincoat, two RAF headwear badges, two pairs of black socks and a number one RAF uniform tunic jacket. The recruits were handed a large blue RAF bag each, which they used to carry the clothing, and they quickly stuffed the items inside the bag.

"Right, you lot, let's get back to the billet, where you can offload all this clobber into your wardrobes, and then we can sort out some sheets and blankets for your beds," stated Sergeant Winner calmly, with no rush in his tone. He was as cool as a cucumber, and nothing fazed him at all.

They returned to the billet, and Sergeant Winner organised the sleeping arrangements for the recruits in alphabetical order, with Jacob Adams taking the first single bed along a row of five on the left hand side of the billet, with David Ephraim in the next bed along, five feet away, then

Stephen Gabriel, Clem Harrison and Joseph Job, all with five feet of breathing space between them. On the right hand side of the billet was Mark Lucas, Timothy Moses, Joshua Peters, John Rufus and Daniel Thomas, also with five feet between them, for personal space. The recruits claimed their beds, and opened the wardrobe doors, placing their kit inside. The keys were in the door and the recruits were able to lock up their new items of uniform, for security purposes.

"Right, if everybody is ready, we shall now go and pick up your bedding, from the Bedding Store," stated Sergeant Winner, clinically and efficiently, like a well oiled machine.

They arrived at the Bedding Store, which was next to the Clothing Store, and they waited outside, beside the door in alphabetical order, like they had done beforehand at the barbers.

"Okay step inside, and pick up three blankets and two sheets, and these must be changed here every Monday lunchtime. If they are not, you shall be in big trouble, and will be back-flighted two weeks, so make sure you adhere to the rules. Cleanliness is a virtue in the Royal Air Force, that is not taken for granted. It has to be earned and worked for, and the same goes for the cleaning nights in the billet every night. It's designed to keep the place in a spick and span condition!" shouted Sergeant Winner, with enthusiasm.

The new recruits nodded in agreement, to the sergeant's advice.

"You can play this game two ways, my way or your way. But there is only one way you can win, and I shall give you one guess which way that will be," informed Sergeant Winner with a grin. "Now take your bedding back to the billet and make those beds, and in the morning, you shall transform these sheets and blankets into immaculate bedpacks, that are better than the one I showed you earlier. If not, then you shall make it again and again, until you get it right! Do you understand what I am saying?" asked Sergeant Winner.

"Yes sergeant!" replied the new recruits in unison.

The recruits returned to the billet, and they made their beds, and Clem was wondering if he could manage to make a bedpack that would pass the sergeant's examination, but he decided not to worry about it, and reckoned that even if he needed some practice, he would be determined to get it right eventually, and he thought positively about the task. He was confident he had the ability to make a success of this adventure at RAF Swinderby, no matter how tough it was becoming.

Chapter 3

At 4pm, the new recruits were dismissed for the day, and introduced to the Airman's Mess, and they witnessed first hand the food on offer from the catering staff at the RAF Swinderby School of Recruit Training, for the very first time, and Clem was impressed. There was a selection to choose from, including; egg on toast, beans and egg, bacon, egg and beans, lamb chops, peas and chips, and meat pie, peas and chips for starters, with apple pie and custard, or blackcurrant and fresh cream flan for pudding, with orange juice, tea or coffee to wash it down with. Clem plumped for lamb chops, peas and chips, with apple pie and custard, and washed it down with a cup of RAF Swinderby tea.

"There's bromide in that tea!" exclaimed Jacob Adams, with tongue in cheek, as they sat down at one of the tables, that had been set for the hungry new recruits.

"What's bromide?" asked Clem innocently.

"It stops you feeling the urge," replied Jacob Adams.

"The urge for what?" asked Clem, just as innocently as before.

"What do you think, you Wally?" replied Jacob Adams, with a chuckle of indecency.

"Oh, that, I get you, now," replied Clem blushing.

"If it works that is, I'm not really sure," admitted Jacob Adams.

"I've never heard of it before, to be honest," stated Clem, tucking into his lamb chop and chips, with relish.

"I've got some mates in the armed forces, and they told me all about it, and they say it's a load of rubbish, so you can make up your own mind," piped up Mark Lucas, joining in with the conversation.

"Really, so it's just a myth then?" replied Jacob Adams.

"There you go, so it's safe to drink!" stated Clem, putting the cup of tea with bromide, to his lips.

"Yeah, it won't poison you, but they say that the bromide is a medicine and keeps you cool, calm and collected in times of stress, and helps stem the flow of blood to reduce the urges," insisted Jacob Adams.

"It's a load of rubbish, I'm telling you!" exclaimed Mark Lucas.

"Well, I'm drinking it anyway, and don't give a toss!" replied Clem.

"You won't, once you've drank that stuff!" joked Jacob Adams, with tongue in cheek.

Clem laughed but didn't take any notice, and he slurped the tea down, and as he did so, he reckoned that it had a different taste to what he was used to at home, with the PG Tips, but he didn't flinch, and finished every last drop.

After their meal, Clem and the others headed back to the billet, and they took a slow meandering stroll there. It was dark and cold, but Clem felt comfortable, and he wasn't homesick in the slighest.

He returned to his bed and attempted to make a bedpack, but he wasn't very successful. He tried again, but it was a disaster, so he gave up, and decided it was going to take him a few attempts to make a perfect bedpack, that would pass the morning inspection, but it didn't faze him. He watched some of the recruits bulling their RAF shoes with Kiwi polish, and saw the effect it had when the polish was set alight, and he realised that he needed some shoe polish of *his own*, from the NAAFI shop, to make an attempt at creating a "gleaming shine" on *his shoes*, as Corporal Cherry would have put it. He remembered he had to call home too, and as it was getting on for six o'clock, he decided to phone his mam and dad, at the same time, as he had promised.

He set off for the NAAFI shop, but had no idea where it was, although he didn't mind, as he wanted to explore his new surroundings and find his bearings in his own inimitable way. There were a lot of people moving around, walking in all sorts of different directions, and Clem assumed they were recruits at various stages of training. He wasn't exactly certain how many billet blocks there were here, or how many recruits were here, but by the look of it, with the amount of pedestrians milling around, Clem estimated that it must have been a fair few dozen.

At long last, Clem reached the NAAFI, after asking for directions, as he got fed up of walking in circles, and it had taken him over half an hour to get there. He purchased a tin of Kiwi shoe polish, and a can of Coca Cola, and then looked around for a public pay phone. He found one, but only after asking for directions again, this time from the female NAAFI shop assistant, who was very helpful. He placed his ten pence piece into the phone box and dialled his parents telephone number, 01482 793358, and got through quickly.

"Hi mam, it's me, Clem! I've called to say I've arrived, and I'm okay," said Clem, swigging back his Coca Cola drink.

"Clem, are you enjoying it?" asked his mam.

"Yes, it's good, don't worry about me, I'm settling in okay," replied Clem, taking another swig from his can of Coca Cola.

"I thought you'd be on the first train back!" joked his mam.

"No, it's not as bad as that mam!" replied Clem, draining the dregs from his can of Coca Cola.

"Okay son, if you say so!" stated his mam.

"'I've been issued with my uniform today, had all my hair cut off, and been deployed to polish all the brass door handles in the billet. Oh, and we got shown how to make a bedpack, and we have to polish our shoes, after setting them on fire!" explained Clem dramatically.

"You what!?" replied his mam, in shock.

"It's okay we don't set fire to the whole shoe, I don't think, it's just the polished bit at the front, to give it a gleaming shine, which is what Corporal Cherry wants, a gleaming shine!" explained Clem.

"Well, it's the first I've heard of it, setting fire to your shoes to make them shine, but hey, each to their own, if that's what you've been told to do, it must be right," replied his mam.

"I'll let you know, when I've done it," said Clem.

"Okay son, so you're not coming home then?" asked his mam.

"No, I'm fine, it's great here, I've settled in quickly. The drill sergeant, Sergeant Winner is funny. He's strict, but he's got a lighthearted way of doing things, and he's had us all in stitches with the cleaning roster, asking if anyone was a good driver, and when the recruits volunteer, he says good, you can drive the irons and press the clothes, and drive the floor polishers across the floor, and when he asked if there was anyone good at kung fu or karate, and a few volunteer again, he says they would be good at cleaning out the toilets, and he mimicks the kung fu and karate hand movements up and down the toilet bowl!" quipped Clem with laughter, as he recalled the funniest bits from his first day at RAF Swinderby.

"He sounds a riot!" replied his mam.

"He is mam, and we've got Corporal Cherry, who is less chirpy, and more stricter, and is always asking for gleaming shoes, he's obsessed with the word gleaming," stated Clem.

"Well, you need somone that is going to issue you with the discipline, otherwise if you're laughing at Sergeant Winner all the time, you won't get anywhere," replied his mam.

"That's true, mam! So that's about it for the first day! Anyway, I've got to go now, as I've got to set fire to my shoes, to get a good shine on them, before lights out, so bye for now, I shall ring you again, later in the week," said Clem.

"Okay son, and for goodness sake, please don't set fire to the whole billet, when you set your shoes alight!" joked his mam.

"No mam, I'll try not to, but I can't promise you anything," replied Clem facetiously, with tongue in cheek.
Clem hung up the phone, and made tracks to the billet room, and found his way there comfortably, and was slowly beginning to find his bearings and working out where things were.

When he got back to the refuge of his own bed, he attempted to make another bedpack, but still couldn't get the hang of it, and was dreading the morning inspection, as he knew he would fail for a fact. But he decided not to dwell on the matter, and he administered a layer of polish on his RAF shoes, with a duster he had brought from home, followed by another and another, until he had half a dozen layers of polish smeared all over the front of his number one shoes.

"Has anyone got a match, please?" called Clem.

"Yeah, I've got a box of them here, help yourself," replied Mark Lucas.

"Thanks, I need to set fire to the polish, and see if it works," stated Clem, with optimism in his tone.

"It'll work a treat, don't worry about that!" exclaimed Mark Lucas.

"I hope so," replied Clem, as he struck the match and placed the flame onto the polished shoes. They caught fire immediately and scorched a gleaming shine on to the top of his RAF number one shoes, resulting in a mirror like finish.

"Wow, they've come up a treat!" exclaimed Clem, as he looked at his newly polished RAF number one shoes, with a bustling pride.

"I told you they would! That was a great little tip that Sergeant Winner let us all in on," replied Mark Lucas, in a broad cockney dialect.

"You can say that again!" exclaimed Clem. "Now for my RAF boots!" He administered more polish onto his RAF boots and followed the same routine as before, setting fire to the polish, and lo and behold, he got the same result.

"Hey presto!" exclaimed Clem. "That is magic! Now for another attempt at my bedpack, while I'm on a roll, otherwise mine will end up being thrown out of the window!" he joked.

"I've heard of that happening before!" piped up Joseph Job. "I know a few recruits that have been through here in the past, and they said some of the drill sergeants sling the bedpacks through the windows, so beware!"

"Really? I'm sure mine will get the same treatment, as I can't make a bedpack to save my life!" stated Clem with a smirk.

"It's just practice, practice practice!" exclaimed Joseph Job. "You'll get there in the end, but at least you've bulled up your shoes and boots, so that's a good start," he consoled with sympathy, in a broad scouse accent.

"Yes, I suppose you're right, I can't do everything on my first day, so I shall just hope for the best, and see if I can make a bedpack at the crack of dawn, after a good night's sleep," stated Clem.

"I wouldn't bank on that! Have you seen the state of the beds?" asked Joseph Job. "The mattresses are as thin as wafers, it's not the Ritz you know!"

"That's okay, I can sleep on a clothes line!" replied Clem, with a grin.

"Good for you, these mattresses look thinner than a clothes line!" quipped Joseph Job facetiously.

Clem shrugged his shoulders and remade his bed, with the two sheets and three blankets, and decided he had done enough for today, and it was time for some sleep. It was getting late, and the lights would be out soon, although Clem wasn't sure when it would be, but he knew it wouldn't be too long.

He picked up his towel, toothpaste and toothbrush and sauntered to the ablutions to brush his teeth. He arrived there and noticed there were five sinks with a mirror, all in a row, back to back with another five sinks, meaning ten recruits could wash and shave at the same time, Clem thought that was efficient and sensible. He had never set foot in an RAF training billet before, and all this was strange to him, but he was coming to terms with it, along with the ten beds in the one room of the billet, with different types of sleeping patterns and various sounds of snoring and the rustling of the crisp white sheets, echoing around the confines of the billet.

He quickly brushed his teeth, before taking a look at the showers and baths that were located in the corner. There were three showers with curtains to keep them private, two baths inside a separate room, with a door lock, and three separate toilet cubicles with flushing bowls, that the kung fu experts would be getting their expert hand movements familiar with, on "bull night", and a row of three separate urinals, that were gleaming, like at the Ritz. The floor was clean and the walls were spotless, and Clem realised that this was going to have to be kept as immaculate as this, for the next six weeks. He returned to his bed and put his towel and toothbrush away, and the tiredness suddenly hit him hard.

The next thing Clem knew, it was 5.45, in the morning, and time to get up, as the loud sound of reveille came through the loudspeaker, in the billet room, rousing the ten recruits in different ways. Some of them sat up in a trance, and listened to it, whilst others turned over and went back to sleep, and the rest jumped out of bed, to take a shower, or have a shave. It was a mixture, but Clem was among those that was up and about, like a dedicated RAF recruit, that he knew he could be.

He raced towards the ablutions, with his shaving gear and towel, preparing for day two. He washed and shaved and quickly got dressed into his RAF uniform, before stripping his bed of the sheets and blankets, and attempted to mould a bedpack. He was alert and composed, as he put the bedpack into place, and he had to admit to himself, that this was by far a better attempt than anything he had tried the previous evening. He straightened out the counterpane on his bed and tucked it in at the bottom perfectly, in a hospital corner, and placed his shoes, hat and belt on top of the bed, ready for inspection, before quickly tidying the contents of his wardrobe.

"Are you ready to go for breakfast?" shouted Joseph Job, in Clem's direction.

"Yes, I'm ready!" replied Clem.

"Come on then, we can always finish our bedpacks when we get back," stated Joseph Job.

"There's no need, I'm fine, I'm leaving mine like this," replied Clem.

"Okay, come on then, let's go!" exclaimed Joseph Job.
Mark Lucas joined them, and they made tracks towards the Airmen's Mess, to sample the delights of the RAF Swinderby cooked breakfasts.

They arrived at the Airmen's Mess and the journey from the billet didn't take them too long, five minutes at the most. They headed towards the fried bacon, eggs, fried bread and sausages, that were sitting on hot plates and they looked and smelled mouthwatering, Clem couldn't wait to tuck in. It was a self service system where the recruits could help themselves to as much or as least as they wanted. Clem helped himself to two fat sausages, three rinds of bacon and an egg, with a piece of fried bread for good measure, and poured himself a cup of tea and bromide from the urn. He looked across at his two friends plates, and saw that they had chosen something similar to him. But they didn't bother with the tea and bromide, they were happy enough with a cold fresh orange juice. They all sat at the table and tucked in, and Clem was impressed with the food. He wasn't used to a fried breakfast at home, as he normally only ate cornflakes or rice crispies, but it was something he knew he had missed out on, and he wished he had indulged in a regular cooked breakfast years ago.

"This aint bad!" piped up Mark Lucas, as he munched on a slice of bacon.

"Yes, it's great!" agreed Clem, nodding keenly.

"I'll third that!" exclaimed Joseph Job, with a huge grin of approval.

"I wonder if we're allowed seconds," stated Mark Lucas, with tongue in cheek.

"I'm not sure about that, but you can always ask," replied Clem.

"Haven't you got enough there, already?" asked Joseph Job.

"Not really, I'm used to twice as much as this at home, but this will do for now, I'll just make sure I'll load up my plate at dinner time," confirmed Mark Lucas.

They quickly finished their food and drink, and set off on the walk back to the billet, to await the morning inspection. Clem wasn't daunted by the pending examination. He was very pleased with his bedpack and was equally impressed with how gleaming his boots and shoes had turned out. He felt positive and confident about all his kit, and his wardrobe was tidy too.

When they arrived back at the billet, there were still some recruits bumbling over their bedpacks, and bulling their shoes and boots at the last minute, and they looked ragged and unkempt, Clem wasn't even sure if they had eaten breakfast. He was amazed at how some people worked, but he didn't judge, he merely observed, and he let them get on with it.

It was quickly 7 am, and the inspection was fifteen minutes away, and only David Ephraim was struggling to make a decent bedpack, and his boots and shoes were as dull as ditch water.

"I'm starving, I've had no breakfast, and I can't get this bedpack into shape!" complained David Ephraim, in a blind panic.

Mark Lucas and Joseph Job, along with Clem Harrison helped him to arrange his kit into order, by polishing his boots and shoes for him.

"Nip over to the Airman's Mess now for some breakfast, and we'll sort out this bulling for you!" exclaimed Mark Lucas.

"Cheers guys, I couldn't sleep on this bed, and I've been awake all night! I only fell asleep when it was time to get up!" replied David Ephraim forlornly.

"Don't worry about it, get some breakfast and be sharp about it, you've only got fifteen minutes!" exclaimed Joseph Job, joining in to help.

"Thanks! I'll be right back!" stated David Ephraim with gratitude.

Chapter 4

The recruits waited nervously, as they stood by their beds, and they watched the clock on the wall ticking down towards 7.15 am. There was a noise in the entrance hall, as the door swung open, but it was a false alarm, it was only David Ephraim returning from the Airmen's Mess. He had just got back in time, as a few seconds later, the drill instructors, Sergeant Winner and Corporal Cherry arrived, with expressions of disdain, confidently carrying their drill sticks in their hands.

"Stand by your beds!" yelled Sergeant Winner.
The ten new recruits each stood rigid, waiting for the inspection to commence, and they daren't move from the spot they were standing on.

"Whose got the best bedpack, and whose got the worst?" asked Corporal Cherry, slowly mooching along the row of beds on the left hand side of the billet. His shoes creaked on the wooden floor boards, and they made an eerie and daunting sound, that unnerved all of the new recruits, even cocky Clem Harrison felt a little scared, merely because he wasn't sure what to expect.

"You can make yours again!" stated Sergeant Winner, dragging the sheets and blankets from Jacob Adams bedpack, and throwing them onto the floor.

"You can make *yours* again!" exclaimed Corporal Cherry, picking up Stephen Gabriel's bedpack, and throwing it across the billet, from one side of the room to the other, with temper and ferocity.

"Your bedpack is a disgrace!" yelled Sergeant Winner, picking up Mark Lucas's bedpack, and hurling it out of the window.

The new recruits gasped in astonishment at this episode, and none of them could hardly believe what they were seeing. It was ironic that one of the recruits that had volunteered to pull another recruit out of the mire with an offer of assistance with regard to the bulling of his shoes and boots, should see *his own* bedpack bite the dust. But this was RAF Swinderby, and the hard work started now, nobody was immune from the harsh reality of strict discipline. Mark Lucas stayed quiet and didn't move a muscle. It wasn't a case of one-upmanship, with him.

"Okay, that's the bedpacks inspected, and if yours is still in one piece, well done, keep it up to that standard! Now for the boots and shoes inspection!" stated Sergeant Winner, with a growl evident in his tone.

The recruits took a sharp intake of breath, almost all at the same time, and waited nervously for the drill instructors to begin their next inspection.

"Very good AC Adams, much better than your poor effort of a bedpack!" exclaimed Sergeant Winner.

"Excellent bulling of both boots and shoes AC Ephraim, keep up the great work!" exclaimed Corporal Cherry. "Gleaming is the word!" he added.

"What's this?" asked Sergeant Winner, picking up AC Gabriel's shoes and boots, and throwing them across the billet. "As poor as your bedpack!"

"Well done AC Harrison, a great effort, they're gleaming!" exclaimed Corporal Cherry.

"Great effort, AC Job, well done!" exclaimed Sergeant Winner.

"Terrible again, AC Lucas! You must do better!" exclaimed Corporal Cherry, as he grabbed the boots and shoes and lobbed them through the same window as his bedpack, earlier. Mark Lucas was having a bad day.

"Brilliant AC Moses, you've got to show the recruits that can't get it right, how to bull a perfect boot!" exclaimed Sergeant Winner.

"Not bad AC Peters, but you can do better!" shouted Corporal Cherry, throwing the boots and shoes through another open window.

"Rubbish AC Rufus and AC Thomas! You two, must do better!" exclaimed Sergeant Winner, throwing two pairs of boots and shoes across the billet floor. "That's five recruits, that need to work harder tonight, on their shoes! If there isn't a marked improvement, you shall be back-flighted one week!"

The recruits nodded in understanding.

"That's no good, just nodding. Who do you think you are, a toy dog on the parcel shelf of your grandad's car?" yelled Sergeant Winner. "I need to hear, yes sergeant!"

"Yes sergeant!" shouted the new recruits in unison.

"That's more like it," stated Sergeant Winner, with a crafty smile.

"All those airmen that have seen their bedpacks and shoes lobbed through the windows, go and collect your stuff, at the double!" yelled Corporal Cherry.

The airmen in question raced outside to gather together their belongings, and they didn't take long to collect what was theirs, and returned in less than two minutes.

"Now, we need to pick a team leader, who will be in charge of this Flight, when we are away. Have I got any volunteers?" asked Sergeant Winner.

Joseph Job and Mark Lucas raised their hands immediately, followed by Stephen Gabriel, David Ephraim and Jacob Adams.

"I said I need a team leader, not a toilet cleaner. We have them already!" joked Sergeant Winner, with tongue in cheek. He glanced around the group of new recruits, and studied each one carefully. "Okay, I digress. AC Lucas, why should I choose you as a team leader?" asked Sergeant Winner.

"Because I can do the job in a similar way to you, sergeant!" replied Mark Lucas.

"Did you assist AC Ephraim this morning, when he was struggling to cope?" asked Corporal Cherry.

"Yes corporal, I did, along with two others," replied Mark Lucas, wondering how he had got to know.

"Who were the two others?" asked Sergeant Winner.

"AC Harrison and AC Job, sergeant!" replied Mark Lucas.

"Okay, but you instigated the noble deed?" questioned Sergeant Winner.

"Yes, I felt I needed to help out a man in distress, as he wasn't coping very well with the pressure, sergeant!" explained Mark Lucas.

"Very good, and you then see your bedpack, boots and shoes go flying out of the window, and you didn't bat an eyelid!" exclaimed Sergeant Winner.

"Yes sergeant, that's correct!" replied Mark Lucas.

"In that case, with your fine leadership qualities, and great temperament under duress, I shall make you team leader, AC Lucas, with AC Job as your deputy," stated Sergeant Winner.

"Thank you sergeant!" called Mark Lucas, with gratitude.

"No problem," replied Sergeant Winner. "Okay, so you now have a new team leader, that will be in charge, when we are not here. He will report back to us with everything that is going on, and he has the power to discipline you, for whatever reasons he thinks fit. AC Lucas can make your life hell, if you don't respect his decisions, and if he does not receive the respect that is worthy of his position, it shall lead to a two week back-flight for any miscreant recruit," explained Sergeant Winner clearly.

"Right you lot, it's time for your jabs, and after that you shall visit the dentist, for a check up, to make sure your dental hygiene is up to scratch," ordered Corporal Cherry.

The recruits were led in a marching formation by the two drill instructors, towards the Medical Centre and they arrived there a few minutes later.

"Okay, roll up your sleeves, and prepare for your jabs!" exclaimed Sergeant Winner.

The new recruits formed a queue in alphabetical order, and with their sleeves rolled up, they waited with baited breath for their jabs and slowly moved forward, as the medical staff carried out the task with clinical efficiency. The recruits were receiving the inoculations as part of the necessary recruitment schedule, that covered them for every type of disease, in case they were deployed abroad in an emergency. It didn't bother Clem Harrison, he was fine with needles. Within half an hour, the recruits were led from the Medical Centre to the Dental Centre for a check-up, after having more pricks in their arm, than a second hand dart board, and they were then provided with expert advice on how to brush their teeth.

"When you are brushing your teeth, make sure you sweep the brush up and down, like this," stated the RAF Swinderby dentist demonstrating how to brush the teeth properly. "In a rolling motion!"

Clem looked on with interest, and was fascinated with the style and manner the dentist used to advise on how to clean teeth. Nobody had ever told him the proper way to brush his teeth, and Clem had suffered a bad experience at the dentist when he was 8 years old, when he had six teeth extracted by his family dentist, and suffered excessive bleeding afterwards, that kept him awake all night. He had to return to the dentist the following day to receive plugs in the wounds, as they would not heal. He remembered swallowing the blood vividly, and the memory of the awful taste had stayed with him until the present day, he was in no rush to have another six teeth removed. It was a nightmare. Why he had six teeth extracted at the tender age of 8 years old was anybody's guess, but it was later discovered that the family dentist that had taken out Clem's teeth was found to be a confirmed alcoholic, and struck off immediately.

After half an hour of tuition by the dentist, the recruits were free to move on to the next item in the training programme.

"Okay, we are now going to the armoury to collect your SLRs," informed Sergeant Winner. "Does anybody know what the SLR stands for?"

"Yes, it's the Self Loading Rifle!" replied Mark Lucas instantly.

"Good man, I knew we made the right decision making you the team leader," stated Sergeant Winner.

"Has anyone stripped a SLR down?" asked Corporal Cherry.

There was no reply.

"Has anybody been in the Air Training Corps?" asked Sergeant Winner.

"I've asked that question already, Sergeant Winner, and didn't get a positive answer," stated Corporal Cherry.

"Oh, have you? I didn't realise, I must have missed that!" replied Sergeant Winner.

"Yes, you was in the middle of the kung fu and karate pitch, looking for some black belt experts to clean out the toilet U bends!" exclaimed Corporal Cherry, with tongue in cheek.

"Ah, was I? But that's a very important part of the training though, Corporal Cherry!" stated Sergeant Winner.

"It certainly is! So when we reach the armoury, we need to have careful diligence with the weaponry, as you will see when we watch a film about the SLR, and how simple it is to shoot someone dead!" stated Corporal Cherry, in a serious tone.

"Make sure you take on board what the film indicates, as careless handling of your SLR can lead to tragedy, and fooling around, however innocently, will not be tolerated. If I find anyone messing with a loaded SLR, they will face an immediate Court Martial!" stated Sergeant Winner. "Is that understood?"

"Yes sergeant!" shouted the recruits, together in unison.

"Okay, fair enough, let's move forward towards the Armoury, left, right, left, right, left, right!" called Sergeant Winner, moving the recruits along in a military style of marching, and beginning their drill practice in earnest.

The marching recruits reached the Armoury a few minutes later, and they filed inside, one by one.

"Remember what I said earlier, no fooling around with these weapons!" stressed Sergeant Winner. "I don't want to have the job of calling your parents with the news that you've been shot dead, or have shot someone else dead!" he added.

The armourer issued each airman with a rifle, after they had signed for them, and they held them tightly in their hands, as if their life depended on it.

"Now you've got your SLR rifles, you need to queue for the loaded cartridges, and one by one sign for them like you did for your rifles," stated Corporal Cherry. "This is when you need to have total respect over your SLR!"

The new recruits understood the reasoning of the corporal, and showed quiet, sober and dignified respect.

"Once you've collected your SLR and cartridges, keep them separate and prepare to march to the rifle range!" ordered Sergeant Winner.

The ten recruits clutching the SLR in one hand, and the loaded cartridges in the other, marched from the Armoury to the rifle range, under the expert guidance of Sergeant Winner and Corporal Cherry.

"Left, right, left, right, left, right!" yelled Sergeant Winner loudly.

The recruits reached the rifle range a few minutes later, which was the beauty of being on a RAF base, everything was situated in close proximity and the venues were only a matter of minutes away from each other.

"Flight halt!" yelled Sergeant Winner, and the ten recruits came to an abrupt stop.

"We are going inside the cinema, which is adjacent to the rifle range, and we are going to watch a film that will educate you in behaving appropriately with regard to the SLR. As we mentioned before, these weapons can kill, as you will see in this film, which is designed to shock you in a way that will make you think about your actions, when handling live ammunition, with a real live rifle. These are not toys!" stressed Corporal Cherry, in no uncertain terms, and he was as serious as he had ever been, since the recruits had arrived there.

The airmen queued up in single file, and in alphabetical order, which was becoming the natural norm, and they placed their SLR rifles on a rack on the wall as they entered the cinema, and placed the cartridges in a metal box nearby, before finding somewhere to sit.

"I'll shall warn you now, if any of you are squeamish, that's tough! What the hell are you doing here? You shouldn't have signed up for the Royal Air Force, get out now, before it's too late!" stated Sergeant Winner.

There was no movement from the recruits, and they all continued to sit on the front row.

"I'm sorry, but there's no popcorn or ice cream in this cinema, Corporal Cherry's eaten them all!" joked Sergeant Winner, with tongue in cheek.

The recruits laughed together at the quip, as Sergeant Winner found his sense of humour again, and lightened up the dark atmosphere, that had suddenly dawned on them.

"No talking, during the film! Anyone caught chatting will be back-flighted two weeks, is that understood?" stated Corporal Cherry.

"Yes corporal!" replied the recruits, in unison.

The film began, and it was a story of ten recruits that had been issued with SLR rifles and cartridges, and had been on the rifle range, firing a number of rounds at the target, with great success, and were now relaxing back at the billet, after a tough day. Somehow, one of the recruits had managed to bring back an SLR rifle to the billet, and was showing off with it, after becoming a Marksman in the shooting, earlier in the day. He was posing with the rifle innocently, with no evil intentions, and pulled the trigger for fun, aiming the rifle at a recruit, thinking because the cartridge was removed, it would be okay to pretend, but when the trigger was activated, it released a bullet that plunged into the chest of the recruit standing nearby, killing him instantly, and the scene in the film was so graphic, it showed the bullet flying through the recruit's body, opening a wound at the back, that was the size of a dinner plate, with blood, intestines, gunge, muscle, sinew, internal organs and other debris flying out of the victim's body, in such dramatic detail, that it unnerved some of the viewing airmen, and made them physically sick. Clem was shocked by the vivid drama of it, and was lost for words, as he looked on with distress, at the scene of carnage. The SLR had a single bullet in the barrel that went unnoticed, and that was all it took, to take the new recruit's life.

When the film ended, it seemed so real, that Clem and the rest of the recruits were wondering if it was an accident that had actually happened, but both Sergeant Winner and Corporal Cherry were staying coy on the matter and simply let the message from the film sink slowly into the brains of the new recruits, so that they would learn a lesson in handling live ammunition and the SLR, in a proper, mature manner.

"That's the film over, I shall let you dwell on it for a moment, and yes I know, it leaves a poignancy, with regard to how simple it is to kill someone, in a matter of seconds," stated Sergeant Winner.

"Okay Flight, we are now going to march across to the rifle range, for a session of shooting, so pick up your SLR's and cartridges on the way out, in a quiet and clinical manner!" ordered Corporal Cherry, changing the subject.

The recruits did as they were told, and they arrived at the rifle range, a couple of minutes later.

"Form a queue as normal, in alphabetical order, and prepare to load the rifle with the live ammunition cartridges, ready for firing!" yelled Corporal Cherry.

The recruits followed the corporal's instructions carefully, and waited for the next order.

"Lie on your front, and prepare to fire!" shouted Corporal Cherry.

The airmen jumped forwards, flat out on the ground, and lay on their stomachs, placing the SLR rifles in a comfortable position against the butt of their shoulders, ready to fire. Clem had never fired a rifle before, in fact he had not fired any type of gun before, so this was all new to him, but he was ready to give it a go, and do his best, as usual.

"If you are all ready! Fire!" shouted Corporal Cherry, and the 10 recruits pulled the 10 triggers of the SLR rifles, and released a round of bullets, that were aimed at the targets in front of them, with varied performances, across the row of the 10 prone airmen.

Clem found it hard going at first, and his shooting was all over the place, with hardly any of the bullets hitting the wooden board, with a drawing of a rampant soldier, equipped in full battle gear, charging before him, in dramatic fashion, and he found the SLR was difficult to handle, and jumping from his grasp, each time he fired a round. He had to make sure that he was in control of the weapon, rather than the other way round. Eventually after a few rounds of bullets, Clem gradually began to hit the target, and although he wouldn't win any Marksman awards for shooting, he knew full well that his aim was improving, with every shot he fired.

"Right, cease fire!" shouted Corporal Cherry, a few minutes later.

The recruits immediately adhered to what the drill corporal had ordered, and they stopped firing, and everything went deadly silent for a few seconds.

"I shall check the results," called Sergeant Winner, moving quickly forward to take down the paper targets that were attached to the wooden soldier cut outs. "Okay in first place, and I am delighted to announce has qualified as a Marksman is, AC Mark Lucas. In second place, and also qualifying as a Marksman is, AC Joseph Job. And in third place is, AC Clem Harrison, also qualifying as a Marksman. The rest are in need of more practice, and shall have that opportunity in the following six weeks training!" added Sergeant Winner.

Chapter 5

Clem could hardly believe his ears, when Sergeant Winner announced he was in third place, and had qualified as a Marksman, on his first ever shooting exercise. It was a miracle, as he expected to finish in last place. It must be beginners luck, he thought to himself. Or someone taking the Mickey!

"Okay, we're going back to the Armoury to return the SLR rifles and cartridges, so get in line and be ready to march there properly and orderly. The three newly confirmed Marksmen will be issued with Marksmen badges, that are needed to be sewed on to their uniform jackets, as soon as possible, so I hope AC Lucas, AC Job and AC Harrison have brought their sewing kit with them, if not, there is some sewing equipment back at the billet, somewhere," stated Corporal Cherry.

The ten airmen marched to the Armoury, in a neat and cohesive manner, that was improving hour by hour, and both Sergeant Winner and Corporal Cherry reckoned that for raw recruits, with no previous experience in the Air Training Corps, these guys weren't doing too bad, although they would never let the recruits know that, as it would go straight to their heads, and make them conceited and lazy. Sergeant Winner was a very experienced drill instructor, and knew that praising a bunch of new recruits after a day or two, was not on the agenda. It could wait until the recruits had finished their "Passing Out" Parade, in six weeks time.

"Flight halt!" called Corporal Cherry, when the recruits arrived at the Armoury.

As soon as the recruits came to a stop and stood at attention, the tinkling sound of metal was heard falling on the tarmac, and each of the recruits stood in silence and shock. A loose bullet had landed at the feet of Clem Harrison, and he was as shocked as anybody.

"What's this doing here?" asked Sergeant Winner, as he walked up to the offending airman, and crouched down to pick up the stray bullet.

"I don't know how *that* got there, sergeant!" replied Clem Harrison quickly.

"You *don't know*?" asked Sergeant Winner, pulling a face of disbelief.

"I don't know sergeant, but I must admit, I felt something ricochet onto my trousers, as I was on the rifle range," explained Clem Harrison trying to dig himself out of a big hole, knowing this could mean instant dismissal, after a Court Martial had taken place.

"You're lucky that it is a spent cartridge, and poses no danger to man or beast," replied Sergeant Winner.

"I didn't try to smuggle in any ammunition sergeant. It deflected from my rifle, after I has shot a few rounds, I distinctly remember being hit on my leg," pleaded Clem Harrison.

"Very well, I shall give you the benefit of the doubt, seeing that it has been spent," stated Sergeant Winner affably, with a smile, and recognising it was a pure accident.

"I'm sorry I didn't realise what it was, at the time, as I was too busy concentrating on my shooting," explained Clem Harrison, desperately trying to prove his innocence.

"I shall let it go, but in future report any foreign objects that happen to hit you, as you've seen the film about the airman that was shot dead by accident, I don't want to see that happen again by careless actions!" exclaimed Sergeant Winner.

"Neither do I sergeant, but I swear, it was a total accident, I didn't intend to smuggle a bullet into the billet, spent bullet or not!" exclaimed Clem Harrison.

"Flight dismiss! Take your rifles and empty cartridges back into the Armoury and sign them in, to officially confirm they have been returned. If you don't sign them back in, you shall be back-flighted one week!" shouted Corporal Cherry loudly, changing the subject quickly.

The recruits moved inside the Armoury, and returned their SLR's and empty cartridges, making doubly sure they signed the items back in, for their own good. None of them wanted to be back-flighted one week. They were looking forwards, not backwards, and they adhered to the corporal's request with a keen passionate fervour, before returning outside.

"Time for lunch now, you shall march across to the Airmen's Mess and have an hour's break, left, right, left, right, left, right!" shouted Sergeant Winner without hesitation, and continuing with the pre-drill practice.

The recruits marched well and were getting the hang of working in time together, and they arrived at the Airmen's Mess, a few minutes later.

"Flight dismiss! We shall meet you back at the billet, at one o'clock!" yelled Sergeant Winner. "Enjoy your lunch!"

The recruits shuffled quickly into the Airmen's Mess with an eagnerness, as they were all starving, and ready for something to eat. Clem chose Yorkshire pudding, roast beef, peas and gravy, and followed it up with rice pudding, with a dollop of jam, and decided on tea and bromide again. He found a seat near the back, as the room was almost filled with other hungry recruits, and without any hesitation he tucked into the food, that was delicious as usual. He was joined by Mark Lucas and Joseph Job, a few minutes later.

"Hey, fellow Marksman, what happened with the empty shell?" asked Mark Lucas.

"I'm not sure, I think it was a rogue bullet shell," replied Clem Harrison.

"You were lucky you weren't charged, as that could easily have been a Court Martial offence," piped up Joseph Job.

"That's very true, but like I said, it was a piece of shrapnel that went haywire, and ended up on my pants!" exclaimed Clem Harrison.

"It's easily done, but next time if you feel anything hit you, shake yourself down, and dispose of any loose spent shells, as if it happens again, I don't think Sergeant Winner will be as lenient," stated Mark Lucas.

"That's very true, and don't worry, I've learnt my lesson. Don't forget, it was the first time I've been on a rifle range in my life, ever," revealed Clem Harrison.

"You're joking!" gapsed Joseph Job.

"I'm not, it's a fact, and I came away with a Marksman award, much to my surprise, as I couldn't hit a barn door at first. The damn rifle was jumping all around, like a fire cracker," quipped Clem Harrison.

"You've done very well, if that's the case," praised Joseph Job.

"I was gobsmacked, when I found out I'd qualified for a Marksman's badge," stated Clem Harrison, with honesty.

"Well done, mate," replied Joseph Job and Mark Lucas in unison.

"Thanks, it's much appreciated," stated Clem Harrison.

The recruits finished their meals and headed back to the billet to relax before the afternoon session began. Clem bought a newspaper from the NAAFI shop and kept up to date with what was happening on the outside world, as although he had only been at RAF Swinderby for a couple of days, it felt like he had been cut off from civilisation, and in a way he had been, because everything was based *inside* the isolated RAF station site.

Clem liked his sport, and he only bought the newspaper, to check up on Hull City Football Club and Hull Kingston Rovers Rugby League Club, that were his home town teams, and also Aston Villa Football Club and Tottenham Hotspur Football Club, that were his out of town teams. He had read in the newspaper that the Ex Leeds United and Scotland international football star, Billy Bremner had signed for Hull City and had been made the captain of the first team immediately, and Clem reckoned that the player could make a big difference to his home town football club, that were nicknamed the Tigers. Clem also read that his out of town team Aston Villa, were doing well in the League Cup competition, and he was hoping for a trip to Wembley to watch them. Hull Kingston Rovers were also having a great run in the Challenge Cup, and he was hoping for another trip to the Twin Towers of Wembley to see them too. Tottenham Hotspur however, were struggling to secure their place in the First Division, and it looked like relegation was on the cards for the north

London football club, after a recent 8-2 defeat against Derby County.

"What football team do you support, Mark?" asked Clem.

"West Ham United!" replied Mark Lucas.

"What about you Joseph, what team do you support?" asked Clem, with intrigue.

"Can't you tell, by my accent?" replied Joseph Job.

"Oh yeah, Everton, of course!" quipped Clem facetiously.

"Wash your mouth out with soap and water, I'm a red! It's Liverpool all the way for me! You'll never walk alone!" replied Joseph Job.

"They're doing well, better than my teams, anyway," stated Clem.

"Who's your teams?" asked Joseph Job.

"Hull Kingston Rovers, Hull City, Aston Villa and Tottenham Hotspur," replied Clem.

"You support four teams?" asked Mark Lucas, with a gasp.

"Yes, Hull Kingston Rovers play rugby league, and along with Hull City are my local teams, and I also support Aston Villa and Tottenham Hotspur, as Hull City don't win anything and haven't been to any finals, although Hull Kingston Rovers haven't won anything major either, so I support Aston Villa and Tottenham Hotspur, to compensate for the lack of silverware, although after having said all that, I'm dropping Tottenham Hotspur soon, when they get relegated to the Second Division, as it looks like they'll be as bad as Hull City, so it's Aston Villa for me, after they won the League Cup final last year!" explained Clem.

"So, really then, what you're saying is that you're a glory supporter, that only follows a winning team?" suggested Joseph Job.

"Yes I suppose so, but coming from Hull, that's what *we all do*. We don't see any glory *in my town*, I'm afraid to say," replied Clem.

"You should stick with Hull City, and support them through thick and thin, as they're your home town team. I'm sure times there will improve," stated Mark Lucas.

"No, I don't think so, they've not won anything in one hundred years, they're a selling club, and when they get a decent player, they sell him. Look at Stuart Pearson, he left Hull City to join Manchester United, and went on to play in last season's FA Cup Final, and now plays for England," stated Clem.

"Yes, he plays for the enemy of Liverpool now," replied Joseph Job.

"He does indeed!" seconded Mark Lucas.

"I thought Everton were the enemy of Liverpool," stated Clem.

"They are, but Manchester United and Liverpool have a deeper rivalry, that goes further than Everton and Liverpool matches, mainly because Liverpool and Manchester United are from different cities, and are arguably the most successful clubs in England," explained Joseph Job.

"Well I never knew that, I thought Everton and Liverpool was the biggest derby in football," stated Clem.

"It is close, I reckon, but not bigger than Liverpool and Manchester United," confirmed Joseph Job.

"Bigger than Rangers and Celtic?" asked Mark Lucas.

"Yes, I would say so," replied Joseph Job.

"You would!" exclaimed Mark Lucas facetiously.

"Bigger than Manchester United and Manchester City?" asked Clem.

"Yes!" exclaimed Joseph Job.

"Bigger than Aston Villa and Birmingham City?" asked Clem.

"Yes, indeed," stated Joseph Job.

"Bigger than Tottenham Hotspur and Arsenal?" asked Clem.

"Even bigger than that match," stated Joseph Job.

"What a load of rubbish, we all know West Ham United and Millwall is the biggest game in football!" joked Mark Lucas, with tongue in cheek.

Clem and Joseph Job laughed at that comment.

"So who will win the league?" asked Clem, changing the subject.

"I don't know, but I would like to see Liverpool win it!" exclaimed Joseph Job.

"They just might, they've got a much better chance than Tottenham Hotspur!" quipped Clem. "But Aston Villa will give them a good run for their money!" he added.

"I bet you that Liverpool finish higher than Aston Villa, at the end of the season!" exclaimed Joseph Job.

"And I bet you that Aston Villa thrash Liverpool at Villa Park, in December!" exclaimed Clem.

"You're on!" exclaimed Joseph Job.

"You're on too!" exclaimed Clem.

"Five pounds for each bet!" exclaimed Joseph Job.

"Twenty pounds for each bet!" exclaimed Clem.

"You're on!" exclaimed Joseph Job.

"You're on too!" exclaimed Clem.

The new recruits shook hands on the deal, and Mark Lucas acted as the third party witness, to the £40 cash bet.

The clock on the billet room wall had come around to five minutes to one, and it was time to move on. The airmen gathered outside and waited for Sergeant Winner and Corporal Cherry to arrive. They appeared at exactly 1 pm, and were ready to take the recruits forward, to the next stage of their training.

"Stand at attention Flight, and prepare to march to the hanger!" shouted Corporal Cherry. "Left, right, left, right, left, right!" he bawled loudly.

The airmen moved forward in time initially, but quickly got out of sync, and they were also veering to one side in a concertina formation, that was sloppy and slack.

"Straighten up Flight!" called Corporal Cherry. "Left, right, left, right, left, right!" he yelled, in a booming voice.

The airmen recovered to form a perfectly straight line, and marched impeccably from there on in, to the designated hangar, a few minutes later.

"Left, right, left right, into the hangar!" shouted Corporal Cherry.

The new recruits marched effortlessly into the hangar, like they had been marching all their lives, instead of two days, and it had surprised Sergeant Winner how quickly they had caught on.

"Have you lot been practising at night?" asked Sergeant Winner, with tongue in cheek, looking on from the side of the marching recruits.

"No sergeant!" replied the airmen in unison.

"Keep it up, left, right, left, right, left, right, left, right!" yelled Corporal Cherry, keeping the flow and continuity of the marching recruits going.

The recruits marched towards the centre of the hangar, and were wondering what would happen, when they came to the corner of the building. They need not have feared.

"Flight halt!" bellowed Corporal Cherry. "And attention!" he ordered, instantly.

The recruits came to a somewhat sloppy and untidy stop, and followed it up with an equally dishevelled stand to attention.

"Smarten up Flight! You're a disgrace to the Royal Air Force!" yelled Corporal Cherry, with an attitude of contempt.

The recruits did as they were told, and tightened up their stance quickly.

"The next exercise needs careful dexterity, quickness of mind and feet, and an abundance of concentration, otherwise you're going to find yourself back-flighted one week, maybe two weeks, if you don't pull it together quickly. Because we can't afford to carry passengers! Is that understood?" asked Corporal Cherry, with a raised voice.

"Yes corporal!" replied the new recruits, in unison.

"Now, we shall begin by shuffling you properly into place. You all need to be an arm's length away from the man next to you, so make sure that is the case! Flight, shuffle into place!" yelled Corporal Cherry.

The recruits, in two rows of five, stretched out their arms to provide the correct space between themselves, and then shuffled their feet quickly to enable them to be positioned in the proper location.

"Flight, stand at ease, and that means hands behind your backs, and your feet slightly apart!" shouted Corporal Cherry.

The recruits immediately adhered to the order of the corporal.

"Attention! Stand at ease! Attention! Stand at ease! Attention!" shouted Corporal Cherry, in bursts of a few seconds in between, to enable the recruits to become familiar with the two separate commands.

"Flight, march forwards, and as we turn the corner of the hangar, work hard at maintaining the gap between you and the next man beside you, and don't concertina! Left, right, left, right, left, right!" shouted Corporal Cherry.

The recruits marched forward and negotiated the corner of the hangar with ease, and managed to avoid a concertina in the line, up to the point when they had to straighten out again, after the corner, and unfortunately, they hit a problem.

"Straighten up Flight!" yelled Corporal Cherry. "Left, right, left, right, left, right!" he bellowed.

The recruits smoothed out the concertina, and continued to march along the straight, at the other side of the hangar, and approached the next corner with apprehension, but completed the task admirably.

"Left, right, left, right, left, right!" shouted Corporal Cherry.

The recruits marched on around another corner, and this time they ironed out all threats of a concertina, and straightened up perfectly, with aplomb.

"Left, right, left, right, left, right!" shouted Corporal Cherry.

The recruits continued marching around the hangar and negotiated the corner again with ease, and continued marching around the hangar for another half an hour, until they had the routine of marching in unison and keeping concertina free around the corners, fixed in their heads.

"Flight halt! And stand at ease!" yelled Corporal Cherry. "Go and take a break for quarter of an hour. There is a tea and coffee machine, in a room over there, with crisps, chocolate and other snacks," added the corporal.

The recruits headed towards the room, and Clem was looking forward to a strong cup of tea, without the bromide, with a bit of luck, although he couldn't be sure whether the vending machine was doctored by the Royal Air Force authorities, or not.

When Clem sipped the cup of tea, it was weak, rancid, but warm and seemed clear of bromide. He stood quietly on his own and enjoyed some restful time, without the screaming voice of Corporal Cherry ringing in his ears. Nevertheless, he was enjoying the training, and it was better than sitting in the office of the local council, making tea for the clerical staff, and sorting out their mail, twiddling his thumbs, being bored out of his skull. This was the reason why he had joined up, spending his day moving around in a hangar and stretching every nerve, sinew and muscle. It had not disappointed him in the slightest.

Some of the recruits lit up cigarettes, and although Clem didn't smoke, it didn't bother him, as he had smoked cigarettes before, for a short while, when he was fifteen, but had stopped completely after a few months, and hadn't bothered with another cigarette since.

Chapter 6

The recruits chatted among themselves, for a few minutes, and made small talk about all sorts of mundane things, like how they were missing their girlfriends and wives, and were looking forward to their official leave, in ten days time, but Clem wasn't among those that were chatting that rubbish. He was not bothered about going on leave, as he knew there wasn't anything back home for him. He had joined up to get away from it all, and although he had a girlfriend at home, for the last three or four weeks, called Ellie. He didn't think it was going anywhere in particular, and reckoned it was early days, so there was no rush to go on leave. At seventeen years of age, Clem thought he had loads of time to settle down with a girl, and form a strong relationship, but for the time being, he was just happy to get as much fun out of life, as he possibly could, and that included learning as much as possible, in his six weeks recruitment training, and to become a capable and valued airman in the Royal Air Force.

"Flight, return to the hangar, we are now going to march from here to the gymnasium, for a spot of circuit training!" yelled Corporal Cherry. "Quickly! At the double! Move it, now! Left, right, left, right, left, right"

The recruits prepared themselves to march from the hangar, and make the short journey to the RAF Swinderby Sports Hall, that held every type of sporting recreation imaginable, including football, rugby, cricket, tennis, table tennis, squash, basketball, volleyball, badminton and weight training. Clem was interested in trying his hand at each and every one of them, eventually, but for now, as Corporal Cherry had stated, Clem and the other nine recruits were going over there to begin a session of circuit training, around the gymnasium.

The recruits marched in time, with impeccable efficiency, to the RAF Swinderby Sports Hall, and arrived there within ten minutes, providing further evidence on how handy it was to have everything so closely situated to each other.

"Flight halt! And stand at ease!" yelled Corporal Cherry, as the recruits arrived at the front door of their destination. "Quickly make your way inside the building!" he added.

The recruits did as they were told, and moved in single file, through the entrance door.

"You shall be issued with PE kit, once you are all inside the changing room, so continue to head along the corridor to the bottom, and enter through the door on your left. Move it, quickly, left, right, left, right, left, right!" shouted Corporal Cherry.

The recruits followed the instructions to a tee, and made their way inside the changing room. As soon as they got inside, they were met by a burly RAF corporal PE instructor, wearing a white vest with two chevrons on both shoulders, blue tracksuit bottoms and white Adidas training shoes. He immediately issued the recruits with a pack of PE kit, nestled inside a cellophane bag, that consisted of a sky blue V neck tee shirt and long navy blue shorts, that were both big and baggy.

"What's your shoe size?" asked the PE instructor, as he handed each recruit a pack. The airmen replied with their individual shoe size, one by one, and were immediately issued with a pair of black plimsolls, to complete their PE kit. "Once you are all changed and ready to go, please move forward into the circuit training room!" shouted the PE instructor.

When the last of the recruits were issued with PE kit and plimsolls, they made their way inside the huge sprawling gymnasium, that was both high and wide, with various pieces of kit situated around the place, including, beams, ropes, vaults, weights and many other implements used in gymnastics.

"Welcome to the RAF Swinderby Sports Hall, my name is Corporal Abraham and I shall be taking you for your training in sports and recreation. You shall have a varied time whilst you are here, and shall participate in football, with a full size pitch outside, weight training, circuit training and general warm up sessions. In fact, we shall begin with a gentle warm up to get proceedings underway, and if I may ask you to find a spot on the floor, we can start with some basic stretching exercises," stated Corporal Abraham.

The recruits were led through some simple routines in stretching, including touching the toes, press ups, sit ups, star jumps and running on the spot, to circulate the blood around the body.

"Now we have warmed up a bit, time for the proper work!" exclaimed Corporal Abraham. "I would like a volunteer to climb this rope, so who would like to take on the challenge of climbing the heights?"

"Me, corporal!" replied Joseph Job keenly, without any hesitation.

"Okay, and what's your name?" asked Corporal Abraham.

"Joseph Job, corporal!" was the reply.

"AC Job is our first volunteer, off you go then, let's see how you do!" stated Corporal Abraham.

Joseph Job was up the rope in seconds, and reached the top, in a blink of an eye.

"Have you done this before, AC Job?" asked Corporal Abraham, in disbelief.

"Not here, I haven't corporal!" replied Joseph Job, with tongue in cheek.

"I didn't mean here. Have you climbed ropes before, somewhere else?" asked Corporal Abraham.

"Yes corporal, in the scouts and cubs, a few years ago. I was the champion rope climber!" revealed Joseph Job.

"Well done! So, is there anybody else that would like to give it a try?" asked Corporal Abraham.

"I will, corporal!" replied Mark Lucas.

"And *what's your name?*" asked Corporal Abraham.

"AC Lucas," replied Mark Lucas, in the correct formal manner.

"Go ahead then, AC Lucas!" exclaimed Corporal Abraham.

Mark Lucas climbed the rope with efficiency and skill, and although he was not as fast as Joseph Job, he still did a pretty quick time.

"Very good, now you know what to do, I want you all to have a go at climing the ropes, and touch the ceiling, before coming back down again," explained Corporal Abraham.

The recruits attempted the task, and only Joseph Job and Mark Lucas could make it to the top. The other eight struggled to get half way. There was a definite knack needed to do this task, and it was lacking in the majority of the recruits, but Corporal Abraham was pleased with the effort that the airmen were putting in, even if they didn't get the results he was after.

"Okay, let's leave the ropes for now, and try something on terra firma," stated Corporal Abraham, moving towards the horse. It wasn't a real live horse, but shaped like a horse, and built of wood.

"Now, I'm sure you must have seen the horse in the recent Olympic Games, held in the summer. It was only a couple of months ago. Anyway I want you to take a long run up, and bounce up and over the horse, without stopping. There is a thick mat at the other side, so there's no danger of breaking any bones. Form a queue in alphabetical order and take your turn, one by one, and let's see how you do!" exclaimed Corporal Abraham.

The ten recruits lined up as requested in alphabetical order, and Jacob Adams was the first to attempt a vault over the horse, and he managed it without any problems, followed by an equally competent effort by David Ephraim, whilst Stephen Gabriel and Clem Harrison also made it over, without any hitches. But somehow both Joseph Job and Mark Lucas struggled to time their jumps properly, and didn't make it over the horse, which tarnished their earlier exploits with the ropes. The other four recruits that followed them excelled on the horse, and cleared it with ease.

"AC Job and AC Lucas, what happened?" asked Corporal Abraham.

"I don't know corporal, I've never done this before," replied Joseph Job.

"Me neither, I couldn't get the timing right, corporal," explained Mark Lucas.

"Try it again, and take your time as you approach the horse. It's all to do with getting the timing spot on!" advised Corporal Abraham.

The two recruits tried again, and Joseph Job went first and put into practice what the corporal had told him, and flew over the horse like a bird. When it was Mark Lucas's turn, he struggled again to get the timing right and couldn't get over. He tried again, but it took him a further two attempts to make it.

"Okay, so that's the ropes and horse. Now it's time for a spot of weight training. Has anyone participated in this before?" asked Corporal Abraham.

There was no reply from the recruits.

"I'll take that as a no then. What happened to your tongues, did the cat get them?" quizzed Corporal Abraham. "I shall ask you again, has anyone tried weight training before?"

"No corporal!" replied the recruits in unison.

"That's a lot better. Don't forget you can talk to me, you know," stated Corporal Abraham.

"Yes corporal!" shouted the recruits in reply.

"So, who wants to volunteer for weight training first?" asked Corporal Abraham.

"I'll have a go," piped up Clem Harrison keenly.

"Very good, it's only a small weight, so don't worry, it won't give you a rupture!" joked Corporal Abraham.

Clem approached the weight, and casting his mind back to the summer Olympics, only a few months ago, he recalled how the weight lifters respected the task ahead, and he tried to imitate their stance, and for a beginner, he did an exceptional job, lifting the weight with ease.

"Well done, I'm sorry, but I don't know your name," stated Corporal Abraham.

"It's AC Harrison," replied Clem, in the proper formal manner.

"Well done AC Harrison. So, who's next?" asked Corporal Abraham.

"I shall have a go," piped up David Ephraim.

"Very good, let's see how you do!" exclaimed Corporal Abraham.

David Ephraim picked up the weight like it was a tube of toothpaste and placed it down like it was an empty cardboard box, with great style and panache.

"Well done, I'm sorry, but I don't know your name, either," stated Corporal Abraham.

"It's AC Ephraim, corporal," replied David Ephraim.

"That was very well executed! Is there anyone else that fancies a go at a spot of weight lifting?" asked Corporal Abraham, but his request fell on deaf ears, and nobody responded. "Very well, I take it nobody wants to chance their arm on the weights?"

The recruits didn't reply, and backed off.

"Lost your tongues again?" asked Corporal Abraham in jest. "That's a shame, as it was break time. But for your insolence, I've decided to cancel it. So I need you to run two laps of the field outside, and the first five back will be allowed a break, but the other five will have to run another lap around the field, to earn their shorter break!" stated Corporal Abraham. "Off you go!"

The recruits raced out of the building and onto the field, and whilst some roared off at a lightning speed, the rest took it easy and paced themselves, in a slow and methodical manner.

Mark Lucas and Joseph Job set the pace by running flat out, but Clem Harrison led the chasing pack in third place, and was determined to finish in the first five. The stragglers struggling at the back consisted of Daniel Thomas, John Rufus, David Ephraim, Timothy Moses, Joshua Peters and Jacob Adams, with Stephen Gabriel pulling away from those lagging, after a slow start, and he was almost on level terms with Clem Harrison.

Mark Lucas and Joseph Job increased their lead at the front, and were neck and neck, with Clem Harrison bravely fighting to hold on to third place, as Stephen Gabriel was closing in. The six stragglers at the back of the field were fighting hard to increase ground, but they didn't make any impression on the leading four, and with only one other place up for grabs to be allowed a long tea break, it was going to be heartbreak for five of the new recruits, who would have to complete another lap.

The first lap of the field was completed by Joseph Job, who had taken a narrow lead over Mark Lucas, and Clem Harrison was still in third place, with Stephen Gabriel still breathing down his neck. David Ephraim had broken clear of the the pack at the back in fifth place, and he looked to have secured the prize of an extended tea break, whilst Jacob Adams, Timothy Moses, Joshua Peters, Daniel Thomas and John Rufus, were all in a seemingly impossible position, and looking favourites to finish in the bottom five. But anything could happen on the second lap.

Suddenly, the front runners Joseph Job and Mark Lucas were beginning to show signs of fatigue, and were being caught up by all of the runners, including the last five, who were quickly gaining ground on all of them, and making the easy paced first lap seem like great tactics.

Clem Harrison found himself in the lead within a few minutes, and he was followed by Stephen Gabriel in second, with David Ephraim racing past Joseph Job and Mark Lucas to take third place, and the five at the back were starting to wonder whether they could overtake Joseph Job and Mark Lucas too. The second lap had sorted out all sorts of questions, and it was only a matter of time before Joseph Job and Mark Lucas were caught up by the remaining eight runners.

Rain started to fall, and a chilly north east wind began to whip up, and it was blowing straight across the massive field that the recruits were racing on. Clem Harrison at the front began to struggle to make any impact in the driving rain and was caught up by Stephen Gabriel, whilst David Ephraim edged closer and closer to Clem Harrison to take second spot, and Clem was looking over his shoulder to see where the rest were. He need not have been too concerned, as the inclement weather had affected those at the back too, and they had lost ground on the leading pack, and it seemed like the places they were all in now had sorted themselves out to be the finishing line up, until Mark Lucas and Joseph Job caught a second wind, and suddenly found their earlier pace, and came up from the last two places to overtake the lagging runners in the field one by one, until they were neck and neck with Clem Harrison. It was a dog fight between the three of them and John Rufus, who had battled hard in the pouring rain to compete for the fifth place. It looked like Stephen Gabriel was home and dry in first place, in the pouring rain, with David Ephraim in second place and John Rufus had paced himself well at the back during the first lap, to grab third place, leaving Clem Harrison, Mark Lucas and Joseph Job to fight it out for fourth and fifth. The wind blew stronger, the rain lashed down even harder and the ground was becoming soggy and slippery, but the ten runners kept on with their task, and with only half a lap left before the end of the race, Clem Harrison battled harder than he had ever done before in his life, and although cross country wasn't his ideal event, as he was more of a hundred metres sprint racer, he stuck to his task well, and rallied hard to finish in the top five, which enabled him to take a tea break, with the first five finishing as follows; David Ephraim pipping Stephen Gabriel on the finishing line, Mark Lucas coming in third, John Rufus finishing in fourth place and Clem

Harrison fighting off Joseph Job with a diving lunge, to grab the fifth place, meaning he was clear to take a mid afternoon tea break, and thankfully, not have to run another lap around the track.

Corporal Abraham was waiting for the recruits on the edge of the field, as they ambled off the turf, in a bedraggled and unkempt state, in the relentless wind and rain, that was refusing to calm down.

"Well done AC Ephraim on that fine performance, and congratulations also to AC Gabriel, AC Lucas, AC Rufus and AC Harrison on finishing in the top five!" exclaimed Corporal Abraham. "But for the rest of you, and that means AC Job, AC Moses, AC Thomas, AC Peters and AC Adams, keep running until you complete another lap, as you know what the conditions were, and if I were you, I would practice cross country running in your spare time, as we shall be having a lot more of these challenges, in the next six weeks!"

The five recruits that finished in the bottom five, continued running around the field in the bitterly cold conditions, but they did it with a typical British stiff upper lip, that epitomised the guts and desire of the 1976 Royal Air Force recruit, at RAF Swinderby.

"Okay, while the others run around the field again, you five have the luxury of an extended tea break, and can go and take some time out. There is a vending machine in the corner of the gymnasium," stated Corporal Abraham, pointing out the direction to the cold and shivering recruits.

Clem Harrison led the way, and couldn't wait to get hold of a hot cup of tea, bromide and all, as he reckoned he was at the point of hypothermia.

Nothing was said between the triumphant five recruits that had managed to claim the extended break. Their brains were not focused enough to string two words together, so they thought it was best to stay quiet, at least until they had slurped on a boiling cup of tea, and they were not disappointed, as the machine churned out piping hot drinks for all five of them.

Chapter 7

When the other five recruits returned, they were exhausted, out of breath, covered in mud, and looked like death warmed up. They needed more than just a hot cup of tea.
  "Okay, you lot, that's it for now! You can all shower and change and prepare yourself for whatever Sergeant Winner and Corporal Cherry have in store for you next. Thank you for your efforts today, and I look forward to the next PE session with you all, in due course!" exclaimed Corporal Abraham.
The ten new recruits dashed through into the changing room and made a beeline for the showers. The recruits that had only just returned from the field, and were freezing cold and wet, charged forwards to take a shower first, as there were only five showers in the changing rooms, and the five that had warmed up on the tea from the vending

machine, graciously let them revitalise themselves under the steaming hot showers, before them.

Within half an hour, all ten recruits were showered, dried and changed and moved from the changing room, to the foyer, at the front of the building, where they were met by Sergeant Winner and Corporal Cherry, a few minutes later.

"Right Flight, you're now going to the Armoury to pick up an SLR each and then you're going to strip it down, clean it and re-assemble it again!" exclaimed Sergeant Winner. "Has anyone stripped down an SLR before?"

"No sergeant!" replied the recruits in unison.

"Well, you will be shortly! Left, right, left, right, left, right, forward march!" shouted Sergeant Winner.

The recruits marched towards the Armoury, for the next instalment of their training.

As they were departing the gymnasium, another group of recruits were hanging about outside the Sports Hall, smoking cigarettes, and joking amongst themselves.

"Oi, you lot, enjoy yourselves whilst you're here, as it doesn't get any better after this!" yelled one of the smoking recruits facetiously, with tongue in cheek.

It struck a chord with Clem Harrison, and he pondered over that remark, with a flashback to what his parents told him when he was little; "Schooldays are the best days of your life," and this in a way, was like going back to school for six weeks. So, that airman had a very valid point, reckoned Clem, and he nodded his head in agreement to what was being pointed out.

"Left, right, left, right, left right!" shouted Sergeant Winner, ignoring the ribbing that his recruits were receiving from the other airmen.

They arrived at the Armoury a few minutes later, and were presented with an oily SLR, which appeared to Clem to have been dismantled, cleaned and put back together again, a million times.

"Okay, so now you've got the SLR, I shall demonstrate how it is stripped down, and you shall follow this method carefully. Once you've got it in bits, make sure you don't discard any pieces. Keep a close watch on where you put them, and then carefully oil the working components, throughly cleaning all the places, with a rag. Once you have done that, you will reassemble the rifle, and I shall time you, and the winner will receive a pat on the back," explained Sergeant Winner, beginning to dismantle the SLR, and showing the recruits how simple it was to do.

Clem watched carefully how the job was done, and tried to remember in his head the correct order. He wasn't very technically minded, and knew he would struggle to put it back together again properly. But he would give it a really good try.

"Okay, your time starts now!" exclaimed Sergeant Winner, after he had showed how the SLR rifle was stripped and then put back together again, in a matter of minutes.

Clem got down to the job with a concerted effort, and put every ounce of energy and determination into stripping the rifle down, and then cleaning each piece methodically. He didn't panic and was cool, calm and collected, especially as this was only the second time he had ever seen a rifle, never mind stripping one down to its bare bones. But he had done well, and he carefully placed the parts back into place again, and finished the job quickly and efficiently.

"We have a winner here!" exclaimed Sergeant Winner. "And it's AC Ephraim, closely followed by AC Lucas in second place, and AC Harrison in third, well done to you guys, that was a fantastic effort, considering you hadn't done that task before," praised Sergeant Winner, keenly.

Clem was pleased with himself, and knew he would be quicker the next time, and realised that practice makes perfect. This RAF recruit training was proving very good for Clem in building up his self esteem, and he was thoroughly enjoying his time at RAF Swinderby.

"Now, do it again, and this time I want it quicker!" called Sergeant Winner.

Clem was ready and he stripped the SLR down, with extra zip in his performance and cleaned around the parts, before reassembling the pieces back on to the rifle, and he knew it was a lot faster than his first attempt.

"We have a winner, and this time it's AC Lucas, in first place, closely followed by AC Harrison, with AC Ephraim in third place. Well done to you three again!" exclaimed Sergeant Winner. "That's it for that. Can you please form a orderly queue and hand the rifles back into the stores, thankyou," ordered Sergeant Winner.

The recruits carried out the order to perfection, and then made their way outside, for the next stage of their training.

"Okay, march forward Flight! We are going back to the hangar for another spot of drill practice," called Sergeant Winner loudly.

The recruits did as they were told and marched towards the hangar. The rain that had been falling during the cross country running had stopped, but the wind had whipped up even stronger, and there was a chilly bite to it. Sergeant Winner and Corporal Cherry marched alongside the recruits, and kept their eyes on the formation of the airmen, making sure they were not falling into the habit of another concertina shape. It seemed alright at the moment, to the two perfectionist drill instructors.

"Left, right, left, right, left, right, into the hangar," shouted Sergeant Winner, a few minutes later, as the airmen approached the vast building.

The recruits wheeled around the bend, and stepped into the hangar, with great aplomb. They were gradually, little by little becoming the finished article, but needed a bit more polish, before becoming near to the standards that Sergeant Winner had set, but all the practice they were having, brought a positive effect on them all.

"Forward march along the straight, and watch your shape, as you all wheel around the corner of the hangar!" yelled Sergeant Winner with passionate fervour. "Keep your shape, remember what I told you, keep your shape, with the next guy in front, and beside of you!"

The recruits listened to what the sergeant was advising, and did exactly as he had ordered, with great success, and their cornering was good.

"Left, right, left, right, left, right, remember to watch your shape as you keep going around the hangar! Left, right, left, right!" repeated Sergeant Winner.

The recruits were shining brightly, as they marched with great gusto and enthusiasm, and it seemed they had been working together for years, not just a couple of days, and Sergeant Winner and Corporal Cherry could see a huge chunk of light at the end of the very dark tunnel. These guys were naturals, they both thought.

"Okay, forward march, back to the billet!" yelled Sergeant Winner.

The recruits followed the sergeant's order to a tee and wheeled out of the hangar, round the bend and up the main road to their billet.

"Left, right, left, right, left, right!" bawled Sergeant Winner, to keep the airmen in check.

Once the recruits were back at the billet, Sergeant Winner ordered them to stand at ease, and the airmen duly obliged.

"Very well done today, I'm impressed with your work rate, keep it up, and no slacking!" shouted Sergeant Winner. "The canteen will be open for tea in a few minutes, so wait in the billet until it opens. We shall see you in the morning, at the usual time, for the bedpack, wardrobe and boots inspection!" he added.

"Sergeant, can we go out in to the village tonight, for a few drinks?" asked Mark Lucas, the team leader.

"Nope, sorry. Nobody is allowed out of camp during their six weeks training, except at the weekend. Besides, there is nothing in the village, apart from a post office, a grocer and a pub," replied Sergeant Winner.

"That's what we're more interested in, *the pub*, sergeant!" stated Mark Lucas.

"It's crap, save your money for the weekend!" advised Sergeant Winner.

"Yes, sergeant," replied Mark Lucas, with disappointment in his tone.

"Flight dismiss!" called Sergeant Winner, and the recruits strolled away, towards the billet block.

"That's a bit tight of him, refusing us a chance of going into the village, for a bevvy or two," grumbled Joseph Job quietly.

"Yes, you're right, it is. But rules are rules, and we have to adhere to them, or face the consequences," replied Mark Lucas.

"Do you think he'll find out, if we go, without telling him?" asked Joseph Job.

"Yes, he'll find out somehow, probably by spies in the pub! So that'll be our RAF career up the swanee, and apart from that, me and you are supposed to be setting an example as team leader, and assistant team leader, to the rest of the group, so forget all about it!" replied Mark Lucas.

"Yes, you're right, I shall put it to the back of my mind," agreed Joseph Job.

"Good, now let's wait for the canteen to open, and sit tight in the billet, until then," stated Mark Lucas.

The recruits returned to their beds, unfolded the bedpacks and made their beds up for sleeping in later, before preparing themselves for tea.

"Come on, it's five o'clock! If everybody's ready, let's go for something to eat. It's been a tough day!" shouted Mark Lucas, ten minutes later.

The other recruits nodded in agreement, and they left the billet block together, making their way to the Airmen's Mess, as quickly as they could, before a big queue developed.

The food was good, but the nerves were strained, as the airmen were exhausted, after such an arduous day, but nevertheless there was banter and joking, as the recruits scoffed their meal, and drank their tea with bromide. Clem chose steak and chips for his main course, followed by lemon meringue for pudding, and washed it down with tea and bromide.

Half an hour or so later, the recruits trooped back single file to the billet, in readiness for the cleaning up, that was part of their training. They got stuck into it immediately, and each airman worked the roster to perfection. John Rufus and Joshua Peters were the designated Kung Fu experts, that chopped up all the turds and worked their magic up and down the U bends of the toilet bowls, Joseph Job and Timothy Moses were the drivers, that drove the heavy polishers across the floor, to bull it up to perfection, whilst Clem Harrison and Daniel Thomas were the brass cleaners of the door handles, light fixtures and fittings. It left Mark Lucas and Jacob Adams to man the irons, driving them over the uniforms, ready for the morning's inspection. Every airman was busy for two hours, fulfilling their chores, to the best of their ability. The builders that would build the bedpacks, Stephen Gabriel and David Ephraim were not required until the morning, so they mucked in with the rest of them, polishing the floors with heavy duty cleaning machines, helping with the brass cleaning of the door handles, and also chopping up the turds in the toilet pans. The recruits worked together in unison and cleaned the billet room up like a new pin. It was gleaming, just as Corporal Cherry wanted it to be, and the team leader Mark Lucas was impressed with the tenacity and drive shown by the airmen, in facing up to the tasks set for them.

The recruits finished their chores shortly before nine o'clock, and Clem decided to go for a stroll to the NAAFI shop to get some fresh air into his lungs, after whiffing brass polish for the last two hours, and he had worked himself into a thirst, for a can of Coca Cola. Some of the others followed him down there too, including Mark Lucas, Joseph Job, David Ephraim and Daniel Thomas. They arrived at the NAAFI, a few minutes later, after the gentle stroll turned into a steady jog. Clem bought his can of Coca Cola, and the others did the same, as they were all under 18.

"Hey, does anybody want to play table football?" shouted Clem Harrison, with hope in his tone, pointing at the table with enthusiasm.

"Yeah, I'll play!" replied Mark Lucas.

"Me too!" piped up Joseph Job.

"And me!" bellowed David Ephraim.

"I'll watch!" shouted Daniel Thomas.

"You can be the ref!" ordered team leader Mark Lucas facetiously.

The recruits took up their positions, with two handles each. Clem teamed up with David Ephraim, whilst Mark Lucas and Joseph Job were their opponents. Clem Harrison and David Ephraim were in red, and Joseph Job and Mark Lucas in blue. The game kicked off, and the reds went into a 1-0 lead immediately, when Clem played a stunning shot straight from the kick off into the back of the net. Joseph Job and Mark Lucas tried valiantly to equalise, but some sterling defensive work by David Ephraim halted their progress, and Clem playing up front, hit another unstoppable shot, from centre forward, to put the reds 2-0 up. This goal was greeted with joy by Clem Harrison and David Ephraim, and they cheered wildly and Joseph Job and Mark Lucas used that as an opportunity to score a sneaky goal, but were left disappointed when Mark Lucas, controlling the strikers hit the post with a vicious shot. Clem replied with a thundering shot of his own, which rocketed into the back of the net to give the reds a 3-0 lead, which amazed Joseph Job and Mark Lucas, and they didn't know what had hit them.

They rallied hard and controlled most of the midfield play, and had the lions share of possession, but David Ephraim was having a blinder in defence, and he did not let anything pass him. Clem was clinical upfront too, and struck another goal with a precision shot that cut through a static defence, as Joseph Job was hesitant with a clearance, and it made the score 4-0, to the reds.

"Swap places, I'll go in defence, and you can play upfront as striker," stated Mark Lucas firmly to a frustrated Joseph Job.

When the players changed places, Joseph Job found a new lease of life immediately, and struck two quick goals, catching David Ephraim cold, to pull the score back to 4-2, and the blues were back in the game. When Mark Lucas tried an ambitious shot from the centre of defence, the ball sailed through a huge gap in the middle of the pitch and ended up in the back of the reds net, to bring the blues within one goal at 4-3, and anything could happen now, after three quick fire goals from the blue team. But Clem Harrison was having none of it, and he eased his team's nerves with a piledriver, to increase the reds lead to 5-3, and David Ephraim got in on the act, hitting an unstoppable shot, that was the goal of the game, from the left hand side of defence, to put three goals between the teams at 6-3. It was entertaining stuff, and great fun, and Joseph Job cracked the ball hard, which whistled off the side, and ricocheted into a gaping net, to give the blues a fighting chance, at 6-4 down.

"How are we going to finish the game, first one to ten?" asked Mark Lucas.

"Yes, that's a good idea!" replied Clem Harrison.

The game continued, and at that stage, it could be anyones to win. David Ephraim hit another goal, to increase the reds lead to 7-4, but Joseph Job, finding his feet as a striker, scored two goals, from close range, and brought the score to a nerve tingling 7-6. Mark Lucas hit a clearance from the full back position, and it had enough power and direction to thump against the back of the net, and bring the scores level, at 7-7. Clem Harrison realising he hadn't done anything for a while, scored a stunning goal that shook the table, and he followed it up with an exact replica, to make the score 9-7. But Joseph Job wasn't to be outdone by Clem, and he found the net twice in a matter of seconds, to equalise at 9-9. The heat was on, the nerves were jangling, the concentration was fixed, and the sweat on the handles of the table football game was excessive. Joseph Job went close with an effort that rocked the goal post. Clem Harrison was narrowly wide with a shot from close range, Mark Lucas hit a deep shot across the ground that was well saved by David Ephraim, in the reds goal, and from the resulting clearance, the ball was hit with venom, and slammed into the back of the net, to give the reds a 10-9 victory, that was hailed with cheering and jubilation from both Clem Harrison and David Ephraim.

Chapter 8

The recruits stayed in the NAAFI for a while, and found some seats at a table in the bar, and although none of them were over the age of 18, it didn't matter, as long as they were not drinking alcohol. The place was warm, friendly and accomodating, with jovial staff that were pleasant and helpful, and they made the airmen feel at home.
Clem Harrison and the others with him noticed an attractive dark haired female in the background, that was

sociable, and appeared to know a few of the recruits. Clem wondered what she was about, and whether she worked in the NAAFI, was a customer, or part of the RAF Swinderby catering staff. She was a mysterious sort of person, that seemed to know everyone, except Clem and his mates, but as they had only been at the RAF station for a couple of days, it was hardly surprising, as they hadn't got to know anybody yet. The pretty dark haired female continued to glance across at Clem's table a few times, but didn't make a move, she was flitting in between tables like an illusive butterfly, that couldn't settle. It was fascinating watching her, thought Clem.

"Does anybody know her over there?" asked Clem in general to anyone that cared to listen to him, sitting at the table.

"I've seen her around a couple of times this week, but I don't know who she is. Somebody said she is the Commanding Officer's daughter," replied Mark Lucas.

"Commanding Officer?" asked Clem.

"Yes, you know, the RAF Swinderby Commanding Officer," explained Mark Lucas.

"Oh, right, I see. She's very confident though, and seems to know a few people in here," replied Clem, glancing across at the energetic female.

"Don't touch her with a bargepole, she's trouble, a prostitute, a scarlet woman, a slag, name her what you will!" exclaimed Joseph Job.

"That's no way to speak about the Commanding Officer's daughter!" snapped Clem Harrison.

"She isn't the Commanding Officer's daughter at all, that's bullshit! She's a bad penny, and is always hanging around the blokes. I don't know whether she goes off with any, but nevertheless, she's bad news, either way," continued Joseph Job, with the bad mouthing of the bubbly female with dark hair.

"Hang on lads, look, she's heading our way now!" piped up David Ephraim.

"Keep shtum," ordered Mark Lucas, taken in by Joseph Job's story about her.

"Hi guys, can anybody lend me fifty pence, I need to put something on the jukebox, so I can have a dance," enquired the pretty dark haired female, who appeared to be about their age.

"No sorry, we're all skint. We haven't been paid yet," replied Mark Lucas, the team leader who thought it was in their best interests to act as the spokesman.

"Oh, come on, you must have a fifty pence piece! How did you buy your drinks?" questioned the observant female with her hand on her hips.

"That was the last of our cash, until pay day," explained Mark Lucas.

"I only want to have a dance to my favourite records, "Dancing Queen," "Play That Funk Music" and "Low Rider." I can get three songs on for fifty pence, someone help me out, please!" exclaimed the feisty female, with insistence.

"Okay, here's fifty pence," piped up Joseph Job, out of the blue.

"Thanks mate," replied the pretty dark haired female, taking the money from the recruit. "Hey, do I know you?" she asked, after a double take.

"No, I don't think so," stated Joseph Job, in denial that they had met before.

"Yes I do, *you know*, we hooked up last night, when you bought me a couple of drinks, and then started flirting with me," stated the female, with a wink of her eye.

Joseph Job blushed profusely, and his face turned a distinctive dark red as the revelation came to light, in front of his airmen mates. They all listened intently to what the female was saying, and nudged each other, as the truth slowly came out into the open.

"To be honest, I can't remember a thing, as I had a skinful of beer," stated Joseph Job, trying to cover up his story with lies and deceit, but the attractive female and his fellow recruits could see right through his story, and all he was doing to himself, was digging a massive hole.

"I don't think so, you were as sober as a judge, and all over me like an octopus!" exclaimed the pretty dark haired female, with a giggle.

Clem Harrison, Mark Lucas, David Ephraim and Daniel Thomas all tried to stifle their laughing, but eventually had to succumb to the laughter, and let it all out.

"Anyway, thanks for the fifty pence! Maybe I shall pay you back in kind later on, if you're in here at closing time!" exclaimed the attractive female with the dark hair, before strolling coolly off towards the jukebox.

The dark haired attractive female put the fifty pence coin into the slot of the jukebox, and as she had earlier promised, selected the three songs, "Dancing Queen," by Abba, "Play That Funky Music," by Wild Cherry and "Low Rider," by War. And when the music came on, she danced alone in the middle of the floor space, writhing her body up and down in an artistic, sexy and seductive manner, and had the men in the NAAFI staring at her with their eyes on stalks.

"That was an interesting conversation," stated Mark Lucas.

"Yes, it was," agreed Joseph Job, nodding his head.

"So much for her being bad news, a prostitute, a scarlet woman and a slag," commented Mark Lucas.

"Erm, *no comment* on that subject," replied Joseph Job coyly.

"So, tell me, what's the correct story. Did you spend all night canoodling with her or not, or was it a figment of her imagination?" asked Mark Lucas.

"I said *no comment*," replied Joseph Job.

"Have you met her before?" asked Mark Lucas.

"*No comment*," replied Joseph Job.

"She's eyeing you up on the dance floor, as we speak!" exclaimed Mark Lucas.

"She's eyeing up *all the airmen in here*, anything for a cheap night," replied Joseph Job.

"What about later, are you staying until closing time?" asked Mark Lucas.

"Yes, I may do, all depends on how I'm feeling," replied Joseph Job with honesty.

"Good luck with that, but I'm sure you'll be fine, she's begging for you!" exclaimed Mark Lucas.

Joseph Job shrugged his shoulders in a nonchalant manner, and didn't seem to have a care in the world, regarding the attractive dark haired female that was having a boogie in the middle of the NAAFI bar, shaking her stuff to "Dancing Queen," and she continued to get down to the next track, "Play That Funky Music," in an equally wild and woolly style, followed by the funky sound of War and "Low Rider," which really got her dark hair moving, as she bopped and grooved to the dance track, with ardent enthusiasm.

"Wow, she's a great mover!" enthused Mark Lucas keenly.

"Yes, she's not bad," agreed Joseph Job.

The recruits that had just walked in to the bar for a pint stopped what they were doing, to watch the attractive female, as she confidently strutted her stuff on the dance floor, and nobody interrupted her as she did her thing, with great style and panache.

"Are you going to join her on the dance floor?" asked Mark Lucas, in the direction of Joseph Job.

"No, I think I'll stay put, as she seems to be in a world of her own," replied Joseph Job, with quickness of mind.

"The records have finished, and she's coming back over here again!" exclaimed Mark Lucas, nudging Joseph Job in the ribs with his elbow.

"Yes, and you know why, don't you?" replied Joseph Job, scrambling in his pockets for another fifty pence coin.

"What's up?" asked Mark Lucas, kindly calling out to the attractive female.

"I need another fifty pence piece!" she exclaimed.

"Here you are then, fill your boots," stated Joseph Job calmly and efficiently, with a fifty pence coin already in the palm of his hand.

"Thanks, you're so kind to me!" replied the attractive dark haired female, with a clear passion.

Joseph Job didn't reply, but played the strong silent type, and tried to pretend he didn't give a toss about the woman.

"She's got the hots for you, mate!" exclaimed Mark Lucas.

"No, I don't think so, she's got the hots for herself! She's the biggest prick teaser I've ever met in my entire life!" replied Joseph Job.

"Do you think so?" asked Mark Lucas, with a frown.

"I know so!" exclaimed Joseph Job, with emphasis. "But hey, we're getting some live entertainment, and at what price? Fifty pence a go, for three dances at a time, so lap it up lads!" he added with a grin.

The attractive female put on three different tracks, "Blinded by the Light," by Manfred Mann's Earth Band, "The Best Disco in Town," by the Ritchie Family and "Don't Go Breaking My Heart," by Kiki Dee and Elton John, which whipped her into a frenzy, as she appeared to really like that particular song. When the tracks had finished, she left the room and there was neither sight nor sound of her for the rest of the night. Clem Harrison, Mark Lucas, Joseph Job, David Ephraim and Daniel Thomas stayed until the end, but the attractive female with the dark hair didn't reappear.

"Looks like your payment in kind has gone down the Swanee!" exclaimed Mark Lucas, patting Joseph Job on the back, in consolation.

"Never mind, I didn't build up my hopes, and I had an inkling what she was like, so I'm not too disappointed," replied Joseph Job.

"As long as you've got your spare fifty pence pieces for her, that's all that matters!" joked Mark Lucas, with tongue in cheek.

"You've got it in one!" replied Joseph Job, and he led the recruits back to the billet.

Clem slept well that night, in between the snoring and the mumbling of some of the recruits, that talked in their sleep, and others that were turning over on the crisp white starched sheets, that made a terrible din, but Clem slept through it all. He was exhausted and he fell asleep as soon as his head hit the pillow. It must have been the cross country running that he had participated in, earlier in the day, as he didn't hear anything until the sound of the reveille, at 5.45 am, the next morning, and he immediately snapped out of his slumber zone and got out of bed.

Like a robot, he stripped his bed of its covers there and then, without any hesitation, and made a pretty decent bedpack, at the first attempt. Then he strolled to the ablutions for a wash and shave, and got dressed into his uniform, before going for breakfast at the Airmens Mess. He chose cornflakes, orange juice and tea, with the usual bromide, which tasted better than ever. Either there was no bromide in the tea, thought Clem, or he was getting used to the taste. Nevertheless, he filled up a second cup and swigged it down in seconds. He helped himself to some toast with jam and another glass of orange juice. When he had finished, he headed back to the billet, to put the finishing touches to his display for the inspection, making sure the inside of his wardrobe was tidy and his hat, shoes, boots and belt were all gleaming to perfection. He need not have worried, as it was all immaculate. When he had completed that task, he waited with baited breath for the clock to travel round to inspection time. Some of the airmen were still in bed, and were struggling to get up to make their bedpacks, but they made it just in the nick of time, although they had to skip breakfast. The two builders in the billet, David Ephraim and Stephen Gabriel helped to build the slackers bedpacks, and also those that were backward with the building skills, and Clem helped along where he could.

Ten minutes later, Sergeant Winner and Corporal Cherry were marching confidently down the centre of the billet room, checking for untidy lockers, scruffy bedpacks, dirty floors, grubby shoes and unkempt recruits, but thankfully for the airmen, they didn't find any faults.

"Well done Flight and good morning to you all, I hope you're okay and slept well. Are there any Rotherham United supporters among you?" called Sergeant Winner, with a facetious grin on his face, looking around the billet inquisitively.

"Yes sergeant, I am!" replied Jacob Adams, red faced.

"I thought as much! So, are you going to the Lincoln City versus Rotherham United match, on 29th October ?" asked Sergeant Winner.

"Yes sergeant!" replied Jacob Adams.

"I can't see Rotherham United doing anything against the mighty Imps!" exclaimed Sergeant Winner.

"No comment, sergeant!" replied Jacob Adams, keeping his opinions to himself, although he wanted to disagree with the sergeant.

"Any score predictions?" asked Sergeant Winner.

"I can't honestly say sergeant, it's too close to call," replied Jacob Adams, playing it cool, calm and collected.

"I shall go for a 2-1 win, to Lincoln City, obviously!" exclaimed Sergeant Winner, with tongue in cheek.

Jacob Adams merely shrugged his shoulders with indifference.

"As you may have guessed Flight, I am a big Lincoln City supporter, and have a season ticket for Sincil Bank, and after watching the club being promoted as champions of the Fourth Division, with a record total of 74 points, I am expecting big things this season in Division Three, from Graham Taylor's squad," confessed Sergeant Winner.

The recruits stayed silent, as they didn't wish to cause unnecessary friction between themselves and the sergeant, as they knew if they aired their opinions on football, it was like a red rag to a bull, and would cause havoc with the remainder of their recruit training, so keeping a low profile where football allegiances were concerned was of paramount importance. Only an idiot would call the drill sergeant's bluff.

"Okay Flight, move outside, it's time to tax your brains. You're going to the RAF Education Department, for a spot of Royal Air Force Knowledge training, so quick march outside, left, right!" yelled Sergeant Winner loudly.

The recruits moved instantly and were marched all the way down the main road to the Education building, which wasn't too far, at the end of a row of buildings. There was a pitter patter of rain in the air, the wind was strong, and the temperature was cool, but it didn't deter the airmen from displaying a fine formation, as they marched from the billet, without any risk of a concertina, which was pleasing to see for Sergeant Winner and Corporal Cherry. The recruits arrived at the Education Centre and found a seat behind a small desk and it reminded them of being back at school again. There was a blue booklet sitting on top of each desk with the Royal Air Force badge in the centre with the words Royal Air Force Knowledge written in gold.

"Now Flight, I shall leave you in the capable hands of Flight Lieutenant Bray, the Education Officer, who shall take you though some elementary stages of RAF Knowledge. Pay attention to what is being said, as you will be tested on your knowledge, and it shall go forward to your overall recruit training result. So don't slack off and don't fall asleep!" exclaimed Sergeant Winner, with a loud bellowing voice.

The recruits prepared themselves for a session of learning, that would need great mental application, and would tax their brains to the limit, as Sergeant Winner had warned earlier.

"Has anyone been in the Air Training Corps?" asked Flight Lieutenant Bray, looking around the room for any eager hands that may have been raised. But he didn't find a single hand lifted into the air. "So all this will be fresh to you, which isn't a bad thing, as you will soon get the hang of it, with study and reading, and this is what you must do in your spare time," he added. He mooched along the floor, with his hands behind his back and was studious in nature and thoughtful in persona.

"Now, if you can open your books to the first page, you will see that it has a display of the ranks of the Royal Air Force Commissioned Officers. The first picture is displaying a Pilot Officer rank, with two narrow dark blue stripes sandwiching a single narrow light blue stripe. Next one along is the Flying Officer, with two broader dark blue stripes running along, with a broader light blue stripe in the centre. The next one is Flight Lieutenant, *which is my rank*, and has four broad dark blue stripes with two light blue stripes sandwiched inside. After this is the Squadron Leader rank, with four broad dark blue stripes, on either side of two broad light blue stripes, and two narrow dark blue stripes sandwiching a narrow light blue stripe. Following this is the Wing Commander rank, with six broad dark blue stripes and three broad light blue stripes inside the dark blue lines. After this is the Group Captain, with eight broad dark blue stripes and four broad light blue stripes sandwiched inside. Following next is the Air Commodore rank, with two very thick dark blue stripes sandwiching a thick light blue stripe. The next picture is the Air Vice-Marshal, with two very thick dark blue stripes and one broad light blue stripe sandwiched between them, and with two broad dark blue stripes sandwiching a broad light blue stripe. The Air Marshal rank is next, with two very thick dark blue stripes, one thick light blue stripe inside and four broad dark blue stripes above them, with two light blue stripes inside the dark blue stripes. The Air Chief Marshal picture is next, with the two thick dark blue stripes, one thick light blue stripe inside, and six broad dark blue stripes, with three broad light blue stripes inside them, sitting above. And finally, the Marshal of the Royal Air Force rank is displayed, with two thick dark blue stripes sandwiching one thick light blue stripe, eight broad dark blue stripes and four broad light blue stripes sandwiched inside," stated Flight Lieutenant Bray.

The recruits studied the pictures and gathered in their minds the information that went with the pictures, regarding the name of the rank.

"Okay, so now we can turn over the page and look at the Non-Commissioned ranks, starting with the Non-Commissioned aircrew, which begins with the RAF Sergeant Aircrew, that has three chevrons and wings above the chevrons, the second picture is the RAF Flight Sergeant Aircrew which has three chevrons, wings and a crown above the chevrons, then thirdly we have a picture of the RAF Master Aircrew, which has a picture of a hat with a coat of arms, wings and a display of white bunting. Following on from this, we shall look at the next picture and see the rank of the Leading Aircraftman and a picture of two propellers, the next picture is the Senior Aircraftman rank and three propellers, swiftly followed by the Senior Aircraftman Technician, with three propellers in a circle, followed by the Junior Technician, that is four propellers, next is the Corporal which is two chevrons, the Sergeant which is three chevrons, then the Chief Technician that is three chevrons with four propellers above the chevrons, followed by the Flight Sergeant, that is a picture of three chevrons and a crown above the chevrons, with the final picture being the Warrant Officer and a picture of a coat of arms," stated Flight Lieutenant Bray.

The recruits studied each of the Non-Commissioned ranks and tried to take on board each individual picture and form a basis in their minds for remembering them. It would all come in time, but for now, with testing and examinations forthcoming on these rank pictures and titles, the airmen knew that the pressure was on to recall each name and rank picture.

"So, that's the ranking system we have in the Royal Air Force, I need you to know these inside out, by the time you leave the training, in six weeks," stated Flight Lieutenant Bray, looking around the classroom at the blank faces of the airmen. "Any questions?"

Chapter 9

Clem and the rest of the recruits stared into space, as the Flight Lieutenant waited for a hand to be raised with a question, but there were none forthcoming. The room was silent.

"That's your initial tuition day with me finished. There will be more in due course, so don't forget to read the booklet and memorise the pictures of the Royal Air Force Commissioned and Non-Commissioned ranks and names and store them in your memory locker, somewhere. I'm sure you're all intelligent enough to recall the information, otherwise you wouldn't be sitting here in this classroom. So I bid you farewell for now, you are all dismissed, and can wait outside for your drill sergeant and drill corporal, who will collect you and take you to the next stage of your training," stated Flight Lieutenant Bray.

The recruits clutched hold of their books and made their way outside, into the drizzly rain swept October mid morning. Sergeant Winner and Corporal Cherry were waiting for the recruits and they marched them off towards the RAF Swinderby Sports Hall.

"Quick march Flight, left, right, left, right, left, right!" called Sergeant Winner, with a loud bellowing voice, as normal.

Clem had a little chuckle to himself, as the drill sergeant was issuing these orders and he couldn't help thinking that Sergeant Winner reminded him of Windsor Davies, the drill sergeant major in the current hit television situation comedy show, "It Ain't Half Hot Mum," which was one of his favourite programmes on the box. The mannerisms of Sergeant Winner was incredibly close to the actor Windsor Davies and Clem was wondering if the other recruits in the Flight thought so too.

When the recruits arrived at the Sports Hall and were having a break, away from earshot of Sergeant Winner and Corporal Cherry, Clem nudged Mark Lucas and Joseph Job in the ribs, to air his revelation.

"Don't you think Sergeant Winner sounds like Windsor Davies from "It Ain't Half Hot Mum," the television comedy show?" asked Clem Harrison, with a little chuckle in his tone.

"Haha, yeah, so he does!" exclaimed Mark Lucas, in agreement.

"I'm sure it's one and the same person!" joked Clem, with tongue in cheek.

"Haha, probably!" piped up Joseph Job.

The three recruits sniggered and chortled privately between themselves.

"This must be his day job, when filming ends, and he uses this wage to pay the rent!" suggested Mark Lucas facetiously.

"Haha, yeah that could be true, it's so funny to compare the two, I was beginning to think it was just me who thought it," revealed Clem Harrison.

"No, I've been thinking that for a couple of days," stated Mark Lucas.

"Me too, but I was too embarrassed to admit it, haha," piped up Joseph Job.

The other recruits were wondering what was being said, as Clem Harrison, Mark Lucas and Joseph Job were sharing their private joke, but they were not going to share it with them, in case it got back to Sergeant Winner and caused complications for the rest of their training.

"What's going on over here?" asked David Ephraim, in frustration.

"Oh, nothing," replied Mark Lucas.

"Come on spit it out, you seem to be enjoying a hell of a joke between the three of you," stated David Ephraim.

"It's okay lads, let's share it with the rest of the group; We were discussing Sergeant Winner and how similar he is to Windsor Davies, from "It Ain't Half Hot Mum," don't you think?" shouted Joseph Job loudly.

As he finished his sentence, Sergeant Winner appeared from around the corner, and overheard the comment.

"Yes, you're absolutely correct!" piped up Sergeant Winner, nodding his head in agreement.

"Sorry sergeant, I didn't mean to take the Mickey out of you!" exclaimed Joseph Job, with a red face of embarrassment.

"It's okay AC Job, don't worry about it. You're not the first to say it and I'm sure you won't be the last, either!" replied Sergeant Winner, with a friendly smile.

"Yes indeed Flight, Sergeant Winner has moulded his style around the skills of Windsor Davies, and owes him for his success, as being the best drill instructor at RAF Swinderby!" piped up Corporal Cherry.

"Wow!" exclaimed Joseph Job, in wonder.

"Yes, so now you know, so come on get yourself in the changing rooms and ready for a session of football training. Grab a pair of shorts, a tee shirt and a pair of football boots each from your locker, and be outside in five minutes!" yelled Sergeant Winner.

The recruits jumped to it and were ready in less than two minutes. They were all looking forward to a game of football and were keen to get stuck in.

"So, as AC Lucas and AC Job are the billet Team Leader and Assistant Team Leader, they will be captaining the five-a-side football teams. And, to get things underway, they shall pick the teams and as AC Lucas is Team Leader, he will have the call of the coin, to ascertain who will pick the first player," instructed Sergeant Winner, tossing the coin into the air.

"Heads!" called Mark Lucas.

"It's tails!" replied Sergeant Winner. "AC Job has the first pick!"

"I'm sorry, but I don't know how good you all are, so this is a bit of a shot in the dark," stated Joseph Job with honesty.

"Hurry up and pick a player, it'll be dark soon!" ordered Sergeant Winner jokingly.

"Clem Harrison," said Joseph Job.

"David Ephraim," stated Mark Lucas.

"Stephen Gabriel," said Joseph Job.

"Jacob Adams," stated Mark Lucas.

"Joshua Peters," said Joseph Job.

"John Rufus," stated Mark Lucas.

"Daniel Thomas," said Joseph Job.

"And last, but I hope, not least, Timothy Moses," stated Mark Lucas.

"Good, that's the teams picked, now wait here for Corporal Abraham to turn up and he shall take you for the Physical Training session," ordered Sergeant Winner.

Corporal Abraham arrived a few minutes later, wrapped up in a thick RAF tracksuit, complete with a football and a very shiny new whistle.

"Okay Flight, let's get the game started!" exclaimed Corporal Abraham.

"Yes corporal!" replied the recruits and nodding in agreement.

"Have you decided on the teams?" asked Corporal Abraham.

"Yes corporal, we've just done that," replied Mark Lucas.

"Well done, that'll save some time, so let's move! I've pumped up the ball to regulation standard, so it's all systems go. Let's see if we have any budding Georgie Best's among us!" joked Corporal Abraham, with tongue in cheek. "Or maybe Bobby Charlton's!"

The corporal led the ten players to the football field, in the middle of the vast green area at RAF Swinderby, situated at the back of the Sports Hall, which had two sets of goalposts, without nets, and there were white lines painted to indicate the touchline, centre spot, penalty area and penalty spot, which appeared to be so professional.

"Let's toss up, to see who kicks off first," stated Corporal Abraham, flicking a coin into the air.

"Tails!" called Mark Lucas, hoping for a change of luck.

"It's heads, so AC Job, it's your decision. Do you want to kick off first?" asked Corporal Abraham.

"Yes, we'll kick off first," replied Joseph Job, taking the ball from the corporal and appearing bemused that he had won the toss again.

"Okay, don't forget, play to the whistle, no dirty challenges, no answering me back, and no swearing! If I book you twice, you're off for an early shower! Understand?" shouted Corporal Abraham.

"Yes corporal!" replied the recruits, together in unison.

Corporal Abraham blew the whistle to indicate the start of the game, and Joseph Job kicked off to Clem Harrison, who appeared to be playing up front together.

The first challenge of the match came instantly from Timothy Moses, when he hit Clem Harrison hard, with a bone crunching tackle, that rocked him to the core. But it was fair and within the rules, according to the referee Corporal Abraham and he waved play on. As Moses carried the ball forward, dribbling across the turf with deft footwork, Clem Harrison was sprawled out on the ground and didn't know what had hit him, as he struggled to get up to his feet. If that wasn't a foul, he thought, he didn't know what was.

"Come on Clem, get up, we need some cover in defence!" yelled Joseph Job.

Clem pulled himself together quickly and jumped to his feet, ready for whatever was thrown at him again. Timothy Moses raced through a wide gap in the defence and looked up to gauge where the goal was, before hitting a shot on the run, with power and precision. Daniel Thomas had volunteered to be the goalkeeper for Joseph Job's team and seemed to have the ball covered, as he watched it with a keen pair of eyes, but with top spin, the ball swerved in mid air and evaded the outstretched arms of Thomas and hit the target to give Mark Lucas's team an early 1-0 lead.

Clem Harrison and Joseph Job prepared to take the kick off, to get the game underway for a second time, and Clem was ready for another hefty challenge from Timothy Moses, as he steamrollered in again. When Moses came forward to hit Clem, with all his might, Clem sidestepped the opponent and left him in a heap on the ground, to totally embarrass him. With a gap ahead, Clem raced through it, with the ball at his feet and headed towards the opponents goal.

He skipped past one, then another and feigned a shot, before thumping the ball hard with the side of his left foot, towards the goal, which gave goalkeeper John Rufus no chance for Mark Lucas's team, and it brought the scores level, at 1-1.

Mark Lucas and David Ephraim kicked off to resume the match and Ephraim sprayed the ball out to Jacob Adams, on the wing, and he controlled well, like a professional, before flicking the ball past his marker, Joshua Peters, to provide some open space for him to gallop in, towards his opponent's goal. Stephen Gabriel was the last man in defence and he crunched Jacob Adams with a sublime tackle, that took both the man and the ball, fair and square, in a perfect tackle, but it resulted in Adams going down like a tree that had been felled, and the referee Corporal Abraham had no hesitation but to award a free kick on the edge of the penalty area, but Joseph Job and Clem Harrison were unhappy with the decision.

"That was a fair tackle ref!" exclaimed Joseph Job.

"Yes! He took man and ball, and also got a touch on the ball!" yelled Clem Harrison, in a loud appeal.

"Shut up, who's refereeing the game?" replied Corporal Abraham.

"You are, corporal," replied Joseph Job.

"Well, let me do my job. I saw that it was an unfair challenge, so it's a free kick, and anymore of your complaining, and you shall both find your names are in my book!" exclaimed Corporal Abraham.

Mark Lucas was preparing to take the free kick and Daniel Thomas in goal for Joseph Job's team was busy organising a two man wall that consisted of Stephen Gabriel and Joshua Peters. The shot came in from Mark Lucas and it cleared the wall and hurtled towards the goal and Daniel Thomas parried with his fists to clear the danger, and he saved bravely.

Clem Harrison raced back to assist his goalkeeper and hacked the ball away with a long punt upfield, that was met by the head of Jacob Adams, who cleared his own area of any unwanted danger. The match was being played at a frantic pace, as both sets of players battled relentlessly for the ball and they were not afraid to go in where it hurt, as the tussles became harder and harder, as the match wore on. Timothy Moses was in the thick of the heated exchanges, that were full blooded and tasty and he was on the receiving end of some bruising challenges from Clem

Harrison, on a number of occasions, as Clem tried to exact revenge for the first minute crunch tackle, which he had not forgotten about.

The referee blew the whistle for half time, and let the players rest for a while, to catch their breath and chat among each other, regarding tactics and formations.

"Keep the ball moving and don't hesitate to clear it away, when in defence. It doesn't matter whether it's pretty stuff we play, as long as it's productive," ordered Joseph Job to his players.

"Pass to feet, not to heads, as we have two feet and only one head, so it's more effective to play to the feet, to continue making progress. Apart from that, shoot on sight, and don't be scared to have a crack at goal, as goals win games!" exclaimed Mark Lucas passionately.

The referee whistled for the match to resume, a few minutes later, and after a short breather, the players were back on the pitch running around the field again, chasing every loose ball and trying to make an impression in front of the goal. Clem Harrison shot at the target, with a half volley from the edge of the penalty area, which thumped hard against the cross bar.

"Keep pressing deep!" shouted Joseph Job.

Clem nodded, but wasn't sure what he meant by pressing deep. But he continued to track the player with the ball and chased long and hard and seemed now to be the lone striker upfront, as Joseph Job appeared to have dropped back in defence, with Stephen Gabriel and Joshua Peters, mopping up any pressure that happened to come their way. Opposing them were Mark Lucas and David Ephraim, who formed a two pronged attack and were outnumbered, but they were hoping for a slip up, or a mistake in their opponents defence, which they could capitalize on.

Clem Harrison waited patiently for a perfect through ball to be despatched to him, which he could latch on to, but it never came, and he had to trundle back into midfield, and plough a lonely furrow on his own, from the centre of the pitch, which he didn't mind. But as the game wore on, the more fatigued he became, but he never gave up trying.

The ball was hit from defence to attack, like a shuttlecock in badminton, and it bypassed midfield, so Clem reckoned it would be best to stay upfront and chase deep, and the plan worked, as a ball came through from Joseph Job which was attainable, from where Clem was positioned, and he managed to reach the ball first, beating Jacob Adams, and he clipped a beautiful shot over the head of John Rufus, to claim the team's and his second goal. His teammates congratulated him, but he knew the game was not won yet. There was still time for Mark Lucas's team to equalise.

Clem chased after another long ball, from an excellent throw by Daniel Thomas, and he threaded the ball past the goalkeeper, with aplomb, in the goal of the game, to earn a well deserved hat-trick, and push the score to 3-1.

Mark Lucas's side didn't give up, and they knew they had the time to score twice in a few minutes, if they played to their strengths, but Joseph Job was magnificent in defence, and stopped everything that came into the penalty area, including blocking, last ditch tackles, heading away, acrobatic clearances and assisting his goalkeeper, by clearing off the line. Joseph Job seemed to be everywhere, and was assisted by two capable defenders in Stephen Gabriel and Joshua Peters, who nullified their opponents attacks by competent defending, that was more than just Sunday League football standards. These three could play, and so could Clem Harrison.

The 3-1 scoreline seemed a big enough margin for Joseph Job's side to clinch the win, but they were caught out by a thunderbolt shot, cracked home by David Ephraim, a few seconds later, when he latched on to a cross by Mark Lucas, and he hit it on the volley and watched it rocket into the top corner of the goal, giving Daniel Thomas no chance, between the sticks.

Mark Lucas's team were looking for an equaliser, but they had no idea how long there was left. It seemed nip and tuck, as the seconds ticked rapidly down on the referee's watch. Would there be enough time for a leveller? Joseph Job and his two co-defenders, Stephen Gabriel and Joshua Peters defended stoutly. Clem Harrison chased after every through ball keenly, and Daniel Thomas kept goal expertly, as the seconds ticked by.

Mark Lucas decided to take the bull by the horns, if he was going to stand any chance of getting a result, and he ran with the ball at his feet, through the centre of the pitch, from the back, without a defender near him. He found some acceleration, which was enough to get him away from his pursuers. With a shimmy and a piece of showboating, as he flicked the ball forward, he managed to beat Daniel Thomas, with a superb low shot, that had the goalkeeper struggling to get anywhere near it, to make the score 3-3. The whistle was blown for full time by Corporal Abraham, a few seconds later.

As the players were making their way off the pitch, Clem Harrison was presented with the ball, following his hat trick, by the referee Corporal Abraham, and as he received the match ball, another ball that had been there as a spare was kicked haphazardly into the air by Timothy Moses, and it hit Clem directly on the back of the head, in a comical manner, with a great thump, as he was walking back to the changing rooms, twenty yards away. Whether there was any malice in the action by Moses, or whether it was a pure accident, nobody knew, but Moses. But it gave everyone a huge lift, and they all screamed with laughter, and Clem accepted it as an accident, because after all, he had scored a hat-trick, and was taking home the match ball, as a souvenir, so it was water off a duck's back to him.

Chapter 10

The recruits showered and changed, and prepared for the arrival of Sergeant Winner, or Windsor Davies, *as he was now known,* and Corporal Cherry. In the meantime they all shuffled off to the vending machine and helped themselves to a cup of hot tea and a chocolate bar each, to fill up a gap in their bellies. It was hungry work this RAF recruit training business. Within ten minutes of hanging around, the recruits were met by their drill instructors.

"How did the football go?" asked Sergeant Winner. "Have we any future stars for Lincoln City?"

"It went well, sergeant!" replied the recruits, in unison.

"Who won?" asked Sergeant Winner.

"It was a three-three draw sergeant," replied the recruits, together in unison again. They were getting used to this type of chatter.

"Who was the man of the match?" asked Sergeant Winner.

"I don't think we had a man of the match, as such, but Clem Harrison bagged the match ball, for a hat-trick of goals," replied Joseph Job, on his own, this time.

"A hat-trick for Clem Harrison, eh? Wow, well done AC Harrison!" exclaimed Sergeant Winner. "I shall be having a word in the ear of Graham Taylor, at Lincoln City and putting a good word in for you, and you never know, you may get a trial," he added, with tongue in cheek.

"Have you had a break?" asked Corporal Cherry, piping up.

"Yes corporal!" replied the recruits, in unison.

"Good, we shall move forward with your training then. It's on to the Armoury, to pick up some ammo, and a SLR. You're all going back on the rifle range!" instructed Corporal Cherry.

The recruits marched smartly from the RAF Swinderby Sports Hall to the Armoury, collected their SLR rifles and each picked up a loaded cartridge of live ammunition, ready to practice with, on the rifle range. Clem Harrison recalled how he had embarrassed himself the last time he was there, when a rogue "spent bullet" had lodged inside his trousers leg. He was certain that wouldn't happen again, as he didn't think the sergeant would be as lenient a second time. When the recruits arrived at the rifle range, Sergeant Winner called for silence.

"Okay, pipe down now, we are here at the rifle range, which is the most dangerous site on the base. Afterwards, I need you to inform me whether you think there are any "spent bullets" on your person, as we need you to be clear of all foreign bodies. Do you understand?" asked Sergeant Winner, with a solemn straight face.

"Yes sergeant!" replied the recruits together, in unison.

"Okay, continue with your task, and I want a one hundred per cent Marksmanship today!" exclaimed Sergeant Winner.

The recruits got down on to their stomachs and prepared to fire away. Within seconds, the whole area was alive with gunfire, as the airmen quickly got into the swing of finding their range. Clem began like a house on fire, and peppered the bullseye with bullet after bullet, as he got his "eye in" immediately. It was a very impressive performance from Clem Harrison, and he was thoroughly enjoying his time on the rifle range, and he would have stayed there all day, if he could.

"Okay recruits, that will do for now, cease your firing!" shouted Sergeant Winner. "Let me check your scores," he added.

The sergeant collected the paper targets from each of the ten cardboard cut-outs and studied each of the markings.

"Right Flight, I have the scores, and first today, is Clem Harrison, with a maximum of one hundred per cent, excellent stuff, AC Harrison! Second is, David Ephraim with ninety per cent, and third is, Mark Lucas with eighty per cent," called Sergeant Winner.

Clem was pleased with himself, as he had had a good day, taking home the match ball earlier, with a hat-trick of goals, in the football, and now 100 per cent in the shooting, on the rifle range.

"Before we depart from here, check your trousers are free of live bullets, shrapnel and empty shells, and also check your shirt cuffs and collars, just in case any loose stuff has flown inside there," instructed Sergeant Winner.

The recruits jumped to the order, and immediately did as they were told, following the unfortunate mishap that Clem Harrison had experienced the other day. After a good rummage and a shake around, the recruits were satisfied they were all in the clear.

"Okay Flight, if you're happy, let's move on for lunch," instructed Sergeant Winner.

The recruits marched impeccably in time, and moved forwards to the Airmen's Mess. It was raining, windy and cold, but the recruits ignored all the elements that were being thrown at them from the skies, and they quickened their step. When they reached the Airmen's Mess, they were thoroughly soaked to the skin.

"We shall meet you back at the billet at one fifteen, and don't be late! Anybody that is late, will be back-flighted one week!" yelled Corporal Cherry, with venom in his tone.

"Yes corporal!" replied the recruits loudly, in unison.

The sergeant and corporal disappeared into thin air, and left the recruits to queue up in the Airmen's Mess for their lunch, and it provided an opportunity for them to dry off, at the same time.

The airmen picked up their dishes and cutlery, and filled their plates with an assortment of culinary delights, including fish and chips for Clem, with peas, and apple crumble and custard, for pudding, and the usual tea and bromide, to wash it all down with. He was famished, and he certainly deserved his dinner, after having such a successful morning. This RAF recruit training was like a walk in the park, thought Clem, and maybe *this was* the best part of the Royal Air Force, like that recruit had

shouted over to them, the other day. There was a whole host of variety, including banter with colleagues, exercise, hard work, learning, sport, comradeship, team building, character building and keeping fit, in body, soul and mind.
The fish and chips went down well, and Clem thoroughly enjoyed them, along with the apple crumble. In fact they were both so delicious, that he could easily have eaten them again. He left the table and bought a newspaper before heading back to the billet, to make his bed up, and rest, before what was sure to be another action packed afternoon. Clem was followed from the Airmen's Mess by the rest of the recruits, and they too rested on their beds.
Sergeant Winner and Corporal Cherry arrived at the billet at exactly 1.15 pm, like they had said. They were sticklers for time keeping, and they were setting the recruits a great example.
  "So, who's ready for the gas chamber?" asked Sergeant Winner facetiously.
There was no reply, and Sergeant Winner smiled in understanding.
  "I hope you all know your service number off by heart, as you shall need to recite it, inside the gas chamber, with your respirator off, and if you struggle to say it, your going to find yourself in a spot of bother," stated Sergeant Winner, with tongue in cheek.
Clem didn't panic, but merely checked inside his wallet for the written details of his recruitment training, and looked at the welcome letter to see if his service number was written on there. It wasn't, but he still didn't fret about it, and coolly and calmly waited for the sergeant and corporal to finish what they were doing, and as soon as an opportunity arose, he was going to address them with the question.

"Where do we find our service numbers, sergeant?" asked Clem.

"Ah, that's a good question, as seeing you haven't been paid yet, you won't actually know them. But I have them all here. So if you bear with me, I shall shout them out, and when your name is called, make sure you record it somewhere, preferably on paper, with ink, so that you can refer to it later," replied Sergeant Winner.

"Thank you sergeant," stated Clem, with gratitude.

Sergeant Winner glanced down at the written list on a sheet of paper, and called out the name and service number of each recruit, and the airmen quickly scribbled down the details, so that they could memorise their service number, for when they were in the gas chamber, and not have a brain freeze in there. Clem wrote down his number, A8129679 and repeated it over and over again, until he got it into his head. He was determined not to stumble and fall, and wanted the day to continue in its successful vein.

"Okay, so now you've all got your numbers, and have memorised them in your brain, let's set off for the gas chamber," stated Sergeant Winner.

The recruits nervously marched from the billet to the gas chamber, that was situated in the middle of nowhere, on a field on the edge of the RAF base. There were worried frowns etched on the faces of all the recruits, and for the first time, they felt insecure and unsure of what to expect. It was like going into the unknown.

"Left, right, left, right, come on don't lose your shape, your like a concertina again, left, right, left, right!" yelled Corporal Cherry in anger.

The recruits were not listening to the corporal's instructions, and were marching like they had never marched together before, and were a complete shambles.

Whether it was the nerves about the gas chamber and what it was going to be like in there, it was hard to say, but this was the worst they had ever been since day one, and it was getting worse.

"Look at your shape, it's a disgrace, if you don't pull yourself together, you shall all be back-flighted one week, and will start this process again. Left, right, left, right!" bellowed Corporal Cherry.

Whether it was the threat of being back-flighted, or a deeper concentration, it was difficult to tell, but somehow the recruits tightened up their formation, straightened their lines, and were perfect again.

"That's better, keep it like that, all the way to the Clothing Stores, to pick up your respirators, left, right, left, right," yelled Corporal Cherry.

The recruits arrived at the Clothing Stores, and were issued with a respirator each, and then they re-formed into their marching group again, and set off for the short journey to the gas chamber on the field, situated on a hill. It looked eerie and it scared the recruits to death. None of them liked the look of the place. It was no wonder it was isolated on a hill, in the middle of no man's land.

"Flight halt!" yelled Corporal Cherry. "Form a queue, in alphabetical order, and place your respirators on," added the corporal.

The recruits adhered to the corporal's order and the first thing Clem sensed, was the strong smell of rubber, and a clear, distinct feeling of claustrophobia.

The recruits lined up as they were ordered to, in alphabetical order, and a chilly wind blew in off the field, that was icy cold, which made the fear worsen, and it sent shivers down Clem Harrison's spine. He was a little scared, but put on a brave face, and to take his mind off the thought of entering a CS gas filled chamber, without a respirator, Clem read his service number over and over again, and tried to get the digits 8129679 into his head, with the letter A at the front, being the correct formation. He wasn't sure what would happen if he froze in the gas chamber, and fluffed his lines, but he wasn't in the frame of mind to find out, he wanted to be in, and out, without any fuss. But he had to admit to himself, that this was the scariest thing he had ever done, in his seventeen years of life. Sergeant Winner piped up, and quickly went through the routine of what would be happening in the gas chamber.

"Okay, so what you need to do when you enter the chamber, is remove your respirator, and recite your service number, name and rank, and then quickly depart, and once outside, run up that hill, across there, to get some fresh air into your lungs, as fast as you can. Is that clear? Now, without any further ado, have we got Jacob Adams ready to enter the chamber, followed by David Ephraim, Stephen Gabriel, Clem Harrison, Joseph Job, Mark Lucas, Timothy Moses, Joshua Peters, John Rufus and finally, Daniel Thomas?" asked Sergeant Winner.

The recruits just nodded in agreement, as they were dressed in their respirators. Jacob Adams slowly approached the gas chamber, and followed Sergeant Winner and Corporal Cherry inside the ugly looking grey building, with each of the drill instructors now wearing a respirator, and Clem watched them disappear inside the flat roofed shack. It wasn't long before Jacob Adams came running out, with his respirator in his hand, running as fast as he could, up the hill.

Clem watched David Ephraim go inside the ugly, flat roofed, grey shack building, and two minutes later he was running up the same hill, with fear on his face, followed by Stephen Gabriel, who looked the most terrified of the three, then it was Clem's turn.

"AC Clem Harrison is next!" shouted Corporal Cherry loudly, which echoed all around the field.

Clem nervously stepped forward, taking his time, thinking about his name, rank and service number, as nothing else mattered to him. He was determined to get the job done in the correct manner, no matter how scared and nervous he was feeling. Clem entered the gas chamber and could see Sergeant Winner and Corporal Cherry standing in the centre of the room. There was an eerie silence, and tension was in the air, as Clem's nerves kicked in. But he quickly pulled himself together, and tugged at his respirator, to take it off, as a CS gas cannister was activated.

"AC Clem Harrison, A8129679!" shouted Clem, at the top of his voice, to make himself heard. He didn't gasp at the air until his feet were outside the door, and he ran up the hill as fast as his legs could carry him. He felt tears flowing down his face. He was certain they weren't tears of sadness, nor tears of joy, but just tears from the CS gas, that had penetrated his eyes. He breathed in deeply, to receive the fresh October air of RAF Swinderby, and he felt relieved and happy, that the ordeal was over. It was another rung climbed on the ladder of the recruit training, which was part of the RAF Swinderby learning curve. The rest of the airmen entered the gas chamber, one by one, and within twenty minutes, the task was completed, without any casualties.

Clem joined the others and found that they too were gasping for breath, with tears running down their cheeks. It had been the toughest assignment yet, but it had been successfully completed, and Clem was certain nothing would beat that for the sheer scale of the unexpected.

"Okay Flight, well done, that's the gas chamber covered. You're going to march back to the clothing stores to hand in the respirators, before heading to the hangar for a spot of drill practice, with a difference, as you shall be learning how to "Present Arms," so yes, we are taking a detour to the Armoury to collect your rifles, and then it's time to sort out the wheat from the chaff!" exclaimed Sergeant Winner. Clem sighed with apprehension. The training was intense. He had seen the military on the television "Presenting Arms," but he never for the life of him expected to be doing that himself, whilst he was here at RAF Swinderby. It was going to be another challenge, not just for Clem Harrison, but the other nine recruits too, as none of them had "Presented Arms" either. Sergeant Winner and Corporal Cherry were going to have their work cut out, moulding these guys into shape. But after a few sessions, both Sergeant Winner and Corporal Cherry were confident enough in the recruits, that they would eventually get the basic hang of it, after all it was practice that made perfect, like everything.

"We shall take a quick break beforehand, as I'm sure you will want to collect your thoughts and senses after that experience, so quick march left, right, left, right, to the refreshment hangar!" yelled Sergeant Winner.

The recruits marched in time, and were quite organised and tight, considering they had just been in contact with CS gas.

On arrival at the refreshments, Clem poured himself a tea and bromide from the vending machine, and quickly drank it, as he was as dry as the Sahara desert. He chose a Mars Bar too, to fill a gap in his stomach. Nothing much was said between the recruits. Everyone seemed exhausted with the intensity of the day. The training was catching up with them, and it was taking its toll on their physical and mental capacity. All the airmen wanted, was to drink their tea and eat their chocolate bars, and a couple of them lit up a cigarette, to calm their nerves.

"Anybody thinking of chucking it?" asked Mark Lucas.

"Nope, I'm sticking at it," replied Joseph Job.

"Me too," agreed David Ephraim.

"And me," piped up Clem Harrison.

The others didn't reply. They were either too exhausted to speak, or they were contemplating whether to chuck it, as Mark Lucas had stated.

"It's been tough today, I'd say the toughest day so far," said Mark Lucas, who had suddenly sprung to life, after the chocolate bar, tea and bromide.

"It has been very hard, and with the "Present Arms" coming up next, it seems like it's going to get even tougher," agreed Joseph Job.

"Yes, but you know what they say; when the going gets tough, the tough get going!" exclaimed Clem Harrison, with tongue in cheek.

"Yes that's true, but it all depends on where you are going; the parade square, or through the exit gate, back to Civvy Street!" joked Mark Lucas.

"I'm not going back to Civvy Street, for a long time yet," stated Clem Harrison.

"Me neither, I've signed on for six years, but I intend to do twelve, and maybe even twenty two," replied Mark Lucas.

Chapter 11

The recruits finished their drinks, chomped away on their chocolate bars, and those that were smoking stubbed their cigarette ends out on the floor, with their boots, when they spotted Sergeant Winner and Corporal Cherry coming round the corner.

"Are we ready Flight? Everything okay? No complaints? No concerns?" questioned Sergeant Winner.

"Everything's fine sergeant!" replied Mark Lucas, the team leader, acting as the spokesman for the recruits.

"Great! So let's make tracks for the Clothing Store, drop off the respirators there, before going to the Armoury to collect the rifles, and then on to the parade ground outside, seeing that's it not raining!" advised Sergeant Winner, at the top of his voice, just like how Windsor Davies would have spoken in, "It Ain't Half Hot Mum."

The recruits got into line and marched forward to their first destination. And they were very tidy, in shape and in timing, with no signs of any concertina anywhere to be seen.

"Left, right, left, right!" called Sergeant Winner, keeping the airmen in time with their footwork.

The recruits arrived at the Clothing Store and returned their respirators, before moving on to the Armoury to collect their rifles for the ambitious task of learning to "Present Arms." It sounded daunting to Clem, but as his mother always told him, practice does indeed make perfect, and the more you work at something, the better you become, so Clem wasn't fazed by the prospect of "Presenting Arms."

"Okay Flight, so now on to the parade ground which is at the other side of the hangar, where we practiced indoor drill, the other day. Left, right, left, right!" shouted Sergeant Winner.

The recruits arrived at the parade ground, and Sergeant Winner was impressed with the way the airmen had marched. They were sublime, confident, showed great poise and swagger, and he had no qualms about the recruits, with regard to taking on board the information on "Presenting Arms," although Corporal Cherry wasn't so sure. He had seen a lot of new recruits struggle with this facet of the training, and had known many to quit the RAF because of it, so he wasn't counting his chickens just yet. He would be surprised to see a full Flight of ten airmen by the end of the week, as usually one or two dropped out, because they were unable to cope.

"Okay, Flight, watch carefully as I demonstrate to you the rudiments of "Presenting Arms," and please concentrate and pay full attention, as I don't want any airmen daydreaming about what they are having for tea tonight, or what they are going to be doing on their first weekend of leave. I need one hundred per cent focus, on what I am showing you. Do you all understand?" shouted Sergeant Winner.

"Yes sergeant!" replied the recruits loudly, in unison.

"Very good," answered Sergeant Winner, taking hold of Mark Lucas's rifle to demonstrate what he needed the recruits to learn.

"This is the "Presenting Arms" in one flowing movement, which you will all be doing in the "Passing Out" parade, at the end of your training," explained Sergeant Winner, before throwing the rifle forward, swinging it into the air, and looking smart, professional and confident, similar to the military people on the television, which Clem could vaguely recall. He was competent, confident and coherent with the rifle, which seemed to be on a piece of string, and the recruits watched in awe.

Clem studied what was going on, closely, watching with a deep concentration the sequence of events, as everything had a sequence.

"Okay, so, let's see if you have taken on board what I have just shown you," stated Sergeant Winner, with a wide grin. The recruits waited with baited breath, at the command from the sergeant. "Flight, "Present Arms," in unison!" yelled Sergeant Winner.

But the recruits were far from being in unison, they were the exact opposite, and it was a total disaster, with rifles thrown into the air like rag dolls, and flying off in all directions, whilst there were other rifles dropped to the ground, in a scruffy, sloppy manner, that was embarrassing to see. In fact, it was a shambles, and it left Corporal Cherry with a wry smile of knowing on his face. But Sergeant Winner was not so understanding. His face was red with rage. He was livid.

"Stop it! Now! Stop what you're doing! You're a disgrace to the RAF! If you don't listen and pay attention to the things I'm demonstrating, then none of you will have any chance of "Passing Out" of here!" bawled Sergeant Winner, in a manner that had not been witnessed previously by the recruits. He was extremely angry. "Listen up, I shall go through the routine again, and if any of you repeat what I have just seen, then I shall pull your arm out of its socket, and hit you on the head with the soggy bit! Do you understand?" screamed Sergeant Winner loudy, at the top of his hoarse voice, in a tone that he surely meant what he said. He grabbed a rifle, and went through the sequence of "Presenting Arms" again, and the airmen were petrified that if they messed up once more, they would be booted off the training altogether.

When it was time for the recruits to "Present Arms" again, it was like watching a different set of recruits. Somehow, everything clicked into gear. The rifles were placed into the proper positions, and the airmen worked like clockwork together, with impeccable timing. It was a joy to watch, and Sergeant Winner had to scratch his head in wonder, as it crossed his mind that the recruits may have been taking the Mickey earlier, and he grinned like a Cheshire cat.

"Well done Flight! That's better, by far! Let's try that again and see if it was a fluke, or just pure skill! Flight "Present Arms" in unison!" yelled Sergeant Winner.

The recruits "Presented Arms" again, in such a confident manner that Corporal Cherry watched in disbelief, and he looked across at Sergeant Winner, with an expression of bewilderment on his face, as if he could not believe what he was watching.

"Did you swap this lot for the Coldstrean Guards?" joked Corporal Cherry, with tongue in cheek.

"These lot are better than the Coldstream Guards!" quipped Sergeant Winner, in jest.

The recruits "Presented Arms" on a further half a dozen occasions, and improved each time, and were on top of their game. In fact by the expression on their faces, it appeared they were enjoying every single second of it too, and it was this that was making them relax and perform to the highest standard. They knew they had nothing to lose, and as the sergeant had stated, if they got it wrong one more time, they would not have had another chance to put it right, so it was all or nothing, and with the correct attitude, everything clicked perfectly into place, for them all.

"Stand at ease Flight!" shouted Sergeant Winner. The recruits relaxed and waited for the next order. "Take a break, to catch your breath, you've had a tough day!" yelled the drill sergeant, in a compassionate tone of voice, which was a great deal softer than earlier.

The recruits dropped their rifles onto the ground, and headed towards the refreshment hangar, that wasn't too far away. It was thirsty work, and the vending machine got another hammering, from all ten recruits.

"I thought we were all goners, earlier!" stated Mark Lucas.

"So did I," agreed David Ephraim, nodding.

"I couldn't get the hang of it, at first, and my rifle was as loose as hell! In fact, I thought I was going to lose control of it altogether, at one stage," joked Clem Harrison.

"Sergeant Winner was losing control of his temper, too!" quipped Joseph Job.

"Yes he was, and to be honest, I thought he was going to have a heart attack!" stated Mark Lucas.

"Yes, so did I! His face went red, then purple, then black! He was in a right state, with himself!" commented Joseph Job.

"He must have been fretting over his bonus!" revealed Mark Lucas.

"Bonus?" asked Clem Harrison.

"Yes, both Sergeant Winner and Corporal Cherry are on a bonus, if they managed to guide us through the recruit training, and the more that "pass out," the more money they'll receive," explained Mark Lucas.

"How do you know that?" asked Clem Harrison.

"I'm the Team Leader, I get to find out everything!" quipped Mark Lucas.

"Take no notice of him, he's having you on!" piped up Joseph Job.

Mark Lucas didn't say anything to defend himself, but he merely smiled cagily.

"If there's one thing you need to learn whilst you're here, it's to stop being so gullible," advised Joseph Job.

"Okay, but he sounded so convincing!" replied Clem Harrison.

"Look Clem. There's no bonus for Sergeant Winner nor Corporal Cherry, they're just desperate to do their jobs properly," stated Joseph Job.

Clem nodded in understanding, but vowed to learn some harsh facts about life in general, not just in the Royal Air Force.

"People are out to get you, in whatever capacity they are working in, and whether they are friendly and sincere, it doesn't matter, as there are tricksters and Mickey takers everywhere," stated Joseph Job.

"Thanks for the advice, I shall take it on board," replied Clem Harrison.

The drill sergeant and corporal returned a few minutes later.

"Everyone okay?" asked Sergeant Winner, looking at the downcast faces.

"Yes, sergeant!" replied Mark Lucas.

"Good, well hang on to your rifles, we're going back to the Armoury to collect the cartridges, and then you're having a go at cleaning the rifles down, and loading the cartridges with bullets, so that should be fun, and it won't be too taxing on your strained and battered muscles!" pledged Sergeant Winner. "So come on let's go, left, right, left, right!" he bellowed at the top of his voice.

The recruits marched tidily in line, although they looked tired and bedraggled in places, but Sergeant Winner wasn't too concerned about that, he had his mind set on the next task, which was the cleaning of the rifle parts, and the loading of the cartridges, with the bullets.

The recruits reached the Armoury, picked up their cartridges and then marched on to the building next door, where there was a room for them to work in. The session went well for Clem and the rest of the recruits, and Clem maintained his record of winning, by finishing first in the timed competition, to find the fastest bullet loader, and he finished second behind Mark Lucas, in the stripping down and rebuilding of the rifle, so it had been a pleasing and satisfying day, for Clem Harrison.

"Well done Flight, and very well done to AC Harrison, for first place in the "loading bullets" section, and congratulations also to AC Lucas for winning the "rifle strip, clean and re-assemble" race. We shall now take the rifles and cartridges back to the Armoury, before heading to the parade square, to sharpen up your drill skills," explained Sergeant Winner.

The recruits quickly formed into a neat and tidy marching group of airmen, and swaggered smartly back to the Armoury, before heading to the parade ground. It was turning dark outside, and the wind and rain was beginning to blow across the RAF station, with an icy blast from the east.

"On second thoughts, we shall use the hangar for the drill practice," stated Sergeant Winner, looking up into the sky and noticing the weather had turned wintry again. "We don't want to catch our death of cold!"

The recruits arrived at the hangar, and were marched in by the sergeant.

"Quick march, left, right, left, right, and iron out the concertina!" called Sergeant Winner.

The recruits marched inside the hangar, and it reminded them of their first marching session, when they were unsure of how to turn a corner, but today, they marched like the Coldstream Guards, with aplomb and panache, and kept a tight, straight line, when cornering.

"Well done Flight, keep your lines straight, and don't concertina round the bends!" exclaimed Sergeant Winner.

The recruits were excellent and didn't show any signs of wavering and they dealt with the corner, with ease, before levelling up and hitting the straight with an impeccable shape. They marched with determination, before cornering another bend, but they began to lose concentration and it led to a slight concertina shape, but they all glanced across at their line and cleaned up their untidiness and became a perfect straight line again. But it was scrappy and inconsistent along the next corner, as their focus appeared to have disappeared once more, and Sergeant Winner was wondering whether it was fatigue that was setting in, after such a busy schedule. But the recruits drove forward and would not be beaten by tiredness, and they entered the next corner with precision, and rounded it with perfection. Their concentration returned and they hit the straight with a great shape, and followed it up with another perfect corner, and came out of the bend with an excellent line and formation.

"Flight halt!" shouted Sergeant Winner. "And stand at ease!"

The recruits followed the command and relaxed. As soon as they stood at ease, they began to feel their muscles tighten, and they appeared to be on fire, and their minds were scrambled like their eggs at breakfast time.

"That was patchy in places, but also very good at times too, so I'm fairly satisfied that you're getting there, although you must cut out the nasty habit of the concertina shape, as it's creeping slowly into your display. The best way of overcoming this, is to keep your eye on your next door neighbour, as you march, and keep in line, it's not difficult, it's just basic concentration!" yelled Sergeant Winner.

"Yes sergeant!" shouted the recruits together, in unison.

"Okay, so let's march to the Airmen's Mess. It's tea time, and I expect you're all feeling rather famished!" exclaimed Sergeant Winner.

"Yes sergeant!" replied the recruits again, in unison.

"Flight, forward march, left wheel. Left, right, left, right, quick march!" yelled Sergeant Winner, at the top of his voice, and the airmen moved forward, in an impeccable formation.

They arrived at the Airmen's Mess a few minutes later, and the sky was pitch black, by the time they arrived. Winter was here, and the wind and sleet blew through the trees, to emphasise that the weather was following suit, to prove that winter had in fact come early this year.

"We shall see you back at the billet, nice and early in the morning at seven forty five, don't be late, and we require bedpacks and full uniform inspection, and oh yes, don't forget, we would like to see the place gleaming from top to bottom! Flight dismiss!" bellowed Corporal Cherry.

The recruits moved quickly inside the warmth of the Airmen's Mess and gathered in the queue, which was quickly forming, as the airmen from other Flights joined the throng. Clem was starving and couldn't wait to pile his plate up with tasty bacon, eggs, beans, fried bread and chips, followed by chocolate sponge and custard, and the usual tea and bromide, to wash it all down with. He wasn't disappointed with the quality of the food, it was as good as ever, and with an empty stomach to fill, it tasted better than it had ever done. Even the tea and bromide tasted good. The recruits sat together on a table and there was a hushed silence, as they all tucked into their meals and reflected on their day.

"I wonder if that bird is in the NAAFI tonight," piped up Mark Lucas.

"Why?" asked Joseph Job sharply.

"I need a massage," replied Mark Lucas.

"Huh?" quizzed Joseph Job.

"She might oblige, if I ask her nicely!" quipped Mark Lucas.

"Only if you pay her fifty pence, for the jukebox!" joked Clem Harrison, piping up.

The recruits laughed, and remembered what she was like.

"That's okay, fifty pence for a massage, is good value!" exclaimed Mark Lucas.

"I don't think she'll accept fifty pence for a massage, to be honest! She will probably expect a week's supply of fifty pence pieces!" stated Joseph Job.

"And how much will a week's supply of fifty pence pieces be?" asked Mark Lucas.

"Oh, I don't know, fifty quid maybe?" replied Joseph Job, with tongue in cheek, plucking a random figure out of the air.

"Fifty quid?" screamed Mark Lucas. "Bugger that, I think I'll make do with a hot bath!"

The recruits burst into laughter again at Mark Lucas's reply, and guffawed all the way through their meals.

"Come on, let's go get this billet cleaned up, and then we can have a evening in the NAAFI afterwards," suggested Joseph Job.

The recruits nodded in agreement, finished their food, before strolling back to the billet, to take on the task of cleaning the entire building.

When they got back, they carried out a vast clean up, and the Kung Fu masters got to work, chopping up the turds in the toilet bowl, the drivers worked the floor polishers all over, to create a gleaming shine on the canvas, and the rest polished the light switches, door handles and anything else that needed some elbow grease. The drivers of the irons hit the ironing boards hard, and pressed the trousers and shirts, so that they would be sharp enough to cut. It was organised, methodical and ran like clockwork, and the whole place shined brightly, like a brand new pin.

"Well done guys!" shouted the Team Leader, Mark Lucas.

"Come on then, let's go to the NAAFI and see if that dancing chick is around, and maybe, just maybe, Mark Lucas might get his massage!" exclaimed Assistant Team Leader Joseph Job, with tongue in cheek.

The recruits screamed with laughter at that quip, and they all followed the Team Leader and Assistant Team Leader, in a ten strong group.

The NAAFI was quiet. There was nobody in there, apart from the bar staff, and a shop assistant. But it was only early, the recruits in the other Flights would still be carrying out their "bull night."

The airmen ordered their drinks, coca cola all round and went to sit down at a table in the corner. There was no sign of the fifty pence piece dancing queen, and Mark Lucas was plucking up enough courage to ask her the burning question, would she give him a massage for fifty pence? The cokes were going down well, and each of the airmen were prepared to buy a round, and with ten recruits present, that was some serious coca cola being drunk. None of them were bothering with alcohol, although some were over 18 years of age, they had decided that booze, and the RAF Swinderby recruit training, didn't mix.

Chapter 12

"Have you got a fifty pence piece, please?" piped up the disco dancing female, from the other night, in the direction of Joseph Job. She had appeared from nowhere, and had surprised the table of ten recruits, who looked on in stark surprise at her audacity and confident nature.

"I'm sorry love, but I'm complety out of fifty pence pieces, but I do know a bloke that can help you," replied Joseph Job.

"Oh, that sounds fascinating, who is it?" replied the disco dancing female.

"My mate here, he will oblige you with fifty pence, but he has a request for you though, love," stated Joseph Job.

"Really? What's the request?" quizzed the disco dancing female.

"I shall let him ask you that, personally," replied Joseph Job politely, glancing across at Mark Lucas and pointing him out to the female.

Mark Lucas suddenly lost his nerve, and went red with embarrassment.

"What's up chuck, cat got your tongue?" teased the disco dancing female.

"No, no, I'm fine, it's just that I'm in need of some nursing and I wondered if you would oblige," stated Mark Lucas, coughing, spluttering and stuttering his words, as he tried to explain his request, the hard way.

"Nursing?" asked the disco dancing female.

"Yes, I need a massage, and I wondered if you would do the honours!" stated Mark Lucas, rapidly gaining his confidence.

"Massage?" asked the disco dancing female, moving forward, toward the impudent airman.

"Yes, and I shall give you a fifty pence piece, for your troubles," quipped Mark Lucas cheekily.

"How dare you!" exclaimed the disco dancing female, slapping Mark Lucas hard across the face, in disgust. "What on earth do you take me for?" she added before turning round, and stomping off in the other direction.

The other nine recruits that were watching, gulped in horror, as the blow caught their Team Leader flush across the cheek, and left a red mark.

"That went well!" exclaimed Joseph Job.

Mark Lucas didn't say anything, but merely rubbed his face, and took a large sip of coca cola, from his glass.

"Never mind, at least I got a reaction, although it was not what I was hoping for," replied Mark Lucas, with honesty.

"No, maybe you should have offered a little bit more," suggested Joseph Job.

"Such as?" asked Mark Lucas.

"I'm not sure really, maybe you shouldn't have said anything," stated Joseph Job.

"It's too late now," moaned Mark Lucas dejectedly.

"It's never too late!" quipped Joseph Job. "Look, she's coming back!" he added, nudging the other airmen around him, in the ribs.

"So, you're offering me fifty pence for a massage are you?" asked the disco dancing female.

"Yes, you asked for fifty pence, so I thought I would offer you that, in exchange for a massage," replied Mark Lucas.

"So, if I asked for another figure, you would have gladly paid it, for a massage?" asked the disco dancing female, raising her eyebrows.

"It all depends on the figure," replied Mark Lucas.

"Okay, I'm prepared to do a deal with you," stated the disco dancing female.

"Oh yes, what is it?" asked Mark Lucas.

"I shall give you a massage in stages, starting with your shoulders, and working downwards, and as soon as the music finishes, you have to give me another fifty pence piece, to select three more tracks, and then I shall continue with the massage, until you've had enough, is that fair?" asked the disco dancing female.

"Yes, you're on!" agreed Mark Lucas, handing over a fifty pence piece, to the disco dancing female.

She moved towards the jukebox and selected three tracks, "Dancing Queen," by Abba. "Blinded By The Light," by Manfred Mann's Earthband and "The Best Disco In Town," by the Ritchie Family. She then returned to Mark Lucas, with a smirk on her face, as the music played.

"Okay, lay on your front, across these three chairs, and I shall start to give you a massage, and then, when the music stops, like I explained, I will need another fifty pence piece, to continue," ordered the disco dancing female.

The other recruits looked on open mouthed, in disbelief, and could not work out in their heads what was happening. There was Mark Lucas, their Team Leader, laying on his front, and having a soothing massage from the disco dancing female, for the price of three tracks, on the jukebox.

"Blimey mate, you're stiff as a board!" exclaimed the disco dancing female, working her fingers into Mark Lucas's shoulders.

"Yes, and it's absolutely agony as well!" exclaimed Mark Lucas, in reply.

The disco dancing female worked her hands over the contours of Mark Lucas's shoulders, and tried as hard as she could to ease the pain that he was suffering, but she found his muscles were extremely tense and it was a tough job loosening up the solid mass of tissue and sinew.

"I think you need at least an hour of massaging, to be honest, just on your shoulders alone!" joked the disco dancing female.

"Whatever it takes, as I'm struggling to cope with the training, in my present condition," replied Mark Lucas.

"Well, I'm no expert, but I would like to say you're in need of a daily massage, to keep the flow of blood moving freely in your tight and taut muscles, as I'm sure that would help a lot," stated the disco dancing female.

"Are you offering?" asked Mark Lucas.

"It all depends," replied the disco dancing female.

"On what?" asked Mark Lucas.

"If I'm any good," replied the disco dancing female.

"Oh, you're very good, don't worry about that!" exclaimed Mark Lucas.

"Thank you!" shrieked the disco dancing female.

"You're welcome!" replied Mark Lucas.

The three tracks played, and suddenly there was a hush around the place.

"Do you want me to carry on?" asked the disco dancing female.

"Yes please, if you don't mind," replied Mark Lucas.

"Okay, but you know the conditions," stated the disco dancing female.

"Yes I do, and here's another fifty pence, for the jukebox," replied Mark Lucas, handing over the silver coin.

The disco dancing female stopped what she was doing, and strolled across the dancefloor with the fifty pence piece, and placed it into the slot of the jukebox. She selected three more tracks to play, "Don't Go Breaking My Heart," by Elton John and Kiki Dee, "Mississippi," by Pussycat and "Can't Get By Without You," by Real Thing, before returning to the prone RAF recruit Team Leader Mark Lucas, laid up on the three chairs, waiting for the next stage of his massage. The other nine airmen watched the disco dancing female, as she continued to work her fingers into the muscles of Mark Lucas's back, all along the spine, and down to his buttocks, where she stopped and then continued to work her hands up along the tense shoulder blades, across, and up and down, until the three tracks had finished playing.

"How's that?" asked the disco dancing female.

"That's a lot better, thank you," replied Mark Lucas.

"Do you want me to carry on?" asked the disco dancing female, with pleading eyes.

"No, I don't think so, I'm fine now," replied Mark Lucas, swinging his legs off the chairs, and standing up on his feet.

"Okay, well if you need another massage tomorrow night, give me a shout, you know what the conditions are," stated the disco dancing female, with a wink.

"Yes, I shall, cheers," replied Mark Lucas, taking a gulp of his drink.

"Is there anybody else in need of a massage?" asked the disco dancing female, looking around at the faces of the other nine recruits that were sat in a row, looking petrified and unable to speak. They all shook their heads in a negative response, and the disco dancing female shrugged her shoulders, before disappearing into the night.

The recruits ordered more drinks, and joked and laughed their way throughout the rest of the evening about Mark Lucas and the disco dancing female. The pair were the brunt of the jokes and Mickey taking all night long, and Mark Lucas took the banter in his stride, all with a pinch of salt. The recruits returned to the billet just before the lights were put out at 11 pm, and were full of exuberance, high spirits and good heart, but as soon as they crashed on their beds, they were out for the count and fast asleep in seconds.

Next morning, when the reveille sounded, with its normal earth shattering din at 5.45 am, the recruits gradually stirred themselves into action. Clem was an early riser again and he galloped to the ablutions for a wash and shave, and dressed quickly, before making his bedpack and displaying the usual bits and pieces of kit, for the morning inspection. He glanced across at the bed that was next in line to his bed, a few feet away, and he saw that it was empty. It looked like it had not been slept in all night.

"Has anybody seen Stephen Gabriel, his bed is empty?" called Clem.

Mark Lucas stepped forward to take a look.

"He's either gone home, or he's spent the night with the disco dancing female!" exclaimed Mark Lucas, facetiously.

"I didn't see him return last night, so you're probably right," replied David Ephraim with tongue in cheek.

"Lucky beggar!" exclaimed Clem Harrison.

"Lucky beggar?" asked Joseph Job.

"Yes, she's fit as a butcher's dog!" replied Clem Harrison.

"Have you got the hots for her?" asked Joseph Job.

"She's alright, I wouldn't say no," replied Clem Harrison.

"Hey Mark, you've got a rival here, Clem Harrison fancies your bird!" exclaimed Joseph Job.

"She's not my bird, she's my nurse, so he's welcome to her!" replied Mark Lucas, with tongue in cheek.

"Ha! There we go, she's all yours, fill you boots Clem! But make sure you've got a hefty supply of fifty pence coins at your disposal!" quipped Joseph Job, facetiously.

The other recruits nearby roared with laughter at that remark, before attending to their priorities, and they prepared for the morning inspection. The bedpacks were made, the kits were laid out, and everyone headed to the Airmen's Mess for breakfast, together.

After breakfast, the recruits returned to the billet and waited for Sergeant Winner and Corporal Cherry to arrive. As soon as they appeared at the door, Mark Lucas approached them with his revelation.

"We appear to have lost a recruit, sergeant," stated Mark Lucas.

"What do you mean?" replied Sergeant Winner.

"I don't think Stephen Gabriel returned to the billet last night, and his bed was empty this morning," explained Mark Lucas.

"Okay, we shall look into that with the admin team at HQ, thank you for the information," replied Sergeant Winner, in an unflappable manner.

Mark Lucas returned to his place, and waited for the inspection to begin.

"Listen in Flight, we appear to be one down on yesterday, as AC Gabriel appears to have gone AWOL. Now if you're thinking of leaving the RAF, please let either me or Corporal Cherry know, beforehand. Just don't do a runner and go missing. We need to know where you are. Is that understood?" asked Sergeant Winner.

"Yes sergeant!" replied the recruits, in unison.

"Okay, now we have the love letters from your wives, girlfriends, mums, grannies and aunties to hand out, so keep you ears pinned back for your name, when I shout it!" called Corporal Cherry, looking at the names on the batch of envelopes, that he was holding in his hand.

The recruits waited with baited breath, and were just as excited now, as they were on Christmas Day, ten years ago.

"Mark Lucas, Joseph Job, David Ephraim, Clem Harrison," shouted Corporal Cherry, handing over the purfumed letters to the four airmen.

Clem looked amazed at receiving a letter, and clutched hold of it in a mystified manner, as he hadn't expected anything at all. He returned to his place and opened the envelope quickly to find out who it was from, and was pleasantly surprised to discover it was from his new girlfriend, Ellie. He keenly read the words, which consisted of two pages, and was taken aback with the content, and it read as follows;

"Dear Clem, I hope the RAF are taking care of you, and treating you well. It's been so long since I've seen you, I can't wait until we catch up, and I find out what you have been doing. Unfortunately, I haven't been well lately. My mum says I'm falling to bits, but I just think it's being away from you. Sorry I sound so slushy, but I have to be honest. I know we've only known each other a few weeks, but it seems like a lifetime to me, and this believe it or not, is the first time I've ever wrote a letter to a boy in the RAF. I haven't even had a pen friend in a different country! Anyway it's good to get things of my chest, according to my mum, so I hope you don't mind me babbling. I hope you write back to me, and that I haven't scared you off, God bless, and the best of luck, love Ellie xxxxx."

It touched Clem in the heart, and he felt loved. He liked Ellie and thought she was an attractive and beautiful girl, but he didn't know if the long distance relationship had the legs to last, as him being away from home was placing a huge burden on their romance, but nevertheless he was keen to write back to her, and was even keener to see her on his first weekend of leave. It was very exciting, and he was ready to "play it by ear."

"Johns Rufus, Daniel Thomas and last but not least, Timothy Moses, and that concludes the mail for today. We shall have some more for you lot, if you're lucky, tomorrow!" exclaimed Corporal Cherry, with tongue in cheek.

"Now, for the inspection," stated Sergeant Winner, mooching slowly around the billet and checking for dust on the light switches, dirt on the window sills and muck on the skirting boards. But thankfully for the recruits, the place was spotless, and not a piece of grime was found anywhere. The inspection of the bedpacks followed straight after, and Sergeant Winner was up to his old tricks once more. "Rubbish, do this again!" yelled Sergeant Winner, at Mark Lucas' bedpack, and sending it airborne.

"Atrocious!" exclaimed Corporal Cherry, at Timothy Moses' bedpack, and he threw it down the centre aisle of the billet.

"Terrible!" bawled Sergeant Winner at Joseph Job's bedpack, and he threw it through an open window.

"Not bad, but could do better!" shouted Corporal Cherry at Clem Harrison's bedpack, and it escaped being roughed up and ragged all over the billet room, much to Clem's relief.

"Fifty fifty!" bellowed Sergeant Winner, at David Ephraim's bedpack.

"Borderline!" called Corporal Cherry, at Jacob Adams bedpack.

"Getting there!" shouted Sergeant Winner, at John Rufus's bedpack.

"Better than the rest!" yelled Corporal Cherry, at Daniel Thomas's bedpack.

"Best of a bad bunch!" yelled Sergeant Winner, at Joshua Peters bedpack.

The recruits stood waiting for the next inspection, which was for the boots, belts, caps, number one shoes and uniforms, and they all held their breath in despair. After the episode with the bedpacks, they were waiting for more items being thrown around the billet, and out of the window.

"Not bad," stated Sergeant Winner, as he approached Mark Lucas's display of his uniform.

"Passable," grunted Corporal Cherry, at Joseph Job's set of uniform items, laying on his bed.

"Needs more elbow grease!" ordered Sergeant Winner, at David Ephraim's display.

"Rubbish!" called Corporal Cherry, at Timothy Moses display.

"Must do better!" exclaimed Sergeant Winner, addressing Clem Harrison's display.

"Get this out of my sight!" shouted Corporal Cherry, at Jacob Adams display of uniform pieces.

"Atrocious!" shouted Sergeant Winner at John Rufus,' and slinging the display over his shoulder, into a pile on the floor.

"As good as any in here!" yelled Corporal Cherry cryptically, at Daniel Thomas's display, but the items remained intact.

"Chronic!" bawled Sergeant Winner at Joshua Peters display, and the uniform was lobbed through the open window.

"Now, those that have either of their displays intact, wait through there, in the lobby, but those that have to collect theirs from the floor, or from outside, wait in here," ordered Corporal Cherry.

Chapter 13

The recruits that were in the clear quickly moved from the billet room to the lobby outside, and only five recruits remained, that consisted of Mark Lucas, Joseph Job, Timothy Moses, John Rufus and Joshua Peters, who nervously waited for their fate to be decided. It was the first time this had happened, as the drill sergeant and corporal usually let it go, but this morning was different. They were pulling up the recruits for poor discipline and cleanliness, in the inspections of bedpacks and uniforms.

"Now, between you and me. I know, and I know, that you all know, we shouldn't be here now, talking about inspections, and bedpacks, and uniforms. You're not newbies anymore. You've been here a few days, and you've been part of ample inspections, but today what I've witnessed in here from you five, is sheer negligence, laziness, call it what you like, but it's not sitting well with either me, or Corporal Cherry. We have noticed a distinct pattern is forming, and I don't know if its complacency, or a couldn't care less attitude, but it needs to stop, and it needs to stop now, from today, and not happen again. I'm very disappointed to see my Team Leader and Assistant Team Leader in this room, being told off for poor results in an inspection, as I thought you two recruits were the men for the job, to bring on the others, and lead by example. It's sad to see that you two are among the laziest and dirtiest recruits in the Flight. It's shocking to be honest, and I expected more from you. So now, what I want you all to do, is have a good think and ask yourselves whether you are cut out for this type of career, or whether you're more suited to Civvy Street. It's up to you to decide what you want to do with your lives!" exclaimed Sergeant Winner, with a scowl on his face.

The recruits were not sure where Sergeant Winner was coming from, because as far as they were concerned they had done exactly the same as the four that were in the clear, but they did not complain. They bit hard on their lip, stayed composed, in the face of adversity, and each of them inwardly vowed to keep their noses clean in the future.

"Flight dismiss, and remember to take on board what I have just said, I don't want to see any repeat of this, and I'm warning you now, if any of you are pulled up again, you shall be back-flighted one week. Is that clear?" asked Sergeant Winner.

"Yes sergeant!" replied the recruits together, in unison.

The five scolded recruits gathered with the other four recruits, to make up a nine strong group, that was now minus one, after Stephen Gabriel had elected to go AWOL.

"Okay, listen in Flight! Now we know where we stand, with the inspections in the morning, it's with great pleasure to announce that the RAF recruit Guard Duty Roster is coming into force, starting at six o'clock, until ten o'clock, tonight and tomorrow night, and you shall be working in tandem with a colleague. There will be two guard duty roles that you shall be covering, which are as follows; Two hours as a static gate guard, and two hours on mobile surveillance, before swapping roles. With four recruits deployed tonight, and five tomorrow. On duty tonight are Mark Lucas and Joshua Peters, working in a pair, with Joseph Job and Daniel Thomas working together. Tomorrow, it's Timothy Moses working with Clem Harrison, and David Ephraim working alongside Jacob Adams and John Rufus. Are there any questions?" asked Sergeant Winner.

There was no reply from the recruits. They looked stunned at the news and didn't know how to digest it. Guard duty? What did it entail? The recruits were baffled, but they decided to remain quiet and not open their mouths just yet, and they took their time, to think things through.

"Fine, no questions. That will do for me. So, now it's time for a spot of gymnasium work, which will help build up your muscles for the guard duty later on!" quipped Sergeant Winner, with tongue in cheek.

The recruits moved outside and marched as a unit in good time, and in fine shape, as they put the thought of the night guard duties clean out of their heads.

"Quick march, left, right, left, right, keep in time, keep it straight," shouted Sergeant Winner.

The recruits continued to show great shape in their marching, and did not concertina once. They arrived at the Sports Hall a few minutes later and headed to the changing rooms, to prepare for the circuit training session.

"I shall leave you in the capable hands of Corporal Abraham, who I'm sure will put you through your paces, in extremely testing circumstances, so no slacking, and no skiving!" exclaimed Sergeant Winner.

"Yes sergeant!" replied the recruits together, in unison.

The recruits changed into their light blue tee shirts, navy blue shorts and black plimsolls, and looked like they were up for a good workout, after the news about the guard duty, and especially for the five that were given the short, sharp, shrift treatment by Sergeant Winner, about the inspections. They were ready to put that to the sword, and work their socks off, as if their lives depended on it.

"Are you ready to participate this morning, recruits?" shouted Corporal Abraham, clapping his hands together quickly, in a display of eagerness.

"Yes corporal!" yelled the recruits in reply, with determination etched on their faces, and anticipation ringing in their tones.

"Good, it's all about your tenacity and willpower today, as you are all about to undergo an endurance test, to find out what your strengths are. Firstly, you shall climb the ropes, followed by a series of press-ups, then you shall move into a number of squat thrusts, before scaling the wall on the climbing frame, and then you shall attempt to clear the horse, before taking on a series of criss-cross beams, before going around for a second time, and this is designed to find the fastest recruit in the Flight, as you are all starting together. So compose yourselves please, before we begin the race of endurance!" bellowed Corporal Abraham.

The RAF Physical Training instructor counted the numbers, and came to eight airmen.

"Just a minute, before you get going, I thought this Flight consisted of ten airmen?" stated Corporal Abraham, with a frown.

"It did yesterday, but we lost one this morning, Stephen Gabriel, as he did a runner, so it's nine now, corporal!" replied the Team Leader, Mark Lucas.

"But, there's only eight of you here," stated Corporal Abraham, scratching his head in bewilderment.

"Eight?" asked Mark Lucas.

"Yes, let me do a roll call, and see who is present and who is not," ordered Corporal Abraham, glancing down at a sheet of paper in front of him, that he had taken out of his briefcase, with the names of all the airmen written down in alphabetical order.

"Listen carefully, and shout, when I call out your name," ordered Corporal Abraham, as he cleared his throat..........
"Jacob Adams?"

"Yes corporal!" replied Jacob Adams.

"David Ephraim?" called Corporal Abraham.

"Yes corporal!" bellowed David Ephraim.

"Stephen Gabriel?" asked Corporal Abraham.

There was no reply.

"Stephen Gabriel is not here, as he has left us," replied Mark Lucas.

"Clem Harrison?" shouted Corporal Abraham.

"Yes corporal!" yelled Clem Harrison.

"Joseph Job?" called Corporal Abraham.

"Yes corporal!" replied Joseph Job.

"Mark Lucas?" bellowed Corporal Abraham.

"Yes corporal!" exclaimed Mark Lucas.

"Timothy Moses?" asked Corporal Abraham.

"Yes corporal," shouted Timothy Moses.

"Joshua Peters?" yelled Corporal Abraham.

"Yes corporal!" replied Joshua Peters.

"John Rufus?" called Corporal Abraham.

There was no reply.

"John Rufus?" asked Corporal Abraham for a second time.

Again there was no reply.

"He's not here corporal!" bellowed Mark Lucas.

"Daniel Thomas?" shouted Corporal Abraham.

"Yes corporal!" replied Daniel Thomas.

"Thank you for that information, so it appears that both Stephen Gabriel and John Rufus are not here," stated Corporal Abraham, scratching his head with bewilderment.

"Yes corporal, that is correct. Like I said earlier, we knew about Stephen Gabriel, from first thing this morning, and reported it to Sergeant Winner. But the disappearance of John Rufus is a mystery, as he was present at the inspection, although he was pulled up for a discrepancy on something or other, but I'm not sure how bad he took it," explained the Team Leader, Mark Lucas.

"That's fine, I shall report his absence to Sergeant Winner, when he reports back here to pick you lot up. Now without any further ado, you shall now compete as a eight team group, instead of a ten team collective, which will make the competition keener, and create more space for you to work in. So, if you are ready, get steady, go!" bellowed Corporal Abraham.

The recruits were off like a shot, racing against the clock, and against each other, and they sped forward like men on a mission, as nobody wanted to finish last. There was no clear leader, as the recruits climbed the ropes together, and it was neck and neck for all eight airmen. Some of those that had struggled before on this, were doing a great job, and when they reached the top, it was difficult to see who was ahead in the race. The next discipline was press-ups, and the airmen were carrying out this task perfectly.

"I would like ten press-ups please!" called out Corporal Abraham, as he watched the recruits begin the second discipline.

The recruits duly obliged with ten press-ups apiece, and David Ephraim finished this discipline in first, followed by Mark Lucas, and Joseph Job.

The others were not that far behind, as they broke from their positions, to begin a series of squat thrusts, which brought those that were trailing, to the forefront of the race.

"I'd like twenty squat thrusts please!" shouted Corporal Abraham.

The recruits once again duly obliged, and Timothy Moses was an expert at this discipline, and he moved ahead in the race from last position, and was striving forward to the wall frame, in a matter of a few seconds. It was an incredible performance from Timothy Moses, as he got stuck in to the tasks set before him. He was followed by Jacob Adams, who excelled at the squat thrusts, and he overtook the early leader David Ephraim, and was also closing in on the current leader Timothy Moses. It was a close run competition between two fine athletes, who knew what it meant to work hard. Daniel Thomas was breathing down the neck of Mark Lucas, and these five recruits were beginning to break away from the other airmen, at this stage. There was no sign of Clem Harrison in the leading pack, at the moment. He seemed to be struggling with the wall frame, but as soon as he got his feet back on terra firma, he shifted into top gear and was over the horse in a matter of seconds, and jostling for first position. He appeared to have come from nowhere, and he was moving forward like an express train, over the criss-cross beams, as he commandeered his way into the lead, at the half way point. It was back to the ropes again, and Clem Harrison climbed as quickly and as efficiently as his body and brain would let him, although he was feeling the burns on his hands from the first encounter with the rope, as he had forgotten to let go, when he leapt from a large height on the first round, and his palms were still smarting and very sore, but he carried on regardless.

He breezed up the ropes at one hundred miles an hour, reached the top, and then endeavoured to make his way back down, which he remembered from earlier, was his Achilles heel. But he put it to the back of his mind, and dropped from a similar height as before, but this time remembered to let go of the rope, and hit the floor with a great thud. He picked himself up, and was pleased to see that he was still in the lead, as the others were struggling to make any real progress with the ropes. It was causing all sorts of problems on the second round. Whether the other recruits were struggling with rope burns, it remained to be seen, but Clem didn't fuss over that, he was grateful to be ahead. He completed his press-ups and squat thrusts, and hit the wall frame with a larger margin than anybody had secured during the whole race, but it was this discipline that slowed him down on the first round. He appeared jittery as he climbed the bars to the ceiling, and could sense the chasing pack were gaining on him, and he wasn't wrong. They were, in their droves, and he began to panic. But somehow, againts all odds, he kept his head, and reached the top, still in the lead. He slowly made his way back down towards the floor, and leapt from quite a height, to hit the deck, and rid himself of this awful discipline, as quickly as he could, picking himself up from the ground, with an expression of relief on his face. He approached the horse, and took care of this discipline, with aplomb and determination, and hit the cross beams, in first position, although he sensed the others were breathing down his neck. He kept a clear mind, concentrated on what he was doing and got his head down in a clinical fashion, to pip Mark Lucas for first place, and take the honours as the winner of the endurance race, with a strong sense of achievement, flowing through his body.

"Well done Clem Harrison, on that fine showing, coming in first past the post, that was excellent work, to maintain your nerve on the wall frame, and congrats to you Mark Lucas, for keeping going under pressure, and for not giving in, as you were up and down in that race, and you could easily have thrown in the towel, so fair play to you!" exclaimed Corporal Abraham.

Clem acknowledged the corporal with a nod of approval, and Mark Lucas did likewise, and they both collapsed in a heap on the ground, after such a gruelling endurance test. The others followed suit when they arrived back, and were all gasping for air, and catching their breath.

"Take five, and cool off for a while, I must admit it's pretty warm in here," stated Corporal Abraham.

The recruits headed for the refreshment corner, and each of them ordered an ice cold can of Coca-Cola, from the vending machine, to help quench their thirst.

"That was seriously wild out there today!" exclaimed Mark Lucas.

"It was worse than that, I can tell you, I thought my lungs were going to burst. I've never felt pain like that, in my entire life! It was like going through the ringer of my grandmother's washing machine!" piped up David Ephraim.

"Where did you finish?" asked Mark Lucas.

"I'm not sure, I lost count of how many were in front of me. Last, I think," replied David Ephraim.

"Oh dear," consoled Mark Lucas.

"Who won?" asked Joseph Job.

"Not me!" exclaimed Timothy Moses.

"Nor me, although I tried my best!" admitted Mark Lucas.

"It was Clem Harrison," stated David Ephraim.

"Well done Clem, you've played a blinder lately! And at this rate, you'll be taking over from me, as the Team Leader!" joked Mark Lucas, with tongue in cheek.

"Ha, possibly! But somehow, I don't think so!" replied Clem Harrison.

The recruits finished their drinks, and waited for Corporal Abraham to return. He was back within a few seconds.

"Alright, recruits? Have you all recovered from the endurance test?" asked Corporal Abraham.

"Yes corporal!" bellowed the airmen together, in unison, which felt like the one hundredth time they had repeated that particular phrase.

"Very good. We shall now continue with the physical training programme, with a gentle game of football. If there ever could be one, among you lot, as you are all very competitive, and the most competitive recruits I've ever had to train, for a long time. Which in my estimation, is a fine thing, and will place you in good stead, for the future years to come. So if you would like to pick players for your teams; Mark Lucas as the Team Leader; and Joseph Job as the Assistant Team Leader," stated Corporal Abraham, standing back with a football in his hands, and letting the two recruits select their nominated players.

"I shall select Clem Harrison first, I think," piped up Mark Lucas.

"And I shall pick David Ephraim," stated Joseph Job.

"I'll select Timothy Moses next," said Mark Lucas.

"Okay, come on Jacob Adams, join my team," stated Joseph Job.

"Joshua Peters, you're in my team," said Mark Lucas.

"And last, but not least, I hope, Daniel Thomas," stated Joseph Job.

"Okay, Joseph Job's team can kick off first, seeing that Mark Lucas picked the first player. So, may the best team win! Don't forget to play to the whistle. No answering back, and no foul play. I have a very low threshold in patience, and if I deem anyone to be going over the top, you will be sent off, understand? Now play smart!" exclaimed Corporal Abraham, as he tossed the ball towards Joseph Job.

The match kicked off through Joseph Job, when he played a pass to David Ephraim, and Mark Lucas was immediately storming in with a hefty challenge that knocked Ephraim for six. But he got up from the floor as if nothing had happened. The referee waved played on, but it looked like a foul to everybody else.

Joseph Job collected a pass from Jacob Adams and hit a low shot towards the goal, to try to catch the keeper Joshua Peters off guard, but he wasn't successful, as Peters was as sharp as a needle. He saved the shot well and immediately got his teammates away into the clear, with a quick low throw to Timothy Moses, who motored sharply down the wing, with the ball at his feet, and he was like a whippet after a rabbit. He slotted a delightful pass into the path of Clem Harrison, who cracked a first time shot at the target, with Daniel Thomas off balance in goal, and the ball rattled the cross bar, and bounced out again to safety. But Mark Lucas was quick off the mark however, and managed to follow up, to head in, and gave his side a 1-0 lead.

The game was open and flowing on the five-a-side pitch, inside the RAF Swinderby Sports Hall, and was being played at one hundred miles per hour, in these early stages.

Mark Lucas trapped the ball under his foot, following a pass from Clem Harrison, and no sooner had he got it under control, then his feet were whipped from under him by David Ephraim, in an act of revenge, and he landed on his back with a thud, and yet again the referee waved play on as he indicated that the player legally challenged for the ball, in a fair manner. Ephraim came away with the ball at his feet, and hit a low, hard shot from the halfway line towards the goal, with swerve, spin and pace, and it bobbled like a balloon in mid-air. Joshua Peters in the goal was mesmerised by the flight of the ball, and it hit the back of the net with venom, to make the score 1-1.

Another crunching tackle on Mark Lucas by David Ephraim, was this time deemed a foul by Corporal Abraham, and he awarded a free kick to be taken, which Clem Harrison volunteered to take. He sized up the distance and the angle, and decided to go for a shot at goal, as it wasn't too far away from the target, and he was pleased he did, as his effort was excellent, and found the back of the net, to put Mark Lucas's team 2-1 ahead. David Ephraim kicked off to re-start the match, and was clipped on the ankle by Mark Lucas, as he passed the ball to Joseph Job. He rolled around the ground in agony, but the referee didn't give a free kick. Job continued forward and dribbled past the whole defence, one by one, and slotted the ball past Joshua Peters for a terrific individual effort, and equalise, at 2-2.

The referee blew the whistle for half time, and the players swapped goals, before having five minutes rest, to regather their thoughts, before getting stuck in again to the battle royal. Mark Lucas kicked off to start the second half, and was shouldered in the face by David Ephraim, as he executed a pass, which was not seen by Corporal

Abraham. Play continued and Clem Harrison received the ball from Timothy Moses and played a one-two with Mark Lucas, before sending an hard accurate shot towards Daniel Thomas in the goal, and he didn't see it coming, but somehow he managed to block the ball with his chest, and it bounced off him and away to safety. It was more of a fluke than skill that he saved, as he had no idea where the ball was. The rebound was controlled by David Ephraim and he looked up to see if there was any danger of being fouled, but he didn't see any evidence ahead of him, until he was tripped up from behind by Mark Lucas, and sent crashing to the floor. The referee awarded a free kick for a blatant foul, and shook his finger at Mark Lucas as a warning to him. David Ephraim weighed up the free kick and placed the ball on the ground, before toe poking it past Joshua Peters, to put his side 3-2 up. The match became scrappy after this, as the players tired and made sloppy challenges, and the referee was the busier man among them. David Ephraim and Mark Lucas continued their feud, and niggled each other throughout the remainder of the second half, but it did not stop Clem Harrison from dribbling through the middle of the pitch and sending a low hard drive through the legs of Daniel Thomas, to level the scores once more, at 3-3. Following this goal, both sides went on the attack to search for a winner, and the two goalkeepers made fine saves to thwart their opponent, then the referee blew the whistle to indicate full time, a few minutes later.

Chapter 14

"Very well played gentlemen, and a thoroughly fair score to be honest! Now go and shower. That's your lot for physical training today. Sergeant Winner and Corporal Cherry will be with you shortly, so don't dilly-dally!" stated Corporal Abraham, in a firm, stern tone.
The recruits showered and changed and nothing much was said. David Ephraim and Mark Lucas stayed well apart from each other, as the other airmen expected a continuation of their footballing rivalry, in the locker room, but nothing materialised.
"That was fun!" exclaimed Mark Lucas towards Joseph Job, as the recruits waited outside for their drill instructors.
"It was the best physical training lesson I've ever been involved in, especially the four-a-side football match," agreed Joseph Job.
"That's what I meant, the football. It was fun," repeated Mark Lucas.
"Even though you spent the whole of it on the deck?" quizzed Clem Harrison piping up.
"Yes, it was just banter, that's all! It adds spice to the occasion!" joked Mark Lucas.
"I wonder if David Ephraim agrees with you?" asked Joseph Job.
"I'm sure he enjoyed the banter too!" exclaimed Mark Lucas.
"Maybe so," agreed Joseph Job.

"I bet you'll both be counting the bruises tomorrow, after your actions," stated Clem Harrison facetiously.

"That's okay, I can live with a few bruises. It's the stiff muscles I can't stand. But now I have a little masseuse to sort out that little problem, everything is rosy!" replied Mark Lucas, with tongue in cheek.

The recruits laughed in unison at that witty remark, and each of them recalled in their minds what happened the other night, when the disco dancing female provided a welcome massage for Mark Lucas, for the price of three songs on the jukebox.

Sergeant Winner and Corporal Cherry arrived at the RAF Swinderby Sports Hall, a few minutes later.

"Stand at ease recruits!" bellowed Sergeant Winner, in full voice.

"Did you enjoy yourselves, in the physical training session?" asked Corporal Cherry.

"Yes corporal!" replied the recruits, together in unison.

"Very good! Have you had a break?" asked Sergeant Winner.

"Yes sergeant!" replied the recruits, together again.

"Good! So, it's off to the parade square we go, with a detour to the armoury for the rifles. Then it's hard concentrated graft all the way, to perfect the art of "Presenting Arms!" Recruits! Quick march, left, right, left, right!" yelled Sergeant Winner, louder than ever.

The recruits marched off towards the Armoury. After they had picked up their rifles, they headed in great spirits, to the parade ground. The weather was cold and cloudy, with a hint of a slight breeze, but it was dry, which was the main thing. The lines were immaculate, with no sign of a concertina anywhere to be seen, which was satisfying to

Sergeant Winner and Corporal Cherry, as they looked on with keen, critical eyes.

"Recruits halt!" yelled Corporal Cherry, when they arrived at the parade square. "Present Arms!" he bellowed. The recruits threw their rifles up in the air, like they were the Coldstream Guards, and "Presented Arms" in a truly magnificent manner, that was close to perfection.

"Very good recruits, stand at ease!" shouted Corporal Cherry.

The recruits did as they were ordered, and stood at ease.

"That was excellent, especially as you have not practised for a while, so well done, keep it up, and no slacking!" bellowed Sergeant Winner.

"Yes sergeant!" replied the recruits together, in unison.

"Recruits, attention!" yelled Corporal Cherry. "Quick forward march, left, right, left, right, keep your lines straight and no concertina's!"

The recruits marched impeccably along the parade square, like true professionals, and their lines remained as straight as a die.

"Left wheel, forward march, left, right, left, right, keep that line straight!" bellowed Corporal Cherry, with a strict sternness in his tone.

The recruits marched with style, swagger and aplomb. They continued around another corner, and worked hard at keeping their lines straight, and their feet in step with one another.

"Recruits halt!" yelled Corporal Cherry. "Present Arms!" The eight airmen "Presented Arms" the best they could, and executed it well, although it was not as good as their first attempt.

"That was rubbish!" shouted Sergeant Winner, facetiously, with tongue in cheek. "What happened?"

The recruits could not reply, as they did not know what had occurred.

"Let's go over it again, and I want it to be better than the first two attempts, otherwise we will be here until midnight, until you *do* get it right!" yelled Sergeant Winner.

"Yes sergeant!" replied the recruits, in unison.

"Forward march, left, right, left, right! Keep those lines straight, and no sloppy slacking!" bellowed Corporal Cherry.

The recruits set off, and were determined to make up for the poor presentation of arms in their previous attempt, and they displayed a great depth of concentration, as each of the airmen knew they had a job to do, and work individually. But they also realised they had to work as a team too, and be synchronized in the way that they moved, both on the parade square, and also in the performance with the rifles, as they "Presented Arms." So it was a tall order for the airmen, as they prepared to tune in to each other's wavelength.

"Keep that excellent line, and maintain those perfect steps forward! That is outstanding! Left, right, left, right, left wheel!" yelled Corporal Cherry, with a loud bellowing voice, that echoed all around the parade square.

The recruits covered a full lap of the parade ground, and were thinking deeply about the next stage of their task, which was the "Presenting Arms," and they gathered their thoughts carefully, to work as a team, and waited for the order from Corporal Cherry.

"Recruits halt!" shouted Corporal Cherry. "Present Arms!"

The recruits "Presented Arms" in a stylish, cool and clinical manner, and were in sync with each other, as their rifles were thrown high into the air, and all around, like a toy, with great aplomb and competency, and they performed exceptionally well, under the weight of great pressure, that had been placed on their shoulders. And they all felt they had come through it with flying colours.

"That was better than your second attempt, but not as good as the first, so we need to try it again!" shouted Sergeant Winner, with a wry smile.

The recruits waited for their next instructions, and were ready to continue. They showed great tolerance and patience, in a very demanding and stressful situation, which would have had many other folk screaming and bawling in frustration. But these guys epitomized calmness, and professionalism, in the face of adversity, and they kept everything to themselves, to maintain strength in nerve and commitment, as they prepared to go again, and improve on their previous presentation of arms.

"Quick march, left, right, left, right! Keep those lines straight, and no concertina's, left, right, left, right!" bellowed Corporal Cherry.

The recruits maintained their excellent conduct, and confidently marched forward with increasing swagger and style. They marched around the parade square twice this time, before Corporal Cherry was ready to bring them to a stop.

"Recruits halt!" yelled Corporal Cherry. "Present Arms!" The recruits worked in unison, like they had been trained to do, and "Presented Arms" in a perfect display of control, synchronization and skill, to show Corporal Cherry and Sergeant Winner that they were not going to be beaten by fatigue and repetition.

"Very good recruits! Stand at ease, that was better than the first attempt and I think it has earnt you a well deserved break! Take five!" shouted Sergeant Winner, with a smile.

The recruits left their rifles on the ground, and made their way towards the refreshments in the vending machine, in a nearby hangar. It had been a tough session, but they had come through it without any hitches or embarrassments.

"Wow, Sergeant Winner was tough to please just then!" exclaimed Joseph Job.

"Yes he was, but you've got to remember that he's only doing his job. If we were crap, and we continued to be crap, he's going to look like a right lemon on our "Passing Out" parade, in a few weeks! Just think about that. He's only doing it to benefit us, and he'll get the glory, as the drill instructor, and look good in front of the guests and dignitaries, but so will we!" explained Mark Lucas.

"Yes, I get that, but he was awkward out there, just then! We know we aren't crap, after the first "Present Arms." But he made us do it three more times, which is cruel in my estimation!" stressed Joseph Job.

"No it's not! He only wanted to tweak out every ounce of commitment from us, to test our strength and resolve. That's what he's paid to do. If we crack under pressure, then we would not be very good as Royal Air Force personnel, when the going gets tough. This is all designed to test us in extreme circumstances," explained Mark Lucas.

"Blooming heck, are you a former drill instructor in a previous life or something?" quizzed Joseph Job, with tongue in cheek.

"No, I'm not! But I can see where both Corporal Cherry and Sergeant Winner are coming from. They are employed to make our six weeks recruit training as hard as possible, but in a good spirit, and to find out what type of people we really are, in both a physical and mental capacity. Then we can move forward healthily in our careers, if we make the grade. But we won't know what our strengths and weaknesses are, if we don't test them to the limits," explained the Team Leader Mark Lucas.

Joseph Job shook his head, and shrugged his shoulders in disagreement, and moved on from there. He didn't agree with Mark Lucas, but he thought that it was no use falling out over it. Joseph Job was, after all the Deputy Team Leader, and he didn't want to cause a rift with the actual Team Leader. The other recruits remained silent and continued to catch their breath, after a gruelling session, and they were thankful that the five minutes break was extended to fifteen minutes.

"Recruits, stand at attention!" shouted Corporal Cherry, on his return.

The recruits immediately jumped to attention at that order, and waited for their next instruction.

"We are now going to head to the Armoury, where you can hand in your rifles, and then it is on to the Education Centre, after that. So without any further ado, let's go! Forward march, left, right, left, right!" bellowed Corporal Cherry, at the top of his voice.

The recruits maintained a good shape, as they progressed along the road to the Armoury, where they handed back the rifles, and then they marched from the Armoury to the Education Centre.

"Recruits halt!" yelled Corporal Cherry, when they arrived at the front door of the Education Centre. "Stand at ease!"

The recruits relaxed and waited.

"Move in an orderly fashion inside the building! No talking and no running! Quick march, left, right, left right!" shouted Corporal Cherry.
The airmen entered through the door, and headed towards the classroom, that was through the first door on the left.

"Once again, I shall leave you in the capable hands of Flight Lieutenant Bray, who will take you through a few things regarding the Royal Air Force education. Behave in there, as we shall be monitoring your performances, and any poor conduct will be reported back to us, with immediate effect. Which could lead you to being back-flighted one week!" warned Corporal Cherry, with a booming voice.

"Yes corporal!" replied the recruits in unison, as they entered the classroom.
Corporal Cherry and Sergeant Winner let the airmen settle in the classroom, and they quickly departed from the Education Centre to catch up on some paperwork of their own.

"Hello airmen, and welcome back to the Education Centre," began Flight Lieutenant Bray. "I hope you're enjoying your time at RAF Swinderby. But more importantly I hope you've been swotting up on the Royal Air Force badges of rank, as I have a little exam for you to complete, to test your knowledge!" he added.
The recruits gulped with worry, as none of them could honestly say with their hand on their heart, that they had thought twice about what the Flight Lieutenant had taught them the other day, but none of them were going to admit it.

"Has everyone been swotting up on the badges of rank in the RAF?" asked Flight Lieutenant Bray.

"Yes we have sir!" lied the recruits, together in unison.

"Very good. I shall soon find out who is telling the truth," stated Flight Lieutenant Bray, as he handed out a Test Paper to each of the eight airmen. "Have we lost someone?" he asked with a puzzled expression.

"Yes sir, two recruits have packed it in," answered Mark Lucas.

"I thought it appeared a little lighter in numbers than before. Okay, these things happen, not to worry! A stiff upper lip and all that. Let's carry on regardless, chaps!" exclaimed Flight Lieutenant Bray.

The recruits looked at the Test Paper, and grimaced with worry at the pictures in front of them.

"Now, this test is in two parts. Part one is the Commissioned ranks, and part two is the Non-Commissioned Aircrew, Non Commissioned ranks and other ranks. It's a fairly straight forward test, to see how well you know the modern Royal Air Force, and who you need to salute on a daily basis, as you're going about your business, and who you don't need to salute, at the same time. So, under each of the badges of rank, place the title that you think is correct, and move on from there. The ranks are in order of importance, and there are no trick questions, or anything to trip you up. So don't worry! On that note, you can begin the test, and you have twenty minutes to complete the exam. So, off you go!" exclaimed Flight Lieutenant Bray.

Clem looked at the pictures closely, and racked his brain to fathom out what rank the first picture was, with two narrow dark blue lines sandwiching a narrow light blue line, and he wrote Pilot Officer. The second picture had a broader light blue line, with two broader dark blue lines than the first picture, and Clem wrote Flying Officer. The third picture was four dark blue lines sandwiching two light blue lines in similar width to the Flying Officer, and Clem wrote Flight Lieutenant. In fact the rank was the same as Flight Lieutenant Bray which gave it away. The next picture, was four broad dark blue lines, sandwiching two broad light blue lines, and one narrow light blue line, sandwiched by two narrow dark blue lines, and Clem wrote Squadron Leader underneath the picture. The next picture which Clem answered, was Wing Commander, with six broad dark blue lines sandwiching three broad light blue lines. After that, Clem worked out that it was the Group Captain, with eight broad dark blue lines sandwiching four broad light blue lines. But it was from here that he began to struggle, as he could not work out what rank came next. He tried to think back to the initial day of RAF Education and work out in his mind what two very broad dark blue lines sandwiching a narrower light blue line, and he wrote Air Commodore as the answer. Following this was a picture of two very wide dark blue lines, with a narrower light blue line sandwiched in the middle, and two narrower dark blue lines above it, with a narrow light blue line inside, and Clem wrote Air Vice-Marshall as the answer. The next one had two very thick dark blue lines sandwiching a narrower light blue line, and four narrow dark blue lines sandwiching two narrow light blue lines, and Clem wrote Air Marshall. The next one was similar to the Air Marshall, except it had six narrow dark blue lines, and three light blue lines sandwiched in between, above two very wide dark blue lines and a light blue line in the middle, and Clem decided to write Air Chief Marshall, and finally, the eleventh picture had eight narrow dark blue lines sandwiching four light blue lines, and two very wide dark blue lines sandwiching a wide light blue line, and Clem wrote

Marshall of the Royal Air Force. He gathered his thoughts together before attempting part 2, as his head began to ache.

After a minute, Clem thought he had better get started on the next part, before he ran out of time, and he looked at the following three pictures, but could not remember who they were. The first was of three chevrons with RAF wings above it, and Clem guessed at RAF Sergeant Aircrew, the second was three chevrons, with RAF wings and a crown, and Clem wrote RAF Flight Sergeant Aircrew, the third was a picure of a hat with RAF wings, and white decoration on it, with a coat of arms, but Clem left it blank. Following on, Clem wrote Leading Aircraftman for a picture of two propellers, Senior Aircraftman for a picture of three propellers, the next picture puzzled him, which was three propellers inside a circle, and he left it blank. The next one was a picture of four propellers in the shape of an X, and he wrote Junior Technician. The picture after that, was two chevrons, which Clem answered as Corporal, three chevrons followed that, which was answered as Sergeant. The next picture was three chevrons, with a picture of four propellers in the shape of an X above the chevrons, and Clem wrote Chief Technician, the next picture was three chevrons, with a crown above them, and Clem wrote Flight Sergeant, and finally, Clem wrote Warrant Officer, for the picture of a coat of arms, and he put down his pen, just as the twenty minutes was up.

"That's it guys, your twenty minutes has elapsed! Stop writing please, thank you very much," stated Flight Lieutenant Bray.

The recruits stopped writing immediately, and the Flight Lieutenant quickly gathered the papers in, and returned to his desk to mark them.

"Okay, take a break, as I go through your papers," instructed Flight Lieutenant Bray.

Chapter 15

They disappeared through the door, and headed to the vending machine, in the room opposite, and helped themselves to tea and bromide, with a chocolate bar. Clem chose a Kit Kat, and munched on it gratefully. He was famished, and thought that all this rigorous training was very hungry work, and he wished he could have a supply of Kit Kats in his locker, back at the billet.

"How did you all get on?" asked Mark Lucas, with tongue in cheek, as he didn't think he would get a positive response.

"Not bad, I reckon," replied Clem Harrison. "There was a couple I didn't know, but I left them blank, and carried on to the next one, so I guess it's just wait and see now," he added.

"I didn't have the foggiest idea of who was what, and what was who, so I guessed every single one. So if my luck is in, it's bingo! But if not, it's the dog house, and I'll probably be stripped of the Team Leader title," joked Mark Lucas, facetiously.

"I wished that I had guessed the two that I left blank, but I suppose it's too late now, never mind. But I've got to admit, I guessed most of the Commissioned Officers," stated Clem Harrison.

"I guessed most of them too!" piped up Joseph Job.

"And me!" shouted David Ephraim.

"I had no choice but to guess them, as I hadn't a clue. I'd only seen them once, and that was during the first lesson. So, I reckon I've failed drastically too!" exclaimed Timothy Moses.

"It seems like we're all in the same boat then!" concluded Mark Lucas, before Flight Lieutenant Bray appeared, with a bemused expression.

"Right guys, can you all return to the classroom, please," stated Flight Lieutenant Bray, sternly.

"Yes sir!" replied the recruits in unison, which seemed like the ten millionth time they had replied together to one RAF superior or other.

The recruits moved from the vending area immediately, and back into the classroom to await their fate, and they were steeling themselves for the worst.

"Okay, I have the results in front of me, and it is not often that I'm lost for words, but I've got to admit, I'm flabbergasted by the results today, and hardly able to speak!" stated Flight Lieutenant Bray, with honesty.

The recruits looked at the officer, with expressions of fear on their faces, and they all expected the worst. They had not swotted up like they said they had. They had purely pulled out a guess on just about every single Royal Air Force rank picture, so now was their time for punishment, and they all wondered what the Flight Lieutenant was going to do.

"In first place, is Clem Harrison, with twenty one correct answers from twenty three. In second position is Mark Lucas, with twenty from twenty three. In third is David Ephraim, with nineteen correct answers. In fourth place is Joseph Job, with eighteen. In fifth place is Joshua Peters, with seventeen correct from twenty three. In sixth place is Daniel Thomas, with sixteen correct answers. In seventh place is Timothy Moses, with fifteen correct from twenty three, and last but not least, is Jacob Adams, with fourteen from twenty three. That is excellent, from first to last, and is the best overall result I have ever had from a Flight, in all my time here, which must be close to ten years!" gasped Flight Lieutenant Bray.
The recruits were stunned into silence, and could not speak. Even Clem Harrison was unable to believe it, especially after what the airmen had said beforehand. Nobody among them had the foggiest idea of the rank badges yet. It was too early in their RAF careers to be able to reel off the rank of Commissioned and Non-Commissioned personnel instantly, especially under the constraints of an examination room. So their silence was deafening.
   "Is everbody okay?" asked Flight Lieutenant Bray, with a frown.
   "Yes sir, we're fine!" bellowed the recruits in unison, with gusto.
   "Good! As a special treat for doing so well in the test, and because I had planned to go over the work again for those that had struggled to answer correctly, but as you can see from the results, you have all reached the minimum pass mark, so there will be no need. Therefore, instead of swotting up, you shall be treated to a film, all about the

history of the Royal Air Force!" exclaimed Flight Lieutenant Bray.

"Whoop whoop!" called out the recruits in unison.
The Flight Lieutenant stepped back to switch out the lights, and rolled the film.

"There's only one drawback chaps! There's no popcorn, or ice cream unfortunately," joked Flight Lieutenant Bray, with tongue in cheek.

The film rolled and the recruits settled back to watch the movie, and for the first time in ages, they were able to relax and take it easy, but each of them were still wondering to themselves how they had managed to pull off such a daring result by mere guesswork. It had them in a quandary, but they didn't dwell on it too long, and enjoyed themselves for a change.

Clem felt his eyelids become heavy, and he was ready to drop off to sleep. That was what watching a film did for Clem. He could never stay awake and see the whole movie. But today he fought back the tiredness, and managed to stay awake throughout the whole forty five minutes. When the film ended, there were one or two airmen *that had managed* to capture forty winks, and catch up on their sleep, as they sat up to attention when the lights came back on, and their sleepy eyes gave them away.

"Alright airmen, did everybody enjoy that little treat? As it's not often that I get to run that film. The recruits are usually in need of extra tuition, but not today, with you lot. So, that's it for the time being. I should think Sergeant Winner and Corporal Cherry will be waiting for you outside, to progress to your next piece of training. So good luck, and once again well done for your efforts today, and keep up the hard work!" enthused Flight Lieutenant Bray, with a sincere smile. "Class dismiss!"

The recruits rose from their chairs, and made their way outside to meet up with their drill instructors, and as the Flight Lieutenant had stated, they were waiting for them in the chilly, blustery, breeze of a typical October morning.

"Welcome back to the hard work!" exclaimed Sergeant Winner. "I hope you all enjoyed your little rest from the exertions of recruit training, now the graft begins again. We are now heading to the rifle range for more practice shooting, so it's off to the Armoury to collect your rifles and cartridges, then let's get down to it again!"

The recruits marched to the Armoury to collect their rifles and were in fairly good shape with their lines, with not a concertina in sight, which pleased both Sergeant Winner and Corporal Cherry immensely.

"Left, right, left, right, keep your shape, and your lines straight, and no concertina's!" bellowed Sergeant Winner.

Those airmen that had just woken up from their slumbering in the classroom, a few minutes ago, were soon brought back to reality, with the booming voice of Sergeant Winner echoing around in their heads.

"We need impeccable standards now, you've been doing this for long enough to know, so keep up the momentum!" called Sergeant Winner.

The recruits improved their lines, and made them straighter, and they moved in time, keeping their arms in synch with each other, and their feet moved in rhythm, like clockwork. It was a joy to see. They arrived at the Armoury a few minutes later.

"Flight halt! Move inside the Armoury quickly and orderly, no running! You know the drill! Sign for your rifle and ammunition, and then move back out here, without any fuss!" shouted Sergeant Winner, louder than ever before.

The recruits did not dilly-dally about, and moved like lightning into the Armoury, collected a rifle and a cartridge of ammo, before returning to their place outside, ready to march forward.

"Has everybody been equipped with all the necessary gear?" shouted Sergeant Winner.

"Yes sergeant!" replied the recruits in unison.

"Very well, quick forward march, left, right, left, right, keep your shape and lines intact!" yelled Sergeant Winner.

The recruits marched on and headed towards the rifle range. Everything was fitting into place in their minds, regarding where each venue was situated.

The airmen arrived at the rifle range, and waited for the order from Sergeant Winner. This marching lark was becoming second nature to these recruits, and they were quickly tuning in to their responsibilities, as a diligent group of airmen, as the drill routine was becoming ingrained in their brains.

"Flight halt!" barked Sergeant Winner, loudly and clearly, which rang around the whole RAF station.

The recruits stopped immediately, and stood to attention.

"Stand at ease!" called Sergeant Winner.

The recruits relaxed, and waited to be dismissed onto the rifle range.

"Flight, move onto the rifle range, grab yourself an appropriate shooting position, and prepare yourselves to fire, with your ammunition cartridge connected to your rifle!" bawled Sergeant Winner, louder than ever before.

The recruits did as they were told, and took up a firing position, laying on their stomachs, with their rifles aimed at the targets in front of them.

"When I shout fire, take aim, and pepper the bullseye with as many bullets as you possibly can, and just like before, we shall be marking your score, and someone will be crowned with glory!" called Sergeant Winner.

The recruits waited patiently for the order to pull the trigger on their SLR rifles, and they were all cool, calm and collected.

"Recruits! Fire at random!" shouted Sergeant Winner, a few seconds later.

Clem was quickly on the trigger, and he got his eye into the game immediately, and covered the centre of the target with bullet after bullet, in a clinical piece of marksmanship. David Ephraim was also on the mark early, with an impressive set of bullet marks visible on his target, with Mark Lucas finding his way, slowly, but surely.

It was fast and furious, and the noise was deafening, as the eight airmen lay prone on the ground, like a bunch of snipers firing at will at a cardboard cut-out, with a picture of a marauding soldier in front of them. But each of the recruits were impressive in their attitude, and they all worked hard at making as many marks on the target, and firing clusters of bullets at the bullseye, and after only a few sessions on the range, these guys were all becoming pretty handy with the SLR. The firing continued, and bullet after bullet penetrated the wooden cut-outs, as the airmen tried their best to be the "Marksman of the Day." Eventually, after a few minutes, the shooting ceased, and there was silence once again, and it was absolutely bliss, and was so quiet, it was possible to hear a pin drop.

"Recruits, no more firing! Place your weapons to one side, and unload your cartridges!" shouted Corporal Cherry, as he made his way towards the score sheets, on the wooden soldier cut-outs. He collected the papers and raised his eyebrows at the amount of markings that were made in the key areas, in a manner to suggest that he was impressed with the accuracy of the recruits, with their rifles. It was a marked improvement on the last time they were here.

"Okay, I have the results, and I'm pleased to say, we have a new winner, with ninety seven per cent, and that person is Daniel Thomas. In second place is the usual name in the frame, and that is Clem Harrison, keeping his consistency going well, with ninety five per cent, and in third place is another new name on the claim for fame glory shout out, in the form of Jacob Adams, with ninety per cent. Well done to you guys, for making the top three today! Now, let's return these rifles and cartridges, and go for lunch!" barked Corporal Cherry loudly.

The recruits congratulated the airmen that made the top three, and Clem Harrison got a greater amount of pats on the back, as it was the third time he had made the glory shout out, and even though he did not win this time, he was pleased with his consistency, and realised he could not make a perfect one hundred per cent, every time.

"Okay recruits, I bet you're all starving hungry, after the morning you've had!" yelled Corporal Cherry.

"Yes corporal!" bellowed the recruits, in unison.

"Well, come on then, form a group, let's march you off to the Airmen's Mess, so you can feed your faces, in preparation for this afternoon!" yelled Corporal Cherry. "Left, right, left, right, forward march, and keep those lines straight, your feet in time, and no concertina's!"

The recruits were exhausted, and did not march as well as they could have done. They were bedraggled, untidy, out of time and a complete shambles.

"Come on Flight, your losing your shape! Keep those lines straight, left, right, left, right!" shouted Corporal Cherry.

The recruits checked to see where their weaknesses were, and quickly rectified them, and in a matter of a split second, they straightened themselves out, and were marching perfectly once more, which was a relief to Corporal Cherry, as he was becoming worried the recruits had lost their mojo.

The recruits arrived at the Airmen's Mess a few minutes later, and were ready to re-charge their batteries, with some nourishing food.

"Flight, halt! Stand at attention! And at ease! Okay recruits, enjoy your lunch, we shall see you back at the billet in one hour's time, Flight dismiss!" called Corporal Cherry.

The recruits darted quickly into the Airmen's Mess, and couldn't wait to load their plates with food. It had been the hardest morning they had ever witnessed at RAF Swinderby, and they all wondered how they had got through it, in one piece. Clem reckoned the days were getting tougher, but he was still enjoying it, and reckoned the training was helping him develop both mentally and physically. He continued with his positive mindset, strength of character and tenacity, and knew these ingredients would pull him through the hard times, during the recruit training. He was ready for anything, that was thrown at him.

"How is everyone feeling?" asked Mark Lucas, conducting his duties as the Team Leader, and addressing the recruits for feedback.

"In a word, knackered!" replied Joseph Job, the Assistant Team Leader, with honesty.

"Me too!" agreed David Ephraim.

"And me!" exclaimed Timothy Moses.

Clem stayed quiet, as he was feeling okay, and he didn't want to give the impression he was fed up. He let the mouthy ones speak, and get things off their chests.

"I didn't think the morning was going to end! It was one thing after another. Talk about packing the itinerary into one morning! It had everything, except the kitchen sink!" replied Mark Lucas.

"I think I even saw that pop up, once or twice!" joked David Ephraim.

"I wasn't expecting lunch today, I thought they'd forgotten all about it!" exclaimed Mark Lucas.

"Me too!" agreed Joseph Job.

"What's the time now?" asked Mark Lucas, who was too tired to look at his watch.

"One fifteen," replied David Ephraim.

"Yes, I thought as much. We've worked an extra hour and a quarter, than normal!" moaned Mark Lucas.

"I thought the morning seemed long!" piped up Clem Harrison.

"That's what I was saying, they've fitted in a whole six weeks training in one morning!" joked Mark Lucas.

"Never mind, there must be a reason for it! That's all I can suggest," replied Clem Harrison.

"Yes, they're trying to kill us off, one by one! We've already lost two by the wayside, and now they're trying to get rid of us all!" joked Mark Lucas.

"What about the bonuses they're supposed to receive, to get us all through the training?" quizzed Joseph Job, with tongue in cheek, pulling Mark Lucas's leg.

Mark Lucas blushed profusely in embarrassment, and didn't say another word on the matter, sending out a message to the other recruits, that his earlier statement about bonuses for the NCO drill instructors, was a fabricated piece of information, and designed to wind them up.

"I wonder what plans they have up their sleeves for this afternoon?" asked Joseph Job.

"Nothing much I hope, as it's guard duty tonight, when we experience the thrills of patrolling the station grounds and also become static guards," replied Mark Lucas, ending his brief silence.

"Yes, it is indeed! I was wondering about that, and it's going to hit us hard in the morning, if we are working late," stated Joseph Job.

"Oh, I don't know about that, it's only like cleaning the billet, except we shall be walking around in the dark, with walkie-talkie radio's, and being policemen for the night, stopping intruders," replied Mark Lucas facetiously.

"I reckon it'll be harder than cleaning the billet! We're outside in all weathers, with all sorts of dangers, and we'll be under duress, with all sorts of pressure to perform professionally!" stated Joseph Job.

"Oh, I'm sure it won't be as bad as that, and it's only for four hours, we'll be fine!" replied Mark Lucas confidently, trying hard to convince himself.

Chapter 16

The recruits finished their meals, and washed the food down with copious amounts of tea and bromide, and Clem reckoned the bromide was stronger than ever, in his tea. He didn't bat an eyelid, and finished off every last drop. He seemed to be getting used to the taste of the stuff, and was being programmed like a robot to accept the change to his palate. After lunch, Clem bought a newspaper from the NAAFI shop, and strolled back to the billet to rest up. His legs were aching and his feet were sore, but apart from that he was in fine fettle. He reached the sanctuary of the billet and stripped the bedpack down, before laying the sheets and blankets across the mattress, tucking them in, and then keenly jumped on the bed to take the weight off his tired feet.

"Looks like we'll have our work cut out tonight, cleaning the billet! We're four men down, six, if you count those that have quit!" exclaimed Timothy Moses, in the direction of Clem Harrison.

"Yes, that's true, but I tell you what, I'd rather be cleaning the billet, six men down, than patrolling the grounds. It's something I'm not looking forward to doing!" replied Clem.

"Why not, that's what being in the RAF is all about, defending your territory and not letting anything pass, that isn't allowed. You shall be doing this regularly once you leave here. They have rosters in all the camps, and the airmen and airwomen are deployed as duty guards, in turn. There's no getting away from it," replied Timothy Moses.

"Really?" asked Clem Harrison.

"Yes, I have friends in the regulars and they're always telling me about their adventures on guard duty, as it gives them a break from the mundane trades they've chosen.

Don't forget, a change is as good as a rest, so they say!" replied Timothy Moses.

"I've never thought of it like that before, but I suppose your right, work does become boring, when you're doing the same thing every day," agreed Clem.

"That's what my mates in the regulars say, the guard duty breaks the monotony and gives them something else to think about. It's not as bad as you think it is, especially if you're on night shift and you manage to get your head down in the Guardroom for a few hours, but it all depends on who the duty sergeant is. If he's a twat, you've no chance, but if he's a decent sergeant, then bingo, you've cracked it and you get a full day off next day, and if you've managed to get some kip, you won't need to sleep off the shift, and you'll have the day all to yourself!" exclaimed Timothy Moses.

"Sounds good, I'm beginning to warm to the idea of guard duty now, especially if it's part of the regular RAF service," enthused Clem.

"Yes, you'll realise that guard duty is designed to bring variety into your life, and who knows, if you really begin to enjoy it, you could re-muster to the RAF police, or even the MOD Police," replied Timothy Moses.

"Cool, but I think I'll take it one step at a time," stated Clem, with sensible reasoning in his tone.

"That's fine, but the opportunity is there for you if you get fed up of your chosen trade, I've known plenty of regulars that have re-mustered. It's very common, in fact once I settle down at my permanent station, I'm applying to re-muster as an RAF Policeman," revealed Timothy Moses.

"Good for you! What trade have you got now?" asked Clem.

"Steward," replied Timothy Moses.

"That's part of the catering team, isn't it?" asked Clem.

"Yes, it's similar to being a waiter in a restaurant, in Civvy Street," replied Timothy Moses.

"Wow, it's a big jump from being a waiter, to becoming a policeman! Do you think you can manage it?" asked Clem.

"I'll shall give it a really good go, but I don't want to spend six years as a steward, so I'll definitely be re-mustering to another trade regardless, and hopefully it will be the RAF Police," enthused Timothy Moses.

"Well, good luck with that!" exclaimed Clem.

"What about you, what's your trade?" asked Timothy Moses.

"Supply," replied Clem.

"That's another name for store basher, isn't it?" asked Timothy Moses.

"Yes, so they say," replied Clem.

"You know what to do if you get fed up of store bashing, re-muster for something else!" exclaimed Timothy Moses.

"Yes, thank you, I shall keep that in mind," replied Clem. A few seconds later, the billet was filled with the loud voice of Sergeant Winner, who had made an earlier than expected visit.

"Flight, stand by your beds! Attention!" yelled Sergeant Winner.

The recruits hopped off their mattresses, and stood at attention like they were ordered, and each of them wondered what was going on, as there was still fifteen minutes left of their lunch break.

"There's been a change of plan to the arrangements we made the other day, regarding guard duty," explained Sergeant Winner. "Instead of splitting into two groups, you shall all be working together as one unit, tonight!"

"Yes, sergeant!" replied the recruits, in unison.

"With that in mind, as you're being deployed as guards, you'll need to work together as a team to clean the billet, and prepare your uniforms for inspection tomorrow morning, and as you're on a four hour duty roster tonight from six until ten, I'm allowing you the time this afternoon to complete the cleaning, and preparation of kit," advised Sergeant Winner.

"Yes sergeant!" called the recruits, in reply together again.

"Very good, enjoy the rest of your lunch break, and begin cleaning the billet in ten minutes. Have tea at four o'clock, under the guidance of the Team Leaders, AC Lucas and AC Job, who will advise of any misdemeanours, and report back to me, and I shall see you all at the Guardroom at six o'clock tonight, to brief you of your guard duties," explained Sergeant Winner.

The recruits watched as Sergeant Winner swaggered out of the billet, with a brash and arrogant confidence.

"That's a turn up for the books!" exclaimed Mark Lucas, when the sergeant had disappeared.

"Yes, I was expecting drill this afternoon, then a quick tea, before darting to the Guardroom at six, totally exhausted, and not in the slightest bit interested in patrolling the station, for four hours!" replied Joseph Job.

"Me too!" stated Mark Lucas.

"Hang on a minute, if you two were deployed on guard duty tonight, who was in charge of the billet cleaning?" asked Clem Harrison.

"You were, if you like! But it doesn't matter now, as they've changed the plans!" replied Mark Lucas.

"That's fair enough, it was just a hypothetical question," stated Clem.

"Hypothetical, have you ate a dictionary for lunch?" joked Mark Lucas.

"Yes, something like that!" replied Clem Harrison.

The recruits relaxed for another ten minutes or so, before the madness started again, and everyone zipped around like a blue arsed fly. The eight surviving recruits tweaked the roster slightly, and compensated for the two that had left the ranks. But it didn't really matter, as everyone was mucking in and helping each other to clean up and make the place as gleaming as they possibly could, and the duty roster was thrown out of the window, like a few of the bedpacks and items of uniform had been, earlier in the week. There was little chatter among the airmen, as each had their own task to complete, and once they had finished it to their satisfaction, they were rolling forward on to the next task. Clem tried his hand at Kung Fu fighting, with the pipes of the toilet bowl U bend, and he came out on top, and successfully cleaned the whole of the row of toilet pans. He was then quickly on to the driving of the large floor polishers that needed a hefty push to move it forward and back, and Clem worked himself into a huge sweat with the effort he was displaying. It was all good, and he was getting through a colossal amount of work, and leaving most of the others standing, and it was a good job Clem was getting stuck in, as some of the recruits became lethargic, lazy and indifferent to the cleaning duties, and on the borderline to being idle, but it did not faze Clem, he had the appetite to cover three airmens tasks, without a bat of an eyelid. He had never shunned hard work in his life. Even when he was younger, Clem liked to get his hands dirty, and showed initiative, in everything he did.

"That's it lads, we're nearly there now, one last push!" yelled Mark Lucas enthusiastically.

Clem continued to work as hard as he had done all afternoon, and was not worried what the others doing. As long as he was getting job satisfaction from the work, that was all that mattered to him.

"There's no medals for cleaning, but the amount of hard graft Clem Harrison has put in today, he deserves the George Cross!" exclaimed Joseph Job, loudly to the whole group.

"Thanks, but it's all part of the job as an RAF recruit, isn't it?" replied Clem Harrison.

"Yes, but the amount of work you've carried out is above and beyond the call of duty as a recruit! You've done two mens work!" stated Joseph Job.

"I hadn't realised. I just got stuck in and went from pillar to post, like I normally do, and as we were two men down, I upped my game. It's no big deal," explained Clem Harrison.

"Yes it is! I shall report everything back to Sergeant Winner," replied Joseph Job.

Clem continued to work hard on the light switches and polished them until they were gleaming, and he worked until every last job was completed. He glanced at his watch and saw it was 4 pm, he couldn't believe how fast the time had passed. But he had enjoyed himself, and he climbed up on his bed and rested, until it was time for tea.

"Congrats lads, that's job done! We've one clean billet, again! Now, let's catch our breath before we go to the Airmen's Mess. I'm sure you're all ready for some scran, as I know, I am!" exclaimed Mark Lucas.

"Here here!" called the recruits in unison, and they followed Mark Lucas to the Airmen's Mess.

When Clem Harrison tucked in to his egg, chips and peas, he reckoned the food was tastier than normal. But that could have been one of two reasons. Either it was because Clem was so famished after such an active day, he was ready to eat anything that looked good, or, on the other hand, the RAF chef had upped his standards and had really pushed the boat out to feed the starving airmen, and had a guilty conscience over what he had dished out in the past.

"Lovely grub tonight!" bellowed Mark Lucas, chewing on a mouthful of egg.

"Yes, it's seems like the food is cooked in oil, rather than fat," replied Timothy Moses.

"How do you know that?" asked Mark Lucas.

"I'm an ex chef," replied Timothy Moses.

"Really?" asked Mark Lucas.

"Yes," confirmed Timothy Moses.

"Are you going into the catering trade in the RAF?" asked Mark Lucas.

"Yes," replied Timothy Moses.

"As a chef?" asked Mark Lucas.

"No, as a steward," replied Timothy Moses.

"A steward, isn't that below the rank of a chef?" asked Mark Lucas.

"It's on a parallel with chef," replied Timothy Moses. "What about you, what's your trade?"

"RAF Police," stated Mark Lucas.

"I'm hoping to re-muster to the RAF Police," replied Timothy Moses.

"Are you, really?" asked Mark Lucas, in surprise.

"Yes, why the shock expression?" quizzed Timothy Moses angrily.

"I'm sorry, you caught me on the hop," replied Mark Lucas, in embarrassment.

"Why?" asked Timothy Moses. "The RAF Police is not a closed shop, you know?" he added, with venom.

"True, I hope you can get in, but it's not easy," replied Mark Lucas.

"I know what you're thinking. Why should the RAF re-muster a steward as an RAF Policeman? Well, let me tell it to you straight, I'm going hell for leather to make this dream come true, because it is a dream, and after spending a couple of years as a chef in a hot kitchen, I knew that catering wasn't my trade, but I accepted the challenge of the RAF, and was offered a role as a steward, and advised by the corporal in the Recruiting Office to re-muster to the RAF Police, if I was serious on changing jobs, and that is what I intend to do, with or without stuck up snobs like you, that look down the noses at people like me, and think that stewards and chefs are the lowest of the low. I will tell you now, I shall re-apply to be re-mustered in to the RAF Police, and keep on re-applying until I am successful, as the RAF Police is the only trade for me," ranted Timothy Moses.

"Why didn't you join up as an RAF Police recruit, from the start?" asked Mark Lucas.

"Because the corporal in the Recruiting Office said there was no current vacancies in that trade," replied Timothy Moses.

"Okay, fair enough, I wish you all the best, and hope to see you wearing the RAF Police uniform, in the not too distant future!" stated Mark Lucas.

"Thank you, but I don't want to hear your sarcasm," replied Timothy Moses.

"Actually, it was intended as a goodwill compliment," stated Mark Lucas.

"Okay, fair enough, point taken," replied Timothy Moses.

"I've got to tell you, if you don't take that chip off your shoulder, you'll get nowhere in the RAF. Whether it's as a steward, or as an RAF policeman," stated Mark Lucas.

"And I need to warn you, if you don't lose your sarcastic attitude, and the belittling of folk, who are trying to make something out of their lives, your nose will be flattened quite a few times, and you may even be sporting a few black eyes too!" replied Timothy Moses, with an irate feeling in his tone.

Mark Lucas walked away from the table and didn't reply, but by the expression on his face, it showed how angry he felt, to that cutting comment. The recruits finished their food and Clem could have had another portion of everything. Even the tea tasted good, bromide or not. It was refreshing and revitalising. His thoughts were now focused on the guard duty that would be taking place in the next hour or so, and he reckoned the best thing was to rest up in the billet, on his bed and take the strain off his legs, in preparation for the unknown. When the recruits returned to the billet, Mark Lucas was waiting for them, with a piece of paper in his hand.

"Listen in lads, just to remind you of who you will be working with tonight, so we don't look like twats, in front of Sergeant Winner. David Ephraim is paired with Jacob Adams, Timothy Moses is partnering Clem Harrison, Joseph Job is working with Daniel Thomas, and last but not least, I shall be patrolling with Joshua Peters. Are there any questions?" asked Mark Lucas.

The room was silent, there were no questions, although Clem had a few in his head, and expected the others to have as well, but nobody said anything, as they did not want to look a fool in front of everybody. Clem reckoned his questions would be answered later on, when he was actually out on patrol, and he would work things out for himself, and if he couldn't, he had "The RAF Policeman to be," Timothy Moses to turn to, who would surely have the answer to anything he could not work out for himself. So, all was good.

"As far as I know, we are working with our designated partners for the duration of the evening, for continuity reasons, and to keep things as simple as possible, but I'm sure Sergeant Winner will explain that to us, in due course. Is anybody nervous, excited, or scared? Don't be frightened! You're only a walkie-talkie call away from assistance, and if you see anything that's suspicious, report it immediately, and things will be taken care of. We can't be too careful nowadays! If in doubt, get the RAF Police out, is my motto!" exclaimed Mark Lucas.

The recruits nodded in unison, but nothing was said among them. They all looked petrified about what the night had in store for them. Four hours of working in pitch black conditions, outside, with all sorts of possible scenario's ready to explode in their faces, and it was the mystery of the unknown that had got them all worried, and on tenterhooks.

"It's alright for you lot, you're only doing this tonight, I'll be doing it every night, when I get to trade training, and then to my permanent posting!" joked Mark Lucas facetiously, with tongue in cheek.

Nobody piped up with a cutting reply, not even Timothy Moses. Everybody was grim faced, and their thoughts were fixed on the guard duty ahead.

Chapter 17

"You're wrong," piped up Timothy Moses, after a few minutes silence.

"What do you mean, I'm wrong?" asked Mark Lucas.

"About the guard duty!" exclaimed Timothy Moses.

"What about it?" asked Mark Lucas.

"We'll continue with guard duty in trade training, regardless of our trade, and we shall also continue with guard duty at our permanent posting, as it's stipulated in the RAF contract. All airmen will conduct regular guard roster duty, whether they are RAF Policemen, Medics, Admin, Stewards, Chefs or Suppliers!" exclaimed Timothy Moses.

"Point taken, I was only trying to make you all feel better, but can I tell you something, Timothy Moses?" asked Mark Lucas.

"What?" replied Timothy Moses.

"You'll make a fine good copper, and that's not bullshit!" stated Mark Lucas.

"Thanks, that's my intention!" replied Timothy Moses, with half a smile.

The recruits waited nervously for 6 o'clock to come around, and it seemed like hours before the hand of the billet clock hit 6 pm.

"We'd better make a move to the Guardroom, and see what the evening has in store," suggested Mark Lucas. "It's pitch black outside, chilly and windy, but at least it's not raining," he added.

"True, that'll probably hit us when we're in the middle of nowhere, with no shelter!" piped up Joseph Job.

"Sod's Law, that's all it is! But hey, we're RAF recruits! We're expected to overcome everything that's thrown at us, even gale force ten storms!" joked Mark Lucas.

"That's true!" agreed Joseph Job.

The recruits left the sanctuary of the billet, and made their way quickly to the Guardroom in a casual manner. It seemed odd to them that they were actually walking at their own pace, rather than the marching in time, like they had been engaged in, over the last few days, and they arrived at the Guardroom, a few minutes later.

"Oi, where have you been, you're two minutes late!" snapped Sergeant Winner, pointing at the clock in the Guardroom office.

"Sorry sergeant, we were late finishing with the cleaning of the billet," replied Mark Lucas, lying through his back teeth.

"Yes, a likely story!" exclaimed Sergeant Winner. "Anyway, in future, if there are any more of these sessions with guard patrols, I would like you all present at six o'clock precisely! Do you understand?"

"Yes sergeant!" replied the recruits, together in unison.

"Good, I shall not stand for sloppiness, lateness, lethargy or indifference in this Flight. And two minutes is a long time! An intruder could have entered the base, and we could all now be under threat from a nuclear bomb! It only takes two minutes, which is exactly those two minutes you were missing for, so remember that in the future, whether here, or at Trade Training, or at your permanent base," expressed Sergeant Winner, with common sense.

"Yes sergeant!" replied the recruits, in unison.

"Very well. Now, we have eight recruits here on duty, four of you will be on static guard and four of you will be on patrol. I have decided to let you continue with your roles, for the duration of the four hours, rather than getting you back here and swapping over and faffing about. You will have plenty of opportunity in the future to experience both of the roles, patrolling and static, so tonight won't make much difference, but what it will do, is give you some idea of what to expect in a real life scenario. Static guarding is important, as it is a way of finding out what is coming inside the RAF station. And patrolling is equally crucial, as it's an opportunity of discovering if there is anybody in the RAF grounds that shouldn't be there, and keeping the security of the base in fine fettle," explained Sergeant Winner.

"Yes sergeant!" agreed the recruits together, in unison.

"So, the static guard roster list is; Mark Lucas, Joshua Peters, Joseph Job and Daniel Thomas, with Mark Lucas and Joseph Job designated as the team leaders, and the patrolling team will be; Timothy Moses, Clem Harrison, David Ephraim and Jacob Adams, with Timothy Moses and Clem Harrison being the team leaders. Are there any questions?" asked Sergeant Winner.

There were no questions from the recruits.

"Now, I shall go through with you the duties for each of the guard roles. For the static team, it's just simply standing at the gate, stopping all the vehicles, and asking for ID, and if you feel inclined, you have the power to search the vehicle, if you are suspicious about the driver. That's all there is to it. It's simple enough. But you must stop all vehicles, all pedestrians and all cyclists from entering the camp, to check their ID. And, as for the patrolling guys, you will be equipped with walkie-talkie radio's and torches and be roving the station, checking that the doors are locked, the windows are closed and that things in general are secure. It's imperative you check every door you come across and make sure it's locked. That includes the office buildings, hangers, the Armoury, shooting range, sports hall, gymnasium. All the places that are not open for business have to be fully secured, which means locked doors and sealed windows. If there is an issue, let the Guardroom know, with your walkie-talkie, and it will be dealt with immediately. Are there any questions?" asked Sergeant Winner.

"No sergeant!" replied the recruits, in unison.

"Another aspect of the patrolling team is, you have the power to stop people and ask for ID, and if there are any problems, get straight on to the Guardroom and they will deal with it accordingly. You have the back up of the RAF Police, that will be on duty, and they shall support you in all cases, so all I can say now is get on with it, good luck and do your best!" exclaimed Sergeant Winner, handing out the torches and walkie-talkie radio's to the patrolling guys.

The static guard recruits made their way to their posts, at the gate outside the Guardroom, and waited there for the traffic to arrive, and the patrolling guard recruits went on their way to check that the buildings were secure, and that there were no unsavoury characters roaming the grounds, with axes or machetes. It was nerve tingling for them all, as none of them had ever done anything like this before, but it was also exciting, and something out of the ordinary, which they knew would put them in good stead for their permanent posting, when they would be doing this regularly, and it made them appreciate the work that the RAF Police executed, on a daily basis.

"This is the life for me!" exclaimed Timothy Moses, towards Clem Harrison, as they left the sanctuary of the Guardroom, and hit the trail of the guard patrol for the very first time, leaving the warmth of the building, with its lights and safety in abundance, with people milling around, and an all round security, that seemed cosy and friendly.

"You must be mad!" replied Clem facetiously, with tongue in cheek.

"No, not mad, but free! This is exactly the job I need, to express my independence, where I can think on my feet, make my own decisions and act accordingly, in the face of danger! It's what I was born to do!" exclaimed Timothy Moses.

"What, walking around a pitch-black airfield, checking doors and windows and looking for mass murderers, in the still of the night, freezing your nuts off?" asked Clem, in disbelief.

"Yes, that's exactly what I mean. When you've been tied to a kitchen stove for two years, with the heat and the pressure, and the constant battering of your self esteem, from the people in charge, you'll know what I mean, when I say this job is heaven, compared to that. We have fresh air, space and the opportunity to make our own decisions, without being given the third degree, by a jumped up Maitre d', that has no scruples!" exclaimed Timothy Moses.

"Point taken, but I still think you're crazy!" joked Clem Harrison.

"I take it you haven't worked in a kitchen before?" replied Timothy Moses.

"I spent a day in the school canteen, as part of work experience in catering, when I was about fourteen," replied Clem.

"Did you enjoy it?" asked Timothy Moses.

"No, not really, it was hard work, very hot and tiring," replied Clem.

"See, that's exactly what I mean!" stressed Timothy Moses.

"I can see where you're coming from, but this job is dangerous, and I reckon you should be paid danger money," replied Clem Harrison.

"I haven't been accepted yet! I'm still a ten-a-penny steward, and think I will be for a few months yet. But one day, I will be doing this job, checking doors, patrolling on foot, or in a jeep, and it'll be my dream come true! Danger money or no danger money, it won't matter to me!" exclaimed Timothy Moses.

"Good for you, I shall still be a Supplier hopefully, and working my way up the ranks," replied Clem Harrison.

"Don't forget, if you ever get fed up of that trade, you can re-muster," stated Timothy Moses.

"Yes, I haven't forgotten," replied Clem Harrison.

The two recruits arrived at a large building, a few minutes later, and began to check that the doors and windows were locked and secured, and they found that they were okay. There were a row of doors along the block of the building, with no lighting on the path, and their torches helped them along the way, in a spooky manner. It was frightening walking in the dark, with the fear of the unknown, just around the corner, and although Timothy Moses was lapping it up, Clem Harrison had his doubts about it, and thought there were better jobs than this, Supplier for instance. Each door was checked with careful aplomb and they were all securely locked, which was satisfying for the two patrolmen, and the windows were secure and closed. The two airmen didn't recognise the building, and assumed it must have been the admin block, where the clerical work was processed. They realised they were right, when the sign above the front door stated its name; Admin Department.

"This place is fully secure," stated Timothy Moses, noting it down in a little black book.

"What are you doing?" asked Clem Harrison.

"Making a note of where we have been, and what we have discovered, so I can report it back to the sergeant," replied Timothy Moses.

"Wow, that's really very organised, why didn't I think of that?" exclaimed Clem Harrison.

"That's because you're a Supplier, and I'm re-mustering to be an RAF Policeman!" replied Timothy Moses, with tongue in cheek.

"Yes, I can't argue with that, point taken! Mark Lucas was right, you will make a brilliant copper!" barked Clem Harrison confidently.

"Come on then, we've a lot to do!" exclaimed Timothy Moses, putting his notebook back in his top pocket.

"Aye, aye captain!" replied Clem Harrison, facetiously.

They continued along a stretch of grassland that was not lit up, and it was difficult to walk on, and seemed to be up and down like a roller coaster, with small hills, and it made Clem lose his footing a few times. He really wasn't very good walking on uneven surfaces in the dark. He had no natural instincts to assist him, and he was beginning to freeze, as the cold wintry wind began to whip up, and blow keenly through the RAF station. Clem could think of a dozen things more appealing than this right now, and if given a chance would gladly swap places with a chef, or a steward, or even the guys on the gate, doing the static guarding. Anything was better than mobile patrolling, in the dark, on uneven ground, and with a force 10 gale blowing in every direction, thought Clem.

"Come on Clem, you're lagging behind, what's the matter with you?" yelled Timothy Moses, who seemed to have motored on ahead, and left Clem yards away.

"I'm freezing!" shouted Clem. "And suffering from hypothermia, I think!"

"Don't be ridiculous, it's not that bad!" replied Timothy Moses, who had stopped walking, and was now waiting for Clem to catch up.

"You walk too fast, as well, I can't keep up with you!" grunted Clem.

"Treat this like it's a game of football, or a session on the rifle range, or even the circuit training in the gymnasium," replied Timothy Moses, in a consoling manner.

"That's impossible, I can't do that! They're all done in the daylight, whilst we're outside in the cold and the dark, right now. It's like chalk and cheese!" exclaimed Clem.

"You've been doing so well too, and looking like RAF Police material, showing an interest, and getting stuck in. Don't forget you're a Team Leader, so you've got to set an example to the other members of the team," replied Timothy Moses.

"Sod that! I can't feel my feet, nor my fingers, and my teeth are chattering, it's like I'm at the North Pole. I need a hot cup of tea, so I can thaw out, as I'm not sure I can move any further," stated Clem, with an uncomfortable frown on his face.

"Okay, we can pop into the NAAFI for a quick cuppa, and you can get yourself warm. I'm fine, I can carry on, but as we're working together, I shall join you for a cup of tea," replied Timothy Moses.

"Thanks," sighed Clem, with a gasp of relief.

"You're welcome, RAF Police do have the best interests at heart for folk that aren't feeling well, and as we've been outside in the bitterly cold weather, it makes sense to catch some respite from the conditions," replied Timothy Moses, with sincerity.

"Are you feeling the cold too?" asked Clem, with intrigue.

"No, I'm fine," replied Timothy Moses.

"How come?" asked Clem.

"I'll give you a little tip on how to combat the freezing cold elements, I'm wearing thermals," advised Timothy Moses.

"Thermals?" asked Clem with a frown, and not understanding the reply.

"Yes, socks, Grandad shirt and Long Johns," explained Timothy Moses.

"No wonder you're not feeling the icy cold temperatures! That's cheating!" yelled Clem, in disbelief.

"No it's not, at all! It's foresight, and when you're on the airfield, in the middle of nowhere, that's the clothing you'll need, so tell your mother you'd like some thermals for Christmas!" exclaimed Timothy Moses.

"Don't worry, I shall, and for my birthday too, if that's what it takes to combat the cold weather!" replied Clem.

"Good man! It's just another learning curve in the development of an RAF recruit," stated Timothy Moses.

"Believe me, I've learnt a lot in the short time I've been here. It's been a series of short, sharp shocks, but I've taken it all on board, and it's put me in good stead for the future.

Now let's have a cup of tea and some time for me to thaw out, before we tread back into the wild!" exclaimed Clem.

The airmen spent a few minutes in the NAAFI, and Clem hugged on to his hot cup of tea, for dear life. He was slowly beginning to feel his toes and fingers again, and although he wasn't totally ready to brave the icy conditions outside, he showed keen enthusiasm, bit his lip, and put the thought of freezing to death to the back of his mind.

"Come on then, are you ready to venture back outside?" asked Timothy Moses, in a hopeful tone.

"Yes, I shall pretend it's five-a-side football, or the rifle range!" replied Clem, with tongue in cheek.

"That's the spirit! If you give it the same enthusiasm as those two disciplines, you won't go far wrong!" exclaimed Timothy Moses.

The airmen trundled back outside, and the weather had worsened. There was sleet and snow in the air, but it did not deter Timothy Moses from continuing, nor Clem Harrison, for that matter, as somehow he had found a second wind. They continued to check the windows and doors of the Armoury, rifle range, sports hall and the offices of an hangar, that was close-by, and found that everything was in pristine condition, with no security breaches, which was satisfactory for the two patrolmen.

"Nothing untoward here, so I shall just make a note of it in my book," stated Timothy Moses.

Just as Timothy Moses was writing out his account of the patrolled area, there was a commotion nearby, which was rowdy and getting out of control. Timothy looked at Clem, and they both tilted their ears in the direction of the squabble. They decided it needed investigating quickly, and they raced to where they thought the noise was coming from.

Chapter 18

When Clem and Timothy Moses arrived at the scene, they were confronted by a group of what appeared to be drunken airmen, as their hair was short and shaved, accompanied by a female, who was instantly recognisable.

"Is that the disco dancer from the NAAFI?" whispered Clem, towards Timothy Moses.

"Yes, I think it is," replied Timothy Moses.

Clem nodded, to acknowledge the fact.

"Oi, what's going on here, then?" called Timothy Moses, using his potential RAF Policeman's "voice of assertiveness."

"What's it got to do with you?" replied one of the drunken airmen, with disrespect flowing through his veins.

"It's got everything to do with me, as I'm on patrol duty, with the RAF Police, so please tell me what you are doing?" repeated Timothy Moses.

Clem stayed quiet, and watched and learned, and reckoned Timothy Moses was doing a fine job on his own, but he was there, in case he needed backup.

"Sod off with your pretending patrol games! It's not real, it's just playing, like you were at school!" exclaimed the drunken airman.

"Is everything okay madam?" asked Timothy Moses, in the direction of the disco dancing female.

"No, not really, these guys were jostling me, and making me feel uncomfortable," replied the disco dancing female, with fear in her tone.

"That's rubbish! It's the other way around!" yelled the drunken airman.

"Get on to the Guardroom, and request RAF Police assistance," requested Timothy Moses, in the direction of Clem Harrison.

Clem instantly called the Guardroom, with the use of his walkie-talkie.

"Hello, it's AC Clem Harrison, out on patrol, and I'm reporting a disturbance, and need RAF Police assistance," stated Clem, slowly and clearly.

"Where are you calling from?" asked the duty RAF sergeant.

"At the front of the NAAFI," replied Clem, glancing up at the building, and recognising it immediately.

"What's the problem?" asked the duty sergeant.

"There are a number of drunken airmen here that appear to be accosting a female civilian," explained Clem.

"Okay, I shall radio through for the RAF Police patrolmen to attend as soon as possible," stated the duty sergeant. "Over and out," he added.

"Over and out," replied Clem.

"Well, what's happening?" asked Timothy Moses, keeping an eye on the airmen.

"The RAF Police are on their way!" exclaimed Clem, in reply.

"Yeah, that's a likely story! Your walkie-talkie probably doesn't work, and you're making it all up!" ridiculed one of the drunken airmen.

"Let's find out, shall we?" asked Clem, confidently.
Within a few minutes, an RAF Police Landrover screeched around the corner, and pulled up to an instant stop, a few feet away, and two RAF Policemen jumped out of the vehicle, and made their way towards the group of people.

"What's going on here, then?" asked one of the RAF Police corporals.

"There's trouble between these guys, and this female, who has accused them of jostling her, and acting inappropriately," explained Timothy Moses. "And to be honest, we did hear a commotion going on," he added.

"Is this true?" asked one of the RAF Policemen, towards the female.

"Yes, it is," replied the disco dancing female, in a quiet, frightened voice.

"Did you see anything?" asked one of the RAF Policemen, in the direction of Clem Harrison and Timothy Moses.

"No, we couldn't see a thing, as it was too dark, but we did hear screaming and shouting," replied Timothy Moses, acting as the spokesman for the two rookie patrolmen.

"Okay, that's fine," replied one of the RAF Policemen.
The RAF Policemen established the names of the four drunken airmen as being; AC Harry Lee, AC Ben Smith, AC Jack Ford and his twin brother AC Tom Ford, who were all due to be "Passing Out" in the morning, and they also made a note of the female's name, as Miss Emily Sawyer.

"Right, we need to take you into custody, and interview you, as part of our investigation, and, madam, if you don't mind, we need an account of what happened in your own words, before we decide what action we shall take, if any. So, if you four guys can sit in the back of the Landrover, with my colleague, I shall accompany Miss Sawyer at the front, as I'm the driver, and make sure she is safe and well," stated the RAF Policeman, with authority.

"Okay corporal, thanks for your assistance, we'll carry on with our patrol, and it's good to be of service!" stated Timothy Moses.

"Yes, well done recruits, we shall make RAF Policemen of you yet!" exclaimed the RAF Policeman, in the driver's seat.

Timothy Moses and Clem Harrison nodded in acknowledgement, and watched as the Landrover drove off towards the Guardroom.

"Job done!" exclaimed Timothy Moses, towards Clem Harrison.

"Yes, and a good job, at that!" replied Clem Harrison.

"Come on then, let's continue with our patrol, and see if we can help more damsels in distress!" stated Timothy Moses facetiously.

"You never know what's around the corner," replied Clem Harrison.

The airmen continued on their way, and Clem came to the conclusion, that the episode with Emily Sawyer and the four drunken recruits, outside the NAAFI building had whetted his appetite for more action, as he realised that the patrol was not just about checking doors and windows were locked and secure, but also that people that lived and worked there, were kept safe. In fact, Clem started to enjoy the role as a patrolman, and could see that the life of an RAF copper would be thrilling and action packed everyday. And something new would be happening throughout the shift, which would break the monotony of the long hours.

"It's seems to have got warmer," stated Clem, as he checked the doors and windows of the Airmen's Mess.

"No, that'll be the adrenaline running through your veins, after the episode with the disco dancing female!" replied Timothy Moses.

"Oi! Her name is Emily Sawyer!" corrected Clem keenly.

"She'll always be the disco dancing female to me!" replied Timothy Moses.

"She's fit!" stated Clem.

"Yes, you've already made that clear, but she's well out of your league!" exclaimed Timothy Moses.

"What do you mean by league? She's not a football club!" joked Clem.

"You know what I mean, she's well out of your reach, and would be perfect for somebody like me!" stated Timothy Moses, facetiously.

"An RAF Policeman to be! What difference is that to a Supplier?" asked Clem.

"Prestige, reputation, skills and intelligence," replied Timothy Moses.

"That's exactly what you'll find in a Supplier, in the RAF! So, what's your point?" asked Clem.

"You'd make a good copper too!" exclaimed Timothy Moses.

"What's that got to do with it?" asked Clem Harrison.

"I'm just saying, you'd make a good RAF Policeman, in just general terms," replied Timothy Moses.

"No, I think I'll stay as a Supplier for now, although an RAF Policeman role is tempting, I shall leave that to you, so you can pull women like the disco dancing female," stated Clem, with tongue in cheek.

"Thank you, that's very kind," stated Timothy Moses.

"You're welcome, and good luck with it!" exclaimed Clem.

The airmen continued with their patrol, and found themselves out on the airfield, where the gas chamber was situated, and it brought back vivid memories to Clem of the time he had to walk in there, with live CS gas filling the room, and take off his respirator, and recite his name, rank and service number. It was one of the many exciting episodes of his time at RAF Swinderby, and he vowed never to forget that experience, for the rest of his life.

"The gas chamber's locked!" exclaimed Clem.

"Good, it can stay locked!" stated Timothy Moses, pulling a face like a bulldog chewing a wasp.

"Why's that?" asked Clem.

"I hate the place!" revealed Timothy Moses.

"Do you?" asked Clem.

"Yes! It provided the worse experience of my life!" exclaimed Timothy Moses.

"How come?" asked Clem, with empathy.

"I gulped a mouthful of CS Gas, and couldn't get my words out. It took me what seemed like an age to finish saying my name, rank and number, and I thought I was going to throw up in there, at one stage! Sergeant Winner had sympathy with me and let me go without me properly saying what I needed to say, clearly, and I didn't need asking twice, I was gone in a shot, and ran for my life!" exclaimed Timothy Moses dramatically.

"Sounds like you had a nightmare in there," replied Clem.

"You can say that again!" agreed Timothy Moses.

"What about your RAF Police duties in the future, won't you be working with CS Gas?" asked Clem.

"I'll be fine with the CS Gas in the open. It's just the gas chamber, I struggle with," replied Timothy Moses.

"Do you suffer from claustrophobia?" asked Clem.

"Yes, I do, a little," replied Timothy Moses, with honesty.

"Do the RAF know about it?" asked Clem.

"No, there's no need for them to know," replied Timothy Moses.

"Are you sure?" asked Clem.

"As far as I know, I can't recall being asked any questions about the condition, so I've kept it to myself," replied Timothy Moses.

"Fair enough," stated Clem.

"That's why I didn't join the RAF Fire Crew, as I couldn't be in an enclosed room, with flames engulfing everywhere. I would probably burn to death," revealed Timothy Moses.

"What about working in a kitchen, how did you manage to do that?" asked Clem.

"That's how it all started!" exclaimed Timothy Moses.

"Really, so is that why you joined the RAF as a steward?" asked Clem.

"Yes, I had to leave the kitchens, before I went out of my mind, as I had panic attack after panic attack, and couldn't cope," explained Timothy Moses.

"Did you inform the RAF of your panic attacks?" asked Clem.

"Are you kidding? No way! It's not something I'm proud of, and as soon as I stopped working in the kitchens, the panic attacks disappeared, except for the episode in the gas chamber!" exclaimed Timothy Moses.

"It sounds like you've got control of your life again. As long as you're not cooped up in a close environment, you should be okay. But let me tell you one thing, don't ever lock yourself up in a prison cell, by mistake, it might be the last thing you do!" joked Clem, with tongue in cheek.

"Don't worry about that, it's something I'm working on, in a postitive way, as I know I shall be locking up prisoners in a cell, sooner or later. But I will cross that bridge, when I get to it," replied Timothy Moses.

"Do you know what?" asked Clem.

"What?" replied Timothy Moses.

"I'd stick as a steward if I was you, as it seems so simple!" stated Clem.

"I might just do that, if I can't get my condition under control. It seems like the easier option," agreed Timothy Moses.

Clem nodded in acknowledgement, and the pair of them continued with the patrol. The bitter wind, that was biting cold earlier, had died down, and it was surprisingly muggy, for an October evening. The sleet and snow had disappeared, and the conditions were almost perfect.

"That's the circuit completed, what shall we do now?" asked Clem.

"Go around again, it's only eight o'clock, so we have another two hours to kill," replied Timothy Moses.

"Is that all it is?" asked Clem, with a frown.

"Yes, so it should take another two hours to walk around again, unless we get a major incident, that takes up the rest of the shift," replied Timothy Moses.

"Is it time for another break for tea?" asked Clem.

"No, I'm afraid not, it's warmed up out here, so we've no excuse for stopping, if we get caught by the duty sergeant," replied Timothy Moses, forcefully.

"Okay, let's go round the block again, and save the world!" exclaimed Clem, with exaggeration in his tone.

"Yes, that's the spirit!" agreed Timothy Moses.

The two recruits continued from the very start again, and checked the same doors and windows, but although it seemed like a waste of time to Clem, it was in fact important to re-trace their steps, in case there was an intruder that had waited for the patrol to pass, and didn't expect them to come back round again and would be caught red handed, as he plundered the goods. It was scientific. But there were no changes to report, and everything remained the same. The RAF Police Landrover pulled up close by, a few minutes later and the driver wound down the window.

"How's it going?" shouted the RAF Policeman.

"Not bad, thanks," replied Timothy Moses, acting as the spokesman for the two recruits again.

"Good, so what you guys up to, now?" asked the RAF Policeman.

"Checking that the doors and windows are locked and secure, for the second time," replied Timothy Moses.

"Have you been round once already?" asked the RAF Policeman.

"Yes," replied Timothy Moses.

"Okay, that's fine, jump on board the Landrover, and I shall demonstrate the mobile patrol to you both," ordered the RAF Policeman.

"Wow, great!" exclaimed Clem Harrison and Timothy Moses in unison.

"Buckle up your seat belts, in case a low flying aircraft makes me carry out an emergency stop. We can never be too careful in the RAF!" exclaimed the RAF Policeman.

The two recruits sat in the front of the Landrover, which had a three seat facility, and they buckled up their seat belts, like they were advised.

"By the way, those four airmen pleaded guilty to being drunk and disorderly, and have been locked up for the night in the cells, to sober up, before their big day tomorrow, with the "Passing Out" parade, and the female was released without any charges made against her. It was a sensitive situation, as apparently the female was romantically linked with one of the guys, and another was trying it on with her, so jealousy ensued and things got heated. There was a scuffle between the two love rivals, with the female in question trying to get in between them, and keep the peace, but she got a belting, by accident," explained the RAF Policeman.

"That sounds like complicated stuff to me," replied Clem.

"Believe me, it goes on all the time. There's always love rivallry between the women and the men in an RAF station, miles from anywhere," stated the RAF Policeman.

"I'm not surprised, as some of the recruits don't drink enough tea!" exclaimed Clem.

"What's that got to do with it?" asked the RAF Policeman.

"The bromide they put in the tea, dulls the urges, apparently!" exclaimed Clem.

"Is that a fact? I didn't know that. You learn something new every day!"
replied the RAF Policeman.

"Or so they say, it's hard to believe, to be honest," stated Clem.

"I'll have a word with my colleagues, and see if they know anything about this bromide in the tea revelation," said the RAF Policeman.

"It could be a fallacy," replied Clem.

"Who knows?" stated the RAF Policeman.

The Landrover covered the perimeter of the RAF Swinderby station in next to no time, and everything was quiet and normal. There were a few drunk recruits, heading out of the NAAFI, staggering back to the billets to sleep off the drink, and it crossed Clem's mind why they lowered themselves to the demon drink. He had never been a big drinker, and aged just seventeen was not even old enough to drink, but he had often frequented pubs with his friends in Civvy Street, but knew when he had enough, and had only ever been drunk once, when he went on a night out with his older brother, aged sixteen, and tasted Newcastle Brown Ale, for the first, and last time, and experienced the curse of the "spinning room," when he got home. He vouched there and then, he would never drink Newcastle Brown Ale again, nor get drunk. And twelve months on, he had stuck by his word.

Chapter 19

The mobile patrol continued, but there was nothing to report, and after half an hour, the RAF Policeman dropped the two recruits off at the Guardroom.

"Continue on foot until ten o'clock, then call it a day," ordered the RAF Policeman, directly to the two airmen.

"Yes corporal!" replied the two recruits, in unison.

They continued to check the doors and windows, for a third time, and maintained a keen enthusiasm for what they were doing, and reported to the Guardroom at 10 o'clock, for a debriefing. Sergeant Winner was waiting for them in the Guardroom, along with the other recruits.

"How's it go?" asked Sergeant Winner.

"Fine, thanks sergeant," replied Timothy Moses, still acting as the spokesman for the pair.

"I heard that you intervened between some drunken airmen, and a woman, is this true?" asked Sergeant Winner.

"Yes sergeant, it is," replied Timothy Moses.

"Well done, this won't go unnoticed in your end of course report, and will follow you to your next posting, at trade training," stated Sergeant Winner.

"We were only doing our job, sergeant," replied Timothy Moses calmly.

"Yes, but you went the extra mile, and that is important in patrol work," explained Sergeant Winner.

"Okay, thanks sergeant," replied Timothy Moses and Clem, in unison.

"The drunks are locked up, and sobering nicely, and should be ready for their "Passing Out" parade in the morning, albeit with a raging hangover no doubt, but hey, that's life!" stated Sergeant Winner.

"Serves them right!" exclaimed Clem.

"That's a bit harsh, isn't it?" replied Sergeant Winner.

"Not really, they shouldn't be getting drunk the night before their "Passing Out" parade, surely. After six hard weeks of slog, they should be looking forward to the "Passing Out" parade, having an early night, and once it's all over and done with, then get drunk, afterwards, and not have to worry about anything, until their trade training begins, after a week's leave," explained Clem.

"Point taken, I agree," replied Sergeant Winner.

"It's common sense," stated Clem.

"But some people can't wait until after the event, they are impatient, and need to celebrate before it, sometimes," replied Sergeant Winner.

"That's stupid. They need some self control lessons, and learn to be patient! As it will save them from a night in the prison cells!" said Clem.

"Good point," agreed Sergeant Winner. "But it takes all sorts, to make the world," he added.

"Those that are due to "pass out," should be banned from going out into the NAAFI, and confined to the billet. That will put an end to their drunken behaviour, and possible assaults on each other, and love trysts between all and sundry, that leads to violence. I'm only suggesting it, as it may help the RAF Police, in the long run," replied Clem, helpfully.

"I shall pass your comments on to the powers that be," stated Sergeant Winner.

"No, it's okay, I don't want to be classed as a troublemaker," replied Clem.

"You won't be classed as that. You'll be regarded as an honourable RAF recruit, that has positive intentions, for a safer environment," commented Sergeant Winner, sincerely.

"I'm not so sure, I know what these guys are like, in the RAF, and if they think I've been snitching to the police, behind their back, they'll have my guts for garters!" exclaimed Clem.

"Think about it," replied Sergeant Winner.

Clem nodded and shrugged his shoulders, both at the same time. He wasn't sure what he was going to do, because he knew how tight knit the RAF rank and file were.

"Okay recruits, that's the shift over and done with, and your first experience with guard duty on the gate, and on patrol. Are there any questions?" asked Sergeant Winner.

The Guardroom went silent, and it was quiet enough to hear a pin drop.

"Alright, that's fair enough, enjoy what's left of the evening, and Corporal Cherry and myself shall see you at the billet, for inspection at a quarter to eight in the morning. Goodnight recruits!" exclaimed Sergeant Winner, and he disappeared out of the door.

Clem and the rest of the recruits trooped wearily back to the billet, and each and every one of them flopped on their beds, fully dressed, and fell asleep, totally exhausted, in next to no time. It had been that sort of day.

Next morning, the recruits awoke in a crumpled state of disarray, still fully dressed, and they ached, from head to foot. Clem felt his head and it ached like he had been on the beer all night, but it was the way he had been laying on his pillow. He looked at the clock on the wall, and could see in the twilight, that it was 5 am, and time to get up. He dragged himself off the bed, and tried to work out what had happened, last night.

"How are you feeling?" shouted Timothy Moses loudly, towards Clem Harrison, across the room, and startling the rest of the billet.

"Shut the hell up, with the shouting!" yelled Mark Lucas, putting the pillow over his head, and going back to sleep.

"Okay, okay, I'm sorry," replied Timothy Moses.

"I'm feeling as rough as a badger's arse!" answered Clem Harrison, just as loudly as Timothy Moses.

The reply brought a few smiles from the listening recruits, and helped to take a little roughness from their morning.

"Yes, me too! Except I feel as rough as two badgers arses," replied Timothy Moses.

"But how come we're all feeling as crap as this? What's wrong with us? We're supposed to be lean, mean fighting machines!" exclaimed Clem.

"The training is taking its toll on our bodies. Don't forget we haven't had a day off for ages. So eventually the body decides to go on strike for a bit, and when we do a treble shift of drill, billet cleaning, and then patrol and guard duty, enough is enough," replied Timothy Moses.

"I suppose so, but I can't see Sergeant Winner, nor Corporal Cherry accepting that as an excuse. They'll be expecting us to be fighting fit at a quarter to eight, and ready to take on the world!" stated Clem.

"And that's what we shall be doing," replied Timothy Moses waking up.

"Yes, let's shrug off the weariness and fight the day with all our might!" exclaimed Clem, as he grabbed his washing equipment, towel and razor and headed in the direction of the ablutions. He showered, shaved and refreshed himself, with a spray of his Brut anti-perspirant, all over his torso.

He managed to avoid cutting his face, as the last three morning's, he had been careless with the razor, and cut himself to shreds. But today, with his new found strength sought from within, after the treble shift yesterday, his mind was in tune with his body, and he was ready to give 100 per cent, at whatever was thrown at him, during the course of the day. After dressing into his RAF uniform, he slipped his shoes on, wiped them over with a greasy cloth and made his bedpack. This had come as a second nature to Clem now, and he reckoned he was that good at making bedpack's, he could do them blindfolded.

"Anyone struggling with their bedpack?" shouted Clem. But he didn't get any immediate reply. He noticed that Mark Lucas had pulled himself from the top of his bed, and although he was looking weary, he moved brightly, and quickly, to catch up with the others, after having an extra twenty minutes lie in. "Do you need any help, Mark?" asked Clem.

"No, I'm alright, but thanks for asking, it's much appreciated," replied Mark Lucas.

"How are you feeling?" asked Clem.

"Crap, and I wasn't helped by you and Timothy Moses, yelling across at each other, in the middle of the night!" snapped Mark Lucas, sharply.

"It wasn't the middle of the night! It was five o'clock," stated Clem, in defence.

"That's the middle of the night, to me!" replied Mark Lucas.

"Don't be ridiculous, it's time to get up for work," stated Clem.

"Not in my world, it isn't. I can easily manage to be ready for a quarter to eight, and still sleep in until seven o'clock," replied Mark Lucas.

"Okay, well good luck with that! But I don't think I would be able to leave it until the last minute," stated Clem, with honesty.

"You would if you skipped breakfast, made your bedpack the night before, and shaved as you dressed," replied Mark Lucas, revealing an immaculate looking bedpack, taken from underneath his bed.

"That's a great idea, what made you think of that?" asked Clem.

"One night, I found it was too warm to sleep in here, with the heating on full blast, and I was tossing and turning for hours. So I decided that I would sleep without any bed covers on, and then it dawned on me that I could sleep in longer in the morning, if I made my bedpack before I went to bed, so I did, and as I'm not one for breakfast in the morning, I skipped that too, and saved some more time, and as for shaving, well, I use an electric razor that doesn't require me to waste time jogging to the ablutions, so voila, I've got longer in bed!" explained Mark Lucas.

"That's resourcefulness for you!" replied Clem.

"You have to be resourceful, if you want to be in the RAF Police, as it could save your life!" exclaimed Mark Lucas.

"That's true!" agreed Clem. "But won't you smell a bit, if you don't wash?"

"No, I have a shower the night before, and spray well in the morning. After half an hour of recruit training, you soon start to perspire, so why waste time washing in the morning, when you can stay in bed longer?" replied Mark Lucas.

"You've got it all worked out, haven't you?" stated Clem.

"I like to think so," agreed Mark Lucas.

"But I reckon I shall stay as I am, with my routine. I'm not skipping breakfast, I'm not going without a good old fashioned wash and shave, nor sleeping without covers, so I think you're on your own, with those ideas," replied Clem.

"Whatever floats your boat! It's horses for courses!" stated Mark Lucas.

"Yes, you're not wrong there!" exclaimed Clem, in agreement.

Clem looked around to see if there was anybody else that needed helping, but everyone appeared to be in control of their situation. Once he was satisfied that his colleagues were okay, he decided to make tracks towards the

Airman's Mess, for breakfast. The weather outside was awful. It was windy, cold and wet, with grey clouds displaying a hint that it appeared to be set in for the rest of the day. Clem decided he needed his raincoat to walk to the Mess, as the rain was not letting up. He didn't hang around for long outside, and jogged quickly along the path, through numerous puddles of rainwater, to make his way to the sanctuary of the Airmen's Mess.

He decided on something different today, scrambled eggs on toast, beans, bacon and sausages, which looked delicious under the glass panel of the serving hatch. He decided against the tea, and chose orange juice instead, and he did not even bother with cereal, neither. It was a completely new choice of menu for Clem, which he was looking forward to, with relish.

"Can't wait for leave!" stated Joseph Job, randomly, as he sat at the table shovelling a spoonful of hot delicious porridge into his wide accommodating mouth.

"When is leave?" asked Clem.

"Tonight!" replied Joseph Job.

"Really?" asked Clem, in disbelief.

"Didn't you know?" asked Joseph Job.

"No, nobody's said anything to me about it. Are you sure?" asked Clem.

"Yes, I'm positive. I've got friends in the Admin Team here, and they've told me that there are rail warrants waiting for eight airmen on this course, to be picked up for a weekend pass," replied Joseph Job.

"Weekend pass? So it's not leave then, just a weekend off?" asked Clem.

"Yes, but it's still leave to me, no matter how long we have off," stated Joseph Job.

"I suppose you're right," agreed Clem, nodding.

"What will you be doing?" asked Joseph Job.

"I'm not sure yet, I'll probably spend some time with my family and then see my girlfriend Ellie, if she's not busy," replied Clem, tucking into his breakfast.

"That's just about the same as me. But whatever happens, I shall make the most of it, as it'll be over in no time," stated Joseph Job.

"That's true. The more fun you have, the quicker the time seems to fly," agreed Clem, munching on scrambled egg and bacon, with delight.

"You can say that again!" exclaimed Joseph Job.

The airmen finished their breakfasts, and headed back to the billet. Clem was pleased that the rain, which had seemed so relentless earlier, had in fact stopped, and the clouds were not as grey and dark as before. He hadn't fancied marching up and down in the pouring rain, now there was a weekend off to enjoy. His thoughts were directed towards Ellie, and he was ready to spend some quality time with her, over the weekend, whether it was Saturday or Sunday, he didn't mind. But he was determined to see her, to catch up.

Clem tidied around his bed, and arranged his boots, shoes, number one uniform and cap, in a presentable manner. He squared up the corners of the bedpack, and was ready for the inspection, hoping his property didn't get the rough treatment from Corporal Cherry or Sergeant Winner, as up to now, he had escaped the embarrassment of seeing his bedpack flying through the window, or his boots, uniform and cap sliding across the floor, and that is what he hoped would continue, for the foreseeable future.

The drill sergeant and corporal were early, and they marched into the billet at half past seven, catching everyone unaware.

"Stand by your beds!" shouted Corporal Cherry.

The airmen obeyed the order, and fortunately for them all, were ready for the inspection, even though it was fifteen minutes earlier than expected.

"It's Friday, so we've decided to start the day a little earlier than normal, so apologies for catching you out. But, as it's nearly the weekend, I'm sure you'll be keen to be off on your jollies for two days, and expecting a flyer. Well, that all depends on how hard you work today, and how focused you all are, so to get proceedings underway, we shall begin with the daily inspection of your kit and bedpacks!" exclaimed Sergeant Winner.

The airmen sighed with apprehension, and took a deep intake of breath, as they waited for the outcome of the inspection. Anything could happen, and they knew that some bedpacks that were perfect had received the rough treatment from Corporal Cherry, and some uniforms that were immaculate had been treated equally harshly by Sergeant Winner. It was a complete lottery, that was determined by the mood of the drill instructors.

"Rubbish, do it again!" called Sergeant Winner, directing his anger at David Ephraim, and slinging the bedpack across the floor.

"Terrible!" yelled Corporal Cherry, directing his wrath at Jacob Adams, and hurling his bedpack out of the window.

"Atrocious!" bellowed Sergeant Winner, directing his annoyance at Clem Harrison, and tipping his bedpack onto the floor, before kicking it like a football, to the corner of the room.

"Poor effort!" shouted Corporal Cherry, directing his frustration at Timothy Moses, and throwing his cap, boots, shoes and bedpack through another open window.

The faces of the stricken airmen, that had just seen their property discarded like rubbish, were a picture, and they gawped open mouthed in disbelief, at the harsh treatment they had been handed, by Sergeant Winner and Corporal Cherry. It did not let up there, and the drill instructors dumped every single bedpack onto the floor, and hurled every uniform through the open windows, in what was a blitz of the airmen's property. Clem was dumbstruck, and could not believe what he was seeing. He had regarded his bedpack as being one of his better ones, and he had only recently been thinking that he was becoming a master in this art, but his hopes and dreams of going through the basic training without seeing his bedpack biting the dust, was over.

"Well, that was a disgrace, wasn't it? Every single piece of property dumped for being inferior, and at this stage of your training too!" exclaimed Sergeant Winner, angrily.

There was silence all around the billet, as the airmen were stunned into submission. There was not one single murmur from any of them, and they all waited with baited breath, to see what happened next.

"Pick up all of your stuff, and prepare for the inspection again. I shall give you a second chance, as I'm feeling generous today, so it's up to you. If you can dig yourselves out of the hole you've created for yourselves, it'll go a long way in character building," stated Sergeant Winner.

The recruits immediately went about their business, to rebuild their bedpacks, with a steely determination, and they did not utter a single word to anyone, but concentrated on the task ahead, taking on one job at a time.

"We shall not cramp your style, by watching you work, we'll be waiting in the foyer. So, good luck! You have fifteen minutes to sort out the mess that you made earlier!" exclaimed Sergeant Winner, ironically.

The airmen did not reply, as they were focused on what they were doing, and Sergeant Winner and Corporal Cherry departed from the billet room, each wearing a wry smile on their faces.

Those recruits that struggled to work under pressure were assisted by those that could work under the high intensity, and all the airmen worked as a team, quickly gathering their property from outside, and from the floor of the billet, with clinical precision. They were efficient, tenacious and diligent in their work, and everyone got stuck into the tasks in a manner that had never been seen before, in all the time they had been there. Nobody was ignored, everbody was part of the well oiled machine, that was ready to show what they were made of, to make this inspection the best ever in their Royal Air Force career.

When the fifteen minutes was up, Sergeant Winner and Corporal Cherry arrived in the billet, and prepared themselves for the inspection, walking slowly around the room and taking in all the changes that had occurred in the previous fifteen minutes. Nothing was spoken by either of the drill instructors, but they nodded and smiled at the display that was set before them. Everything was presented in an immaculate manner. It was perfect. There was no need for the drill instructors to throw anything across the room, and they did not not. They merely inspected every single bed, and every piece of uniform, before walking out of the billet, and leaving the airmen to ponder on what had just happened.

Chapter 20

Sergeant Winner and Corporal Cherry returned to the room a few minutes later.

"Well done recruits! That was a great effort, and the best inspection yet. Both myself and Corporal Cherry are very impressed. But the question I need to ask you all, is why did it take a total blitz of your property to be able to reach these standards?" piped up Sergeant Winner.

There was no reply from any of the recruits, even the noisy ones remained quiet.

"I shall tell you why, it's because you are all becoming blase', taking things for granted, and not working hard enough. It's plain to see, that when you're in a corner and up against it, you can turn on the style, but until then, you're showing signs of apathy and indifference, which is not very healthy! This needs to be cut out immediately," explained Sergeant Winner, with feeling.

The recruits remained silent, and let the words from the drill sergeant settle into their brains.

"Okay, that's the inspection done and dusted, now let's see how good you are on the rifle range, as its time to check out what your shooting skills are like, and see if there is any room for improvement there too," stated Sergeant Winner. "Recruits dismiss, and wait outside!" he ordered.

The airmen moved quickly and formed a tidy looking formation ready to march to the Armoury, to collect their rifles and ammunition.

"Quick march, left, right, left, right, and keep a straight line!" yelled Sergeant Winner loudly.

The recruits were buoyed by the results of the second inspection and were ready to give their all on the rifle range.

They arrived at the Armoury, signed for their rifles and ammunition, and left the building in an orderly and efficient manner. This morning's shock at seeing their property and equipment hurled through the window and across the floor had done the recruits a big favour, as it had brought them down to earth with a huge bump and made them think deeply about what they were doing, and they were all determined not to be slap happy again.

"Forward march, towards the rifle range!" ordered Sergeant Winner, when he noticed that each of the airmen had returned with their rifle and ammo.

The recruits marched with impeccable style, and made this the best performance to date, which had both Sergeant Winner and Corporal Cherry purring with satisfaction. The airmen arrived at the rifle range a few minutes later, and they waited for the next order.

"Recruits halt! Attention! Stand at ease!" yelled Sergeant Winner quickly, in a loud brash voice.

The airmen did as they were told, and were very receptive to the sergeant's requests.

"Recruits dismiss, and head into the rifle range in single file, in an orderly manner, with no running, no chatting and no jostling!" ordered Sergeant Winner.

The airmen carried out the order to a tee, and made their way inside the rifle range, without any fuss or friction.

Everyone knew what the other was doing, and there was no arrogance from any of them. They were all in this together, and they were ready to work as a team, and make this a successful exercise, for their own job satisfaction, as well as impressing Sergeant Winner and Corporal Cherry.

"You know the drill by now. When I say load, do as I say, and when I say fire, do likewise! I need to see some sharp shooting today, to build your confidence up, after the dismal first inspection this morning. But I'm sure you don't need me to tell you that. Now recruits! Ready! Load! And fire!" shouted Sergeant Winner loudly, across the rifle range, which echoed all around the RAF Swinderby airfield, and beyond.

The recruits instantly loaded their rifles with their ammunition cartridges, and immediately began to pull the trigger on their SLR rifle, with a keen determination. Every recruit was eager to get a great start with their shooting, and the focus on the targets by each and every one of them, was fixed closely, like it had never been before. The recruits meant business, and there was no sloppy, slap dash, slap happy attitude this morning. This was ultra-serious.

The bullets were fired at an extremely quick rate, and Clem knew he had got his eye in rapidly, as the centre of his target seemed to have a hole in the centre, where he had peppered his bullets with frequent ferociousness. Each round was fired by Clem with careful aplomb, and he worked the rifle as hard as he could, to get the maximum output from it, as he reckoned that it would be great to go on a weekend break, with the thrill of finishing top of the class in the shooting, so he could tell Ellie all about it. He had just as good a chance as anybody among the recruits in finishing first, but it was all about the concentration and focus. If Clem could continue throughout the session with the same determination at the end, as he had showed at the beginning, then he knew he had a great chance of topping the group standings.

The bullets flew like lightning, the noise was incredible, this was the most intense session of shooting that the recruits had ever been involved in, and there was no letting up from any of them, including Clem, who was as determined as ever to finish strongly and take the first prize, *with a bit of luck*. After the commotion and din of the firing came to a halt, it was silent again and there was ringing in Clem's ears, following the huge amount of noise. But he didn't mind. He could live with that. He was waiting for the results. That was all that mattered to him.

"Well done recruits! That was a good session!" acclaimed Sergeant Winner with sincerity. "Cease firing now, and I shall check the results on the score boards," he added, ambling slowly towards the targets. He unpinned each of the marauding soldier pictures and looked at the peppering of the bulls eye with interest. He quickly tallied up the scoring, and the airmen waited with baited breath for the announcement of the results.

"In first place today, we have Clem Harrison with one hundred per cent, excellent marksmanship Clem! In second place is Timothy Moses, with ninety nine per cent, and in third place is David Ephraim with ninety eight per cent," announced Sergeant Winner.

Clem was chuffed to bits with the result, and attaining one hundred per cent accuracy was something he had not expected, although he realised his concentration levels were magnificent today, as he had focused hard, so he knew he would be close.

The other recruits congratulated Clem Harrison, Timothy Moses and David Ephraim, with the customary pat on the back, showing that there were no hard feelings among any of them.

"That's the rifle range then, and it's now on to the parade square, for a spot of drill. Keep hold of your rifles, as you shall be needing them for practice, but we shall report back to the Armoury to drop off the cartridges," informed Sergeant Winner. "Recruits forward march, out of the rifle range and head towards the Armoury, left, right, left, right," called Sergeant Winner.

The recruits formed into a decent looking marching team, and headed off to the Armoury, with style, panache and swagger. They arrived a few minutes later, and despatched the cartridges back, and signed to say they had been returned.

"Very well Flight, now to the parade square! Forward march, left, right, left, right, keep the lines straight and even," shouted Sergeant Winner.

It was another great effort by the recruits to continue with their impeccable shape, and it impressed Sergeant Winner and Corporal Cherry immensely.

"Keep this up recruits, all they way to the parade square! Let's banish the memory of the nightmare inspection first thing this morning, to the history books!" exclaimed Sergeant Winner with sincerity.

The airmen continued their great shape, up until the parade square, when things started to go slightly awry. Sergeant Winner looked at Corporal Cherry and they could not believe what they were watching. Two recruits, David Ephraim and Mark Lucas accidentally crashed into each other on a left wheel, and they both mistimed a kerb and were sent hurtling to the ground. If it hadn't had been so crucial to the day's parade practice, it would have been funny to watch. But nobody was laughing.

"Recruits halt!" called Sergeant Winner.

The recruits pulled up, and waited for the crumpled forms to get to their feet.

"What's your game?" asked Sergeant Winner, calmly and coolly towards the two stricken airmen, that had bitten the dust.

The recruits did not answer. They were gobsmacked, and in shock.

"It's a good job you've done this today, and not on the "Passing Out" parade, as I think if you had have done, you would not have lived it down," stated Sergeant Winner, in an unflappable manner of understanding.

"Sorry sergeant!" replied Mark Lucas.

"Yes, sorry sergeant," echoed David Ephraim.

"You had better get yourself cleaned up at the Medical Centre. It looks like you've grazes and abrasions, that need some treatment," stated Sergeant Winner.

"Yes sergeant!" replied the two recruits in unison, and they left the group immediately.

"Okay recruits, comedy half hour is over, and without further ado, we shall continue with the "Presenting Arms" practice, until you get it perfect!" yelled Sergeant Winner.

The recruits re-formed into a smaller team, and prepared to march around the parade ground.

"Only six of you left now, so I think I'll need you to merge with another Flight, to make this a better balanced unit, as six is ridiculous!" stated Sergeant Winner. He moved across to Corporal Cherry, and discussed the issue with him. "Can you arrange another Flight to merge with this lot, as we are low in numbers, and it's going to affect their performance on "Passing Out" day," stated Sergeant Winner.

"I shall see what I can do," replied Corporal Cherry.

"I will leave it with you, then," stated Sergeant Winner, confidently expecting Corporal Cherry to come up with the solution. "Whilst Corporal Cherry is away sorting out the merging with another Flight, we can press on with the drill practice!" shouted Sergeant Winner.

"Yes sergeant!" exclaimed the recruits, in unison.

"Flight, forward march!" yelled Sergeant Winner.

The recruits continued where they had left off, and were impeccable in shape and form, and showed how composed they were, despite being restricted to only six in the team. They marched along the straight, and were perfect, as they turned around the corner, and wheeled with grace and aplomb, in a confident and assured manner. It was a joy to watch for Sergeant Winner, and he was only hoping the merging with another Flight, would not have any drastic consequences.

"Flight, "Present Arms!" shouted Sergeant Winner, when the recruits came around to the front again.

The airmen "Presented Arms" in time, in unison and in a professional manner, that was hard to fault.

"Forward march!" shouted Sergeant Winner, and he watched as the recruits set off for another excursion, around the parade square.

They continued in the identical manner as they had marched before, and hit the corners without any problems, marching straight and true, with a perfect shape. When they came around to the front of the parade square, and were waiting for the orders to "Present Arms," they did not come, as Sergeant Winner wanted them to continue with the marching, to make sure it was fine tuned to perfection. He let them go around three more times.

"Flight, "Present Arms!" shouted Sergeant Winner, as the recruits came around to the front.

The airmen "Presented Arms" impeccably again, with a greater urgency, style and swagger, and were confident in each other, as their timing was perfect.

"Flight, stand at ease!" yelled Sergeant Winner.

The airmen relaxed, and got their breath back, and it was no more than they deserved.

"That was one of your best performances to date, Flight. Don't slacken off now, keep pushing forward and make it even better. The onus is on you to focus even harder, because when the Flight merges, we shall be going back to square one again. But if you put into practice what you've learned in the last few days, and rally round as a team, it will be like a walk in the park!" exclaimed Sergeant Winner, with a determined passion in his tone.

The recruits listened with a keen interest to Sergeant Winner's words of wisdom, and they took on board everything that he said.

"I'm not certain how good the other recruits will be, when they arrive, and I'm not sure whether they have worked hard, or been slackers in the time they've been here, but one thing I do know, and that's the benchmark that you have reached will be tough for the newbies, no matter how hard they have trained. You lot have attained a very high standard in next to no time, and it will be my job to integrate the team quickly and efficiently, to reach the heights that you have reached. It's going to be tough, and it's going to be painstaking, but I'm clear in my mind, that it can be done!" exclaimed Sergeant Winner, with a positive vibe pouring out from him.

The words sunk into the minds of all the airmen, and they believed that Sergeant Winner was speaking sense, and they were determined to put into practice his brave enterprising theories.

Within seconds, the peace was broken by Corporal Cherry's loud brash voice, as he cajoled the new Flight into shape, with his usual bellowing tone.

"Left, right, left, right, keep your shape! It's a disgrace, left, right, left, right!" shouted Corporal Cherry, towards the eight recruits.

"Oh no! This is my worst nightmare!" stated Sergeant Winner to himself, as he glanced across at the shambles in front of him.

"Flight, halt!" called Corporal Cherry, and some of the recruits stopped, whilst the others carried on marching, and they bumped clumsily into those that had obeyed the order from the drill corporal. It was a complete mess. "Flight, stand at ease!" yelled Corporal Cherry.

The recruits were unsure what this meant, and it ended up in a mishmash of "Attention," "Stand at Ease" and "Forward March," rolled into one.

"What do we have here?" asked Sergeant Winner, rubbing his eyes in disbelief.

"The only Flight that was gash, at this present moment in time, and they haven't had much drill practice, as you can see," replied Corporal Cherry.

"Yes, I can see very clearly indeed, and by the look of it, these guys haven't seen a parade square in their lives!" answered Sergeant Winner.

"They've been neglected, somewhat," agreed Corporal Cherry, nodding.

"You can say that again! But never mind! Welcome recruits!" exclaimed Sergeant Winner, enthusiastically.

The recruits looked scared, unsure, nervous and ready to bolt for the gate, as they wondered what they were doing among this Flight.

"How many have we got here?" asked Sergeant Winner.

"Eight in total," replied Corporal Cherry.

"Okay, fine, so that will be fourteen airmen presently, and sixteen when the other two return from the Medical Centre," stated Sergeant Winner.

The eight new recruits swallowed hard, when they heard the sergeant speak of the Medical Centre, and they all wondered in unison what on earth they were letting themselves in for.

"Medical Centre?" asked one of the new recruits cheekily, in the direction of Sergeant Winner.

"Oh yes, sorry, you lot were not here when the incident happened. But two of our airmen stumbled heavily onto the tarmac and received substantial grazes and abrasions. It's nothing serious, but they needed to report to the Medical Centre for a check up, and a cleaning of the superficial injuries," explained Sergeant Winner, with courtesy.

"So your guys are not as hot with the drill, just like us, then?" replied the cheeky new recruit, with tongue in cheek.

"It was a one off! But you're correct, we are not as hot as we like to think we are, so you lot should fit nicely into a routine around here, where we can all start from basics, and work our way up slowly, but surely to the pinnacle of "Presenting Arms," in a clinical and efficient manner, and be professional, in every facet. That is my aim, and I shall do my damned best to make sure that this works out in our favour!" exclaimed Sergeant Winner, in a positive and determined tone, that impressed everyone present.

Chapter 21

The two injured recruits, David Ephraim and Mark Lucas returned from being patched up at the Medical Centre, and joined the group of sixteen airmen, that were ready to start from the beginning, and go over the old ground again, after the merging of the two Flights. One that was inexperienced and naive, and the other that was overconfident, arrogant and brash.

"Fall in Ephraim and Lucas, and take up your places!" shouted Sergeant Winner. "And I don't mean that literally!" he added with tongue in cheek.

The other fourteen recruits laughed out loud in unison, at the funny quip from the drill sergeant, and it broke the ice among the eight new recruits, that were quickly beginning to settle down and relax.

"You have to work hard, and concentrate like your lives depend on it, in the next few weeks, or otherwise, you could find yourselves back-flighted one week, or even two, and I'm sure none of you will want that. However, I'm sure you're all intelligent enough to pick up the basics and develop accordingly, otherwise you would not be here. But if you would like to bail out now, before the hard work commences, please raise your hand, and we can make arrangements for your demob!" called Sergeant Winner.

There were no takers on that issue, everyone was ready, willing and able to give it a go and embark on the new adventure, which would sure to be a rollercoaster of blood, sweat and tears, mixed with excitement, fatigue, grit and determination. The airmen were ready to go the extra mile and test themselves in the toughest of circumstances, and take on the challenge of moulding themselves into a lean, mean fighting machine.

"So, are we all in?" asked Sergeant Winner.

"Yes sergeant!" replied the recruits, in unison.

"Good! Those with rifles place them down on the side, and let's get started on some basic drill practice, for the benefit of our new group members!" yelled Sergeant Winner, returning to his old self again. "Flight attention! And, forward march!"

The recruits worked hard on their shape, and tried as best as they could to march in time. It was tougher than before, as the group had grown twice in size, and there were some very shaky moments. But on the whole, the airmen did well, especially the new recruits, who were keen to make up for their poor first impression. After all, they could not get any worse.

"Keep up that standard, it's excellent!" shouted Sergeant Winner loudly, and the words rang around the parade square, and across the whole of the RAF station, and they were firmly instilled into the minds of the sixteen airmen, which spurred them on to improve even further.

They marched around and around the parade square, wheeling round the corners, with style, panache and aplomb, and Sergeant Winner could see things were clicking into place. He realised the new members of the

Flight *had received some drill training* whilst they were here, and it was just the case of tweaking it slightly, with the guidance of Sergeant Winner's skill, patience and knowledge. But he could clearly see there was light at the end of the tunnel.

"Flight halt! Attention! And, stand at ease!" yelled Sergeant Winner, after the recruits had marched around the parade square half a dozen times.

The recruits came to a satisfactory stop, and stood at attention in time, before standing at ease.

"Okay, that was better! And I've got to say it looks like the new additions to our group *have had a little drill practice*, and know the fundamentals of what is needed, which is encouraging. And, I am pleased to say, I'm confident that you can all reach the necessary requirements, if you continue in this manner," stated Sergeant Winner.

"Thank you sergeant!" replied the airmen together, in unison.

"Now, we have eight new recruits on board, which has doubled our numbers, but I don't know any of your names, so if you can shout out your rank and name in the order you are standing in, then I shall do my very best to remember each and every one," called Sergeant Winner.

"AC Ray Lord!" shouted the first airman.
"AC Walter Phillips!" called the second.
"AC Ken James!" yelled the third.
"AC Denis King!"
"AC David Isaac!"
"AC Jordan John!"
"AC Abraham Jude!"
"AC Jacob Marks!"

"Thank you for that, I've made a mental note of your names and will link them to your faces in due course, although it might take me a little time, as I'm still coming to terms with the other eight recruits. So please, bear with me!" stated Sergeant Winner, with tongue in cheek.
The eight new recruits laughed and were amused by Sergeant Winner's sense of humour.
"It's time for lunch, so you need to return the eight rifles to the Armoury and have them signed in, and then you can take an hour's break, and replenish with food and drink, and be ready for another long session of drill this afternoon. Flight forward march!" yelled Sergeant Winner.
The recruits marched to the Armoury in good style and handed in their SLR rifles. There was a pattern emerging among them that looked promising, and it filled Sergeant Winner with optimism. They then headed towards the Airmen's Mess for lunch, and arrived a few minutes later. The recruits dispersed towards the serving hatch and were ready to fill up with a hot curry, as it was the Chef's Speciality for the day. It had been a tough morning's workout, with the eight new additions to the group, and all sixteen were mentally and physically shattered, and counting down the hours to the weekend, which was just around the corner. It could not come quick enough for them all.
Clem headed to the serving hatch first, and ordered a beef curry and rice, and he could not wait to tuck in. The weather was chilly and damp, and Clem knew that a curry would take away all the frost from the air around him, and warm him up beautifully. He chose apple crumble and custard for his pudding and poured himself a cup of bromide and tea, to wash it all down with. He was famished and headed straight for a large empty table,

which would accomodate the other fifteen recruits. The curry hardly touched the sides, as he made light work of the delicious meal, and the Chef certainly knew how to balance the seasoning, with the red hot chilli peppers, black peppers and curry powder complimenting each other perfectly. It certainly was the Chef's Speciality, and Clem reckoned it was one of the best curry's he had ever tasted in his life.

"How's everyone finding the training?" asked Clem to the new guys, who had joined him at the table.

"Fine!" replied Ray Lord.

"Yeah, not bad, so far," backed up Walter James.

"The drill sergeant is a nutter, but is making the transition easy," piped up Ken James.

"You're not wrong there, mate! But he gets the results, and before you lot joined us, we were world class at drill," replied Clem.

"Are you sure about that? I noticed you were two men down, due to them falling over on the parade square and injuring themselves badly enough to receive treatment from the Medical Centre," retorted Ray Lord.

"I can't lie, you're right, but apart from that isolated incident we were looking red hot," stated Clem proudly.

"I'll believe that when I see it," replied Ray Lord, with tongue in cheek.

"I can't argue with that, but we were all looking the part in the latter stages of this morning, when everyone settled down and began to work as a team," stated Clem.

"But we haven't "Presented Arms" as a team yet, that will be the biggest test, because it will require perfect timing, guile, skill and a smidgen of luck," replied Ray Lord.

"Very true, indeed, but when the going gets tough, the tough gets going," stated Clem.

"Let's hope it includes us lot when it comes to the "Presenting Arms" bit!" joked Ray Lord facetiously.

Clem finished his beef curry and rice and set upon the apple crumble and custard. It didn't disappoint neither, and he made light work of it with keen, eager, exuberance. He washed it down with a mouthful of tea and bromide, which appeared to have more bromide than tea, but it didn't deter Clem and he sunk the cupful. He had enjoyed the meal so much, he reckoned he could go back to the servers and have seconds of everything.

A few minutes later he headed back to the billet to switch off his brain for a while, and find some time for himself. He bought a morning newspaper, of the tabloid variety on the way out, from the NAAFI vendors and read it as he had his routine lunchtime dump. He did not buy the newspaper for the front page news, it was just for the back page and the rest of the sports pages. He was finished within ten minutes. Half an hour later, Sergeant Winner and Corporal Cherry arrived at the billet, with a small cardboard box.

 "Stand by your beds!" yelled Corporal Cherry. "And attention!"

The recruits looked puzzled. They were wondering what on earth was going on. Was this another inspection? No, it couldn't be, they surmised, after a little thought.

 "Okay, stand at ease! It's the best part of the week!" called Corporal Cherry cheerfully. "Pay day! And yes, before you ask, you do get paid for this recruit training malarkey, surprising as it may seem!" joked the corporal.

The recruits laughed together in unison, but they were shocked. They had not expected to be paid today. But having contemplated a while, it was the weekend, and the guys were being issued with a weekend pass later.

"When I call out your name, come and collect your pay packet and don't spend it all at once!" quipped Corporal Cherry with tongue in cheek.

The corporal yelled out the names one by one and the airmen eagerly approached their paymaster to receive their wages. It was over and done with, in the space of five minutes, and was similar to opening presents on Christmas Day.

"If there any discrepancies with your pay, let me know and I shall inform the Wages Department later in the afternoon, and it can be addressed before you go home for the weekend break. But I think you will find that everything is fine and above board, as the Wages Department never make mistakes!" exclaimed Corporal Cherry facetiously.

Clem opened his wage packet eagerly, and found seven crisp one pound notes nestled inside. He didn't think he had ever had so much money in his hand at one time, apart from when he was working as a part time gardener a couple of years ago, and had saved twenty five pounds, but that had taken him five weeks to accrue. He folded the cash, and placed it back into the brown envelope and tucked it safely into his pocket.

"Flight attention! Move quickly outside. We're heading back to the Armoury for rifles for you all, and you know what's coming next, don't you? Yes, it's "Presenting Arms" time again!" shouted Corporal Cherry loudly. "But first we need to collect the other eight recruits, that are in a different block, so let's make headway, and reunite with them!"

The recruits formed a neat and tidy group and marched to the billet to pick up the other eight, and they were ready to take on the world. This was it. The moment they had been waiting for. Time to prove to themselves they could handle the pressure and perform as a team of sixteen, to produce an impeccable display of synchronisation, as they embarked on their biggest challenge to date.

"Flight, forward march to the Armoury to collect your rifles!" yelled Corporal Cherry, after they had picked up the other eight recruits.

Their lines were tidy. Their shape was intact. Their footwork was in time, and there was no evidence of a concertina. The sixteen recruits were marching as good as they had ever done, and it was impressive to watch. Each of the airmen looked across at the column of recruits beside them, and with a glimpse at their positioning, they managed to keep in time with each other. It was the trick of the trade, glancing across at the people next along, and staying in shape with them, was the key to success.

The recruits arrived at the Armoury and waited for the orders from Corporal Cherry, with eager ears.

"Flight halt! Attention! Stand at ease!" yelled Corporal Cherry.

The orders were immediately carried out by the sixteen airmen, with immaculate timing.

"Very good! That was better than earlier! Keep up this standard!" called Sergeant Winner, watching from the side.

The recruits waited patiently for the next string of orders.

"Move forward in single file into the Armoury, pick up and sign for your SLR rifle and make your way back out here, in an orderly fashion!" yelled Corporal Cherry loudly.

The recruits entered the Armoury, collected their rifle, signed for it, and made their way outside, ready to march to the Parade Square, as requested.

"Flight, forward march to the hangar!" yelled Corporal Cherry, looking up at the sky and noticing the rain was beginning to fall very heavily. The airmen continued to march in time and kept a decent shape, with no dreaded concertina in sight. It was pleasing for Sergeant Winner and Corporal Cherry to see the continued progress being made, even in this dreadful October weather. They arrived at the hangar a few minutes later.

"Flight halt! Attention! And stand at ease!" bawled Corporal Cherry.

The recruits stopped on a one penny piece, in stunning style and were in time with all the three disciplines that had been ordered.

"Now is the time to show your mettle! You've improved your marching! You've improved your line and shape! You've improved on halting, standing at attention and standing at ease. But the biggest challenge to overcome now, is marching and then "Presenting Arms," on the hoof!" yelled Sergeant Winner.

The recruits listened and nodded, but stayed silent. They knew what they had to do and they were all determined to make the best of their first opportunity to impress with a rifle on the"Presenting Arms" discipline.

"Flight attention! Quick forward march!" bawled Corporal Cherry.

The recruits hung on to their rifles with all their might and marched in time, keeping an eye on their neighbour marching next to them, to stay in shape. It was paying off well, as the group of sixteen were lined up in an excellent formation and in tip top condition.

"Left, right, left, right!" encouraged Corporal Cherry, helping the recruits to maintain the fine rhythm they had gathered up.

The square yard dimensions of the hangar were smaller than that of the parade square outside, and the recruits reached the first corner quicker than they normally would have done, if it had been the parade square, but they did not panic and negotiated the bend in a first class manner, with style, aplomb and panache, and careered the corner like they had been marching together for years, rather than hours. It was the first test passed with flying colours.

Their minds were fixed firmly on the next big test, "Presenting Arms." They knew what they had to do. The eight newer recruits among them had limited experience with "Presenting Arms" in their previous Flight, but they knew the basic requirements, whilst the eight original airmen in the Flight had ample experience and it was now just a question of moulding together the limited amount of practice of the newer guys to the greater experience of the established recruits, that had been given more opportunity to hone their skills.

The recruits marched around another corner, followed by a second and then approached the third bend. Their faces were fixed hard like concrete, in concentration, as they went over in their minds what the precise drill for "Presenting Arms" consisted of. The third corner was negotiated in a fine shape and their lines were excellent and they quickly approached the spot where they would be "Presenting Arms."

The moment of truth had arrived, and the airmen waited with baited breath for the orders that would see the sixteen recruits "Present Arms" for the first time as a group.

  "Flight halt! Flight attention! Flight "Present Arms!" yelled Corporal Cherry.

The airmen were nervous at first, as they grappled with their rifles, and they all seemed at sixes and sevens for a second or two, but they soon got the jitters out of their system and settled down nicely, to make a good fist of the discipline, and they sent their SLR weapons high up into the air, and twisted and turned the rifle in all sorts of different shapes, to put on a heart-warming display of style, skill and synchronisation. It didn't take long to complete, just a minute or two, but it was the most important couple of minutes in the lives of the sixteen airmen, that would decide the destiny of their Royal Air Force careers. They completed the discipline and waited for the reaction from Corporal Cherry and Sergeant Winner, with flushed cheeks, a booming heartbeat and intrigue running through their veins.

"Very good!" praised Corporal Cherry. "That was almost perfect!"

"Yes, I agree. It was a little iffy at the beginning, which is understandable, but you carried on regardless and got stronger, and it was better than the previous attempt the other day, so congrats to you all!" enthused Sergeant Winner.

The airmen gasped with relief, and were pleased with the outcome, although they knew they had to sharpen up at the start, as it was ropey and could have cost them their RAF careers.

Chapter 22

The remainder of the afternoon was a blur for Clem Harrison and the rest of the group, as they were stunned by their performance in the "Presenting Arms" discipline, and they knew that could not be beaten for satisfaction, in any way shape of form, no matter how hard they tried. It was something for Clem to tell his parents and maybe his girlfriend Ellie, when he returned home, as he reckoned the "Presenting Arms" success was the greatest achievement of his entire seventeen years.

At four o'clock, Sergeant Winner led the weary recruits back to the billet, after numerous circuits on the parade ground, to iron out the rough patches.

"Well done on today Flight! Enjoy your weekend, and don't forget your travel warrant, which you will need to collect from the Admin Block, on your way out. Oh, and by the way, even though you're on leave, and it's the weekend, you are still members of the Royal Air Force, so remember your responsibilities and no horseplay, whilst your on your break. You need to continue to remain lean, mean RAF fighting machines, with discipline, and not get drawn into any controversy with civilians. Flight dismiss!" bellowed Sergeant Winner.

The recruits raced inside the billet room, grabbed their kit bags and placed all their belongs inside. They changed into their immaculate number one Royal Air Force uniform, and swapped their headgear, from a beret to a peaked cap, with a light fluorescent band sitting around the centre, that was fondly known as the "Twat Hat." Clem shrugged off the label, as he knew every airmen that passed through RAF Swinderby would have donned a "Twat Hat" sooner or later, in his career.

After picking up his travel warrant from the Admin Block, Clem was free to make his way towards the bus stop outside the base, and he joined the others that were queuing up for the next bus. It didn't take long to arrive, and within ten minutes Clem and the other fifteen recruits from his Flight were settled in their seats on the bus and travelling towards the Newark railway station. Clem boarded the train for Hull half an hour later and was satisfied that things were going to plan. There had not been any snags as yet, and that was how he hoped it would stay, for the rest of the journey.

Clem arrived home shattered, at seven o'clock in the evening, and felt like going straight to bed, but he refrained from being so pathetic and stayed up to have a bite to eat, graciously cooked for him by his adoring mother. He had missed his mum's cooking more than he realised, and no matter how delicious the RAF Swinderby food had been, Clem had to admit that nothing beat his mother's grub.

"So son, how's it going?" asked Clem's mum, with baited breath.

"It's going better than I ever imagined!" exclaimed Clem, with enthusiasm.

"Is it really? Wow, that's terrific! What have you been up to?" asked his mum, with intrigue.

"You name it and I've done it! Marching, shooting, running, cleaning, climbing and jumping, among others too numerous to mention," replied Clem.

"Your hair is short!" commented Clem's mum, changing the subject.

"Yes, it's a regulation Royal Air Force recruit haircut," replied Clem.

"It suits you though," stated his mother.

"Thanks mum," replied Clem.

"So, what have you got planned for the weekend, then?" asked Clem's mum.

"I'm not sure, really. Hopefully I'll spend some time with Ellie, if she's not busy. *I have been receiving post from her*, well, one letter actually, but she seems keen to see me, so I'll just have to wait and find out what happens there," replied Clem.

"Lovely, that's nice! I hope it all goes well for you, and Ellie," stated Clem's mum.

"Yes, so do I. It's tough being away from her, but I decided to join up for the RAF before I met her, so I was committed. But only time will tell how things pan out between us," replied Clem.

"Yes son, that's true. Well, it's good to have you back home again, and I hope you have an enjoyable weekend, whatever you decide to do!" exclaimed Clem's mum.

"Thanks mum," replied Clem.

The rest of the evening was spent in front of the television, and Clem unwound and relaxed, as best he could. There were some tacky comedy shows on, and a James Bond film, but he didn't catch the end of it, as he fell asleep before it finished. He stumbled up the stairs at midnight, and crashed out on his bed, for a good night's rest.

Next day, Clem's elder brother Grant phoned from his flat to see how he was doing. Clem explained to his brother that he was doing well, and they arranged to meet up at the Hofbrauhaus German beer garden, in Hull city centre, for a catch up at lunchtime. The Hofbrauhaus was a popular drinking venue for the public, with clientele mainly aged under twenty five, and Clem being seventeen and his brother Grant, twenty three, it suited them down to the ground, although Clem was not old enough to consume alcohol, he played by the rules, and remembering the advice from Sergeant Winner, the day before, chose orange juice instead.

"What's up with you, *you're not drinking lager*?" asked Grant, with a frown, as he ordered the drinks from a busty female barmaid, working behind the bar.

"I'm under age, and if found out, would get into trouble with the law, which would not go down well with the RAF, so I'm playing it safe," explained Clem.

"That's fair enough," replied Grant, taking a keen swig of his two pint German beer beverage, that was the best in the house. "But, you're missing a taste of nectar here though!" he added.

"Oh well, I'll have to wait until my eighteenth birthday in January, when I'm legally able to drink," stated Clem coolly, calmly and confidently.

"Are you sure, you're not even having a pint?" asked Grant.

"I'm positive, I'm looking after my RAF career, and not falling foul of drinking underage. It's a mugs game!" stated Clem in reply.

"That's fair enough," replied Grant.

"So, what's been happening at home, whilst I've been away?" asked Clem.

"Nothing much. But, I'm returning back there, having put in my one month's notice at the flat I'm living in," replied Grant.

"Why's that? I thought you enjoyed living at the flat!" exclaimed Clem.

"I do like it there, but it's too expensive, and I can't afford it. Besides, I'm thinking about getting married next year," replied Grant.

"Are you? Who to?" asked Clem facetiously.

"Who do you think? Caroline, of course!" replied Grant, in a ruffled manner.

"Oh yes, of course, I forgot," quipped Clem, with tongue in cheek.

"Cheeky bugger!" joked Grant.

"So, have you set a date yet?" asked Clem.

"No, not yet, I haven't even popped the question. But I'm going to, and I'm thinking of a September wedding next year, if she accepts," replied Grant.

"Oh, I'm sure she will! So, have you decided on a best man yet?" asked Clem hopefully, and waiting with baited breath for the reply.

"No, not yet. I might ask one of my colleagues from work, and see if they'll do the honours. But it's early days yet. I need an answer from Caroline first, before I make arrangements for a best man," replied Grant.

"Fair enough," said Clem in disappointment, after he expected to be offered the role.

"It all takes time, I suppose. But I'm in no rush. I've got a year to plan everything, if we can both agree on a wedding date, that is," stated Grant.

"Yes, that's true. By the way, I think you're drinking that strong lager too quickly! Are you in your car?" asked Clem.

"Yes I am," replied Grant.

"Don't you think that's rather a stupid thing to do? You might not make it to your wedding, if you're drinking and driving! You'll either be dead, or serving time in one of Her Majesty's prisons!" exclaimed Clem.

"I'll be fine, I've had a big breakfast, have a strong constitution, and will take the side roads home," replied Grant.

"That's not the point! You might kill somebody!" exclaimed Clem.

"Shut up grandma, and drink your orange!" replied Grant facetiously.

Clem shrugged off the criticism and continued sipping his ice cold fruit drink. They stayed for a further hour, and Grant bought some food, but did not order any more drinks. Clem bought himself another glass of orange and Grant declined another two pint glass of of lager, when asked by Clem. His conscience had been pricked with regard to drink driving, and he decided to behave responsibly.

"Do you want a lift home?" asked Grant.

"No, I'm alright thanks, I'll get the bus," replied Clem.

"Okay, fair enough! See you around bro!" answered Grant.

"Yes, see you later, and for goodness sake, drive carefully!" exclaimed Clem.

"I'll do my best," replied Grant.

Clem headed to the bus station and Grant walked to his car, a green mini with white stripes on the bonnet, roof and boot. Clem was home within half an hour and wondered if his brother would make it back in one piece. He hoped so. Even if he had not been chosen as his best man. He still didn't want him dead, or arrested.

He phoned Grant after his tea to check he had got home okay, and was relieved when he found that he had, and then he called Ellie up and nervously waited for her to answer the telephone, as the ring tone buzzed incessantly.

"Hello," replied the softly spoken female voice, at the other end of the line, eventually.

"Ellie?" asked Clem.

"Yes, who's this?" replied the female.

"It's Clem, from the RAF!"

"Oh, hi Clem, I didn't recognise your voice, sorry," replied Ellie.

"That's okay, how are you?" asked Clem.

"I'm fine thanks, how about yourself?" replied Ellie.

"Yes, I'm good. I'm on a weekend off, and at home now, and wondered if you're able to meet me sometime over the weekend?" asked Clem.

"Yes sure, that'll be great! But I can't meet up tonight, as I'm going out on a hen do, although I'm free tomorrow," replied Ellie.

"That's brlliant! I shall see you tomorrow! What time is best for you?" asked Clem.

"Any time in the afternoon, as I have a family dinner on a Sunday," replied Ellie.

"Okay, shall we say two o'clock then? I will call for you," suggested Clem.

"Yes, that sounds perfect," agreed Ellie.

"See you tomorrow at two o'clock, then," replied Clem, and he replaced the telephone handset back on to its holder.

The rest of the evening was spent on the settee, with his feet up, as Clem waited for his favourite television programme, Match of the Day to come on, at 10 pm, and he waited patiently to see his favourite football teams, Aston Villa and Tottenham Hotspur, who both had fine victories today.

As usual, Clem fell asleep before the programme came on and he missed the majority of the football matches, but he wasn't too concerned, as his two favourite teams were two of the last matches to be shown, so it was a relief for Clem, and he thanked his lucky stars for that.

Tottenham Hotspur beat Chelsea 2-0, and Aston Villa came out on top against Manchester United by two goals to one. It was an extremely satisfying couple of results for his two favourite teams, but he knew they both had a lot of work to do to climb the table, as their form was patchy and inconsistent, and both clubs were languishing at the bottom end of the First Divison table. More points were needed to lift them both up, but that was easier said than done, although today was a good starting point, thought Clem.

Chapter 23

Next morning, after having a relaxing sleep in his single bed, in his single room, Clem woke up at 10 am, refreshed and relaxed and was looking forward to calling for Ellie. He washed, shaved and dressed and went downstairs for breakfast, which consisted of toast, cereal and a glass of fresh orange. He picked up the Sunday morning newspaper from the table, and browsed through the pages, towards the sport and in particular the football reports of his two favourite football teams, Tottenham Hotspur and Aston Villa, and he read with interest.
After breakfast, Clem sat down at his desk in his bedroom, and jotted down some notes for a book he was writing. He had been writing stories and novels since he was five years

old, and he always found time to write a few pages, and couldn't find anything better than to be creative with pen and paper, and bring the pages to life, with vivid, entertaining and enthralling adventures, and he often wrote until the early hours of the morning. When Clem had a pen in his hand, he wrote for hours and hours, and tried to bring his ideas to the forefront of his mind, and unearth his subconscious thoughts into a paperback masterpiece. He wrote until it was time for lunch, and his current project was a story he had began before he joined the RAF, about a forest that was reputed to be haunted, and unable to be developed into anything worthwhile. But a local man, Tom Bay had other ideas, and he decided he was going to transform the forest into a leisure amenity for the town, with all the facilities needed to provide the residents of the community with endless hours of entertainment and fun.

Clem enjoyed his lunch, of Yorkshire pudding, beef, sprouts, carrots and mashed potato and it was similar to a Christmas dinner. Clem's mum always pushed the boat out on a Sunday and treated the family to a delicious Sunday roast. It was followed by apple pie and custard and a pot of tea, that was strong and tasty. Clem was clock watching throughout lunch, and counted down the seconds to half past one. He had arranged to call for Ellie at 2pm and didn't want to be late, so he needed to give himself half an hour to make his way on foot to her house, as she lived opposite his old high school, and he knew how far it was there, and how long it would take, which was roughly thirty minutes.

"What are you doing this afternoon, son?" asked Clem's mum.

"I've got a date at two with Ellie. I'm calling for her at her house," replied Clem.

"Oh lovely! That's nice! I hope you have a fabulous time!" answered Clem's mum.

"Thanks mum, I haven't seen her for ages, so we'll have a lot to catch up on," replied Clem.

"I'm sure you will," agreed Clem's mum.

Clem glanced at the clock again, and saw that it was 1.15pm, so he quickly wolfed down his roast beef and Yorkshire pudding, and tucked into his apple pie and custard. He washed it all down with a cup of tea, minus the bromide, and left the table. He nipped upstairs and brushed his teeth, rinsed his face, and ran the Brut anti perspirant spray over his body, before combing his short hair and slipping on his jacket. He was ready, and he was nervous, but he was looking forward to seeing Ellie, and was filled with excitement.

"Bye, I'm going now, see you later!" shouted Clem, as he left the house.

"Bye son, have fun!" replied his mum.

Clem's dad was also preparing to go out, to watch the local rugby league team Hull Kingston Rovers play, and he offered him a lift.

"Thanks dad, that would be handy. As I'd rather be early than late," replied Clem.

Clem arrived at Ellie's house at 1.45pm. He knocked at the the door, and was pleasantly surprised to find Ellie answering.

"Hi!" called Ellie.

"Hey!" replied Clem.

"Your hair's short!" stated Ellie.

"Yep, it is. What do you reckon?" asked Clem.

"It's nice, I like it, it suits you!" replied Ellie.

"That's good, thankyou," stated Clem.

"So, what have you got planned for this afternoon?" asked Ellie.

"Spending quality time with you. It doesn't matter what we do, as long as we're having fun together," replied Clem.

"That's nice. But I can't invite you in here, the family are in, and are all having a Sunday afternoon kip," stated Ellie.

"Let's go back to my parents place then, we can listen to some music, watch tv, or chat," replied Clem.

"That sounds fun. Okay, let's go, I'll get my coat, as it's a little chilly outside," said Ellie.

"Okay, and by the way, it's nice to see you again!" exclaimed Clem.

"And you too!" replied Ellie.

The couple walked hand in hand to Clem's parents house, and the weather was fresh, sunny and dry, which were ideal conditions for a steady walk. The atmosphere between them was amicable, and the attraction they had felt from their first encounter at the Youth Club Disco a few weeks ago was still intact, so the signs were good.

"What have you been doing, whilst I've been away?" asked Clem.

"Nothing much really," replied Ellie.

"Have you been taking things easy?" asked Clem.

"Yes, I've not been feeling too great, to be honest. I've been falling apart," replied Ellie.

"What do you mean?" asked Clem.

"Oh, it's a long story," replied Ellie, with a sigh.

"Well, I'm all ears, and I've got the time to listen. Let me see if I can help you," suggested Clem.

"It's personal, really. I'd rather not talk about it," replied Ellie.

"Okay, I understand," consoled Clem, with empathy.

"I'm sorry, but I'm not being secretive. It's just that I've had a bad year and have some issues, which I'm trying to get my head around, but I'm doing okay. It just takes a little time to adjust," explained Ellie.

"That's fine. You can take as long as you need to sort out your troubles, I'll be here, if ever you need to talk about it. I shall be completely supportive, and sympathetic to your needs," replied Clem.

"Thank you, that's very kind of you," stated Ellie.

The couple continued to stroll along the pavement, and there was a slight lull in the conversation. Clem thought deeply about what was being said over the course of the last few minutes. He was okay with it. He realised Ellie had things on her mind, and when they reached the solitude of Clem's parents house, Clem showed Ellie the way in.

"Nice house!" exclaimed Ellie.

"Thanks, but it's not mine!" joked Clem.

"It's better than the house I live in. This seems a properly built house, whilst I live in what appears to be a rabbit hutch," joked Ellie.

"It's a modern style that you live in, that's all, which is designed to save room," commented Clem.

"It's ugly!" teased Ellie.

"Come and move here, on this estate," suggested Clem.

"I can't afford it! I'm not working!" replied Ellie.

"I didn't mean you. I meant your parents. Talk them round," stated Clem.

"I'll have a word with them," replied Ellie.

The couple headed through to the living room, and startled Clem's mum.

"Who's that?" shouted Clem's mum.

"It's okay mum, it's only me," yelled Clem.

"What are you doing back here, I thought you were seeing Ellie?" replied Clem's mum.

"I am," stated Clem. "She's here with me!" he added.

"Oh sorry, I didn't realise," replied Clem's mum in embarrassment.

Ellie giggled out loud, finding Clem's mum hilarious, in the way she replied.

"We are just going upstairs, to listen to some music," said Clem facetiously.

"Okay son!" replied Clem's mum nonchalantly.

Clem led Ellie by the hand along the hallway, and upstairs to his single room, with the single bed, and with a radio and record player sitting in the corner. Ellie looked at Clem and Clem looked at Ellie, and passion quickly overtook them, as they embraced lovingly on the bed, after they had flopped down in a twirling, entwining and spinning mass of flesh coming together. Their lips locking frantically, with a longing to explore the delights of carnal desire, and both were eagerly discovering the contours of each of their bodies, as hands clasped flesh and ran smoothly over the various shapes and outlines of one another. It was a moment of discovery for them both, as they came to terms with the goods on offer, and they warmly and eagerly petted, grappled, grabbed and grasped at the squirming and rolling torso of their partner on the bed, as they rapidly embraced, with arms, legs, and hands twisting, shifting and turning to feel what the other had to offer. The love-in lasted for half an hour, as the cavorting couple snogged and caressed each other in a variety of ways. It was hot, romantic and pumped with passion, as the two lovers went for it hammer and tong. They were embroiled in a fervent and steaming clinch, that had no boundaries, as they rolled and reeled over the full width of the single bed. The springs creaked, the headboard banged against the wall, but the passionate couple were oblivious to everything around them.

"How was that for you?" asked Clem.

"Grrrrrreat!" exclaimed Ellie.

"Ditto!" replied Clem.

"You could be useful to me, in the future!" stated Ellie.

"And you could be useful to me, too!" replied Clem.

"Touche!" joked Ellie.

"Sounds good to me!" stated Clem.

"Shall we meet up again, this time next week?" asked Ellie.

"Yes, that goes without saying!" exclaimed Clem.

"Nice one, I shall look forward to it, with all my might!" screamed Ellie.

"Me too!" replied Clem, laughing.

The cavorting couple sat up on the bed, and Ellie's hair was everywhere. They looked at each other and laughed.

"Come on, let's go downstairs and have a cuppa! Unless you want something stronger?" suggested Clem.

They stepped keenly downstairs, and headed into the kitchen.

"Tea, or coffee?" asked Clem.

"Coffee, please," replied Ellie.

"Okay, coming up!" answered Clem.

Clem put the kettle on, and when it had boiled, he brewed up two strong cups of coffee.

"That's a lovely cuppa, love," blurted Ellie.

"Nice!" replied Clem.

They sat opposite each other, sipping their coffee, and making eyes at each other. They only had eyes for one another.

"I can't wait for next week!" stated Ellie.

"Neither can I!" replied Clem.

"We can go further, if you want!" stated Ellie confidently. Clem smiled, nodded, and by the expression on his face totally agreed with Ellie's suggestion, without having to say a word. They finished their drinks, and Clem looked at the clock on the wall. It read 5pm.

"Wow, time flies, when you're enjoying yourself!" exclaimed Clem.

"It certainly does!" agreed Ellie.

"I've never enjoyed myself as much as this, in my entire life!" stated Clem.

"That's sweet, and the feeling's mutual!" replied Ellie.

"Wow, thanks!" said Clem.

"Right, it's time for me to head home now, for tea, and a bath, so are you ready to walk me back, honey?" asked Ellie.

"Yeah, sure, it'll be a pleasure!" exclaimed Clem.

"Come on then, I'm ready to go!" stated Ellie eagerly. "And I'm sure you're ready to get back to the billet, and to your RAF mates!" she added.

"I wish you could come back with me," replied Clem slushily.

"Maybe I can fit in your suitcase?" quipped Ellie, with tongue in cheek.

Clem raised his eyebrows, and nodded positively.

Chapter 24

Clem stepped on the train at Paragon Station at 8pm, for the 8.06pm direct train to Newark, to embark on his journey back to RAF Swinderby. The train left exactly on time, and pulled slowly away to take Clem the airman back on his RAF adventure. It had been a good weekend, and as usual went as quickly as sand through a sieve. His biggest memories were the Match of the Day football programme, catching up with his mum, having a drink with his eldest brother at the German pub Hofbrauhaus, and last but not least, the rendezvous with his girlfriend Ellie, which stood out head and shoulders above the others. His head was filled with the vision of his short time with her during the Sunday afternoon hot passion session. It had all the hallmarks of being one of his most cherished memories ever in his life to date.

An hour later, and the train pulled into the Newark railway station, and Clem disembarked from the carriage, and he lumped his bag with him towards the taxi rank outside. He jumped into a cab and provided his destination to the driver. The taxi zoomed off within seconds and headed towards the RAF Swinderby campsite. He arrived twenty minutes later, paid the cab driver, and made his way to the billet block. He was relieved to be back and happy to reach the safety of the accommodation block once again, and was ready for anything that was going to be thrown at him.

He entered the billet block, unpacked his RAF kit bag and quickly hung up his freshly laundered clothes that his mum had kindly washed for him during the weekend, in his billet wardrobe. It smelled fresh, clean, and of home. He grabbed his washing kit, and headed towards the ablutions for a shower and a shave. It was 9.45 pm and most of the other airmen were already back and relaxing on their beds, waiting for "Lights Out," all with their own individual memories from their weekend break. There was laughter, banter and joking on some of the beds, as the other recruits talked of their events during the last couple of days, in an amiable manner. Clem kept himself to himself and didn't join in with the "wide heads" that had crowded around a couple of beds in the corner. He remained aloof, just like he usually did. The banter, laughter and revellry continued, but Clem took no notice, and he let them get on with it. He slipped into bed, covered himself up with his covers, and drifted gently to sleep.

Next morning, at the strike of 6.15am, the sound of reveille woke the whole billet room, with a thundering boom, and the recruits were ready, willing and able to take on the new day. Clem was the first up, and he breezed through the room with his washing kit, to freshen up and shave. He dried, dressed and was making his bed pack within minutes, and he made a perfect specimen that he was proud of. He had to admit to himself that it was one of his best efforts. He looked around the room to see if anyone needed help, but everyone seemed to be managing okay. He tidied his wardrobe, arranged his kit on the bed and waited for the others to complete their tasks, before making his way for breakfast. Within five minutes, the majority of the recruits were ready to go down to the Airmen's Mess for breakfast.

After breakfast, the airmen returned to the billet, and waited for the drill instructors to arrive. The recruits were keen, eager and ready for another tough week ahead, without having a clue what was in store for them.

The front doors of the billet flew open, half an hour later, and Sergeant Winner and Corporal Cherry breezed inside, with a cocky and arrogant attitude.

"Recruits, stand by your beds!" yelled Sergeant Winner. "And attention!"

He walked slowly around the billet, keeping a keen eye on the bedpacks, and Corporal Cherry followed closely behind, focusing on the kit that was displayed on the bed. There was nothing for them to complain about, as each airman had made the "perfect bedpack" and all of the kit seemed to be in fine condition as well, and it would have been harsh if either of the drill instructors happened to sling the bedpacks, or the kit across the floor. Fortunately for the recruits, they escaped with the embarrassment, and Sergeant Winner and Corporal Cherry kept everything intact on the beds, which was appreciated by all of the recruits.

"Okay airmen!" shouted Sergeant Winner. "Good morning to you all, and well done on the presentation of your kit and bedpacks. They are all very good!" he added.

"Thank you sergeant!" replied the airmen in unison.

"This week is going to be different, as we are going to travel to Sherwood Forest for R and I, which stands for Resources and Initiative, and it will test your skills in various amounts of endeavours, including diligence, intelligence, mental strength, awareness, navigational skills, map reading, courage and night time searching skills. It won't be easy, and it won't be a walk in a park. It's going to be tough, and it's going to be stressful. It won't be any place for the faint hearted! You're all going to need balls in abundance, and if you weaken at any stage, you shall find this experience very difficult indeed. So I would like to advise you to be on your mettle at all times, stay as focused as you possibly can, listen to the instructions from both Corporal Cherry and myself, and concentrate on the tasks ahead. If you adhere to the orders, this will be one of the most enjoyable experiences you shall ever witness in your lives!" stated Sergeant Winner.

The airmen listened carefully to the instructions that Sergeant Winner kindly provided, and took everything on board. They all realised the importance of adhering to the advice of somebody that had expert knowledge on "Resources and Initiative." It was imperative that they carried out all these orders from Sergeant Winner, to help make the tasks in Sherwood Forest as enjoyable and productive as possible.

"Okay Flight! We shall be setting off in ten minutes, so prepare yourself to board the bus, and change into camouflage uniform and steel toe capped boots. Everything else will be issued to you when we have arrived there!" bellowed Sergeant Winner.

Ten minutes later, the recruits filed slowly but surely onto the RAF bus, and found themselves a seat. There was also the other small Flight that had been attached to this Flight to make up the numbers, that would be going along with them.

Five minutes later, the bus driver started the engine, and the vehicle rumbled forward to its destination, Sherwood Forest, Mansfield in Nottinghamshire. The atmosphere on the bus was of a low tempo. It was so quiet, that it was possible to hear a pin drop, as each of the recruits settled back into their shells, contemplating the events ahead of them, as they wondered what was in store, in the next few days. They were excited, nervous and anxious, but committed and thoughtful, all rolled into one. The bus travelled along the A614, and then on to the A1 for the 24 miles journey, which would take 50 minutes to complete.

Sherwood Forest was the legendary stomping-ground of Robin Hood, and set in a 450 acre country park, which had 900 veteran oak trees including the historic Mayor Oak, and with way marked trails amongst the leafy glades, adorned by birds that included jays, woodpeckers and redstarts, it was a beautiful setting for the "Resources and Initiative" experience. But the airmen from RAF Swinderby were more concerned about where they were living, with no sign of tents or shelter anywhere to be seen.

"Right recruits, when you've disembarked from the bus, head towards the rear of the vehicle and prepare to unload the boot, of boxes of food and drink!" called Corporal Cherry loudly.

"Yes corporal!" replied the airmen in unison.

The boot was emptied of the heavy luggage, which consisted of tinned food, tin openers and tinned drinks. There was still no sign of shelter, and it worried all of the recruits. They were wondering where on earth they were going to stay. The place was only full of trees, bushes and shrubs, and it seemed to be an uninhabitable place to live.

"I expect you're all wondering where you will be living whilst you are here, but I'm afraid to disappoint you that there isn't any four star hotels around, neither caravans, tents or huts. But there are plenty of branches, leaves, shrubs and bushes, and that will be your shelter in the form of a bivouac!" exclaimed Corporal Cherry. "You shall construct a framework with natural materials, like tall branches and then cover with leaves, ferns and similar items for waterproofing, and leaf litter for insulation. The more leaves you lay down, the drier you'll be, especially if we have a rainstorm whilst we are here. But it's going to be

chilly at night, so it's important to fully insulate your bivouac, and make your frame strong, sturdy and solid, with thick leaves and fern on top!" continued Corporal Cherry.
The airmen were full of appreciation for these tips from the drill instructor, and it eased their minds slightly, but they were still concerned about how to gather enough strong branches, without a saw or hammer, as there didn't appear to be those tools anywhere near them.
 "Excuse me corporal, but how do we cut down these strong branches?" asked Clem Harrison.
 "Resources and Initiative is the name of the game, use your initiative to become resourceful, that is why you're here!" replied Corporal Cherry.
Clem frowned, and wasn't particularly satisfied with the answer he received from the corporal, but he didn't let it get him down. He simply nodded, smiled and backed away, without letting the corporal know that he reckoned it was an empty reply. If a job needed doing properly, thought Clem, it had to be done by himself, and he was as determined as ever to make the best bivouac of the year, and to make sure there would be no leaks, draughts or damp problems. He owed it to himself and to his health to make sure these next few days in Sherwood Forest were comfortable, at the very least.
 "Any more questions, regarding the bivouacs?" asked Corporal Cherry.
There were no replies. The airmen fully understood what they had to do. The "Resources and Initiative" subject explained itself, and each recruit knew they were being tested for diligence, mental strength, intelligence and resourcefulness, as well as initiative. The corporal hadn't lied to them. It was all about *resources and initiative*.

They could not argue. All they had to do was gather enough strong branches, thick leaves and large fern, and there would be no complaints from them. Clem put the matter into a "positive" box in his mind and broke the problem down into pieces. First he reckoned he needed a tool to break the branches, and he produced an axe that was made out of the strongest branch he could find, and he used the sharpest part of the implement as a cutting tool, to enable him to shred the branches from the trees, with as much ease as possible, and it worked a treat, although it was hard, laborious work and very tiring.

But Clem stuck at it and made inroads into the trees, to gather enough sturdy branches to construct a decent sized bivouac. He worked on the branches for over half an hour and was making great progress, and it then suddenly dawned on him that the job was becoming easier, as the leaves on the gathered branches were coming in handy as insulation and damp proofing for the floor, so he was killing two birds with one stone.

The work became easier, as Clem quickly built up a plethora of sticks, branches, leaves, fern and shrubs, of all different shapes and sizes, and his morale was raised at the sight of the pile of the natural commodities he had collected, and he continued to break down many more branches, to help him in his quest to build the best bivouac in the world. He was a man on a mission, and he would not be satisfied until he collected another large pile of materials. Eventually, after another hour of toil and labour, he decided that he had gathered enough raw material to enable him to begin work on his bivouac.

He started by placing the branches in order of size and length, with the largest separated from the smallest, then he placed the fern in a separate pile, followed by the leaves, in another pile, to keep the material in order. He gathered the largest branches and carried them over to a secluded part of the forest, with plenty of shelter available, and immediately began work on building a bivouac, as best he could.

He had no previous experience in working with raw building materials, like wood, and scratched his head on how he could bind the material together. But he quickly came to terms with what was required, and he remembered watching a programme on the television a few years ago, about Robinson Crusoe, and recalled how he built a house from branches, and how he used strong twine that he found in the wild, which was sturdy enough to hold the branches together.

Clem leant the dozen or so large branches across to a gigantic oak tree that was strong and sound, and this acted as the main pillar and he secured them with twine. He then covered the dozen or so large branches with smaller sized sticks and filled in the gaps, to make the roof as solid as possible, with hopefully little chance of springing a leak. He criss-crossed the smaller pieces of branches across the longer shafts of wood, and tied them together with the strong twine, to fully secure them into place, and then he carefully located the fern, leaves and other foliage on the top, to fully cover the entire roof. After he was satisfied there would be no risk of leakage, he went to work on the floor insulation, and gathered the rest of the leaves and fern, to make the bivouac as snug and cosy as he possibly could.

Clem had to admit to himself that the bivouac would be too small to share, as there was little room to spare for another person, but he wasn't bothered about that, it was every man for himself, and nobody said anything about sharing with fellow recruits, so Clem was happy enough with his efforts.

The roof appeared to be wind proof, and Clem added extra strong twine to the edges to bolster the branches that were holding the leaves and fern in place, and he added further branches to secure the loose foliage. He also wrapped further strong twine around the branches that were leant against the tree trunk, just in case they might slip and crush him in the night.

When he had added the extra support, he stood back and admired his work, and was impressed. He contemplated whether he should gather further amounts of floor insulation material, as it looked a little thin on the ground, and his conscience got the better of him, and having an attitude of "better safe than sorry," he decided that it would be a good idea to bulk up on the ground materials.

He searched the area for loose leaves and fern, and collected the material that was conveniently available nearby. As it was autumn, the trees had began to shed their leaves, and it was fortunate for Clem that there was plenty of foliage available which was dry and crisp, and ideal to place on the floor of his bivouac.

Ten minutes later, Clem had finished, and he was satisfied with his efforts. He was a lot happier about his living quarters now, than he had been two hours ago, and he was positive he could get some well earned rest underneath the makeshift house, when it came to turn in for the night, no matter how wild the wind blew, or how rapid the rain fell. This bivouac of his was the best in the world, he thought.

Sergeant Winner and Corporal Cherry appeared a couple of minutes later, and inspected Clem's handiwork. They had a good look around, testing the construction for weak spots.

"Very good effort, Clem, well done!" exclaimed Sergeant Winner, keenly.

Chapter 25

"Come along now Clem, it's time for the ration hand out," stated Corporal Cherry.

"Ration hand out?" asked Clem.

"Yes indeed. Each airman will be issued with food three times per day, and this will be handed out at the Catering HQ," replied Corporal Cherry.

"Okay, I'm on my way!" stated Clem, following the two drill instructors.

They arrived at a long wooden table, dressed in a white line table cloth, with an array of tinned food and drink displayed in all its glory, sitting on top. Clem looked closely at the merchandise on offer and tried to work out what to choose. He had not experienced food like this before, and it was all novel to him. But he didn't let it get him down. If it was food and he was hungry enough, he would partake in consuming, no matter what it tasted like, and being in the middle of Sherwood Forest, with only this fare on offer, he realised beggars could not be choosers.

"Pick your main meal from this pile, your pudding from here and your drink from there," pointed out the cook complete in white overalls, and a chef hat.

Clem looked at the tins and tried to decipher what each of them had inside, by reading the small print on the back. He chose beef for the main course, jam sponge for pudding, and cola for a drink. He grabbed a tin opener and a fork and spoon from the tray at the edge of the table and as soon as he had managed to open them, tucked gleefully in. The taste was different, but it was palatable, although cold, but he didn't have any complaints.

He quickly wolfed down the main course, and then started on the jam sponge, which was sweet and tasty. Then he washed it down with the cola drink, and there wasn't any sign of bromide anywhere to be seen. If this was lunch, Clem wondered what was for tea.

"Once you've finished, please move away from the table, to enable those that haven't eaten, to collect their tinned food!" shouted Corporal Cherry.

Clem shuffled forward and stood away from the long table, and he let in those that were starving hungry, to pick up their scran.

"Has everyone managed to build a bivouac?" asked Sergeant Winner.

"Yes sergeant!" called the recruits together, in reply.

"Are they safe enough?" asked Sergeant Winner.

There was no reply from the airmen, only shrugs of the shoulders of indifference.

"We need to inspect each and every one, before anyone steps underneath, for obvious reasons, as we don't want to be scraping up bodies from the ground in the morning!" stated Sergeant Winner facetiously, with tongue in cheek.

The recruits grimaced at this comment, and they were not sure whether to laugh or cry. But it was only a joke, as per usual from Sergeant Winner, albeit in a crude manner.

"Once every one has eaten and has filled up again, we shall endeavour to inspect the bivouacs, before proceeding with the afternoon's activities," stated Sergeant Winner confidently.

The recruits that were eating were given ten minutes to finish their food, and then Sergeant Winner and Corporal Cherry proceeded forward to check the bivouacs for safety. He checked Clem's bivouac again for security reasons, in case anything had slipped since before lunch, and it was passed as fit for purpose. In fact, each and every recruit had built a safe and habitable bivouac, all constructed with great care and diligence, which was unusual for a Flight to achieve, as there was usually one or two that was slipshod and slapdash. But Sergeant Winner's beaming smile said it all, every single recruit had taken their time and shown great effort to construct a bivouac of the highest calibre, and every one was different.

Joseph Job constructed his bivouac in a hole in the ground, and built a sturdy roof over the hole, whilst Mark Lucas had built his bivouac independent of any trees or shrubs, and linked three branches together at both ends of the construction to form two frames, which were able to accommodate a roof of branches, that was secured by reed and twine, in an ingenious manner. Timothy Moses built a bivouac in the shape of a teepee, that was cone shaped, and similar to an Indian wigwam in the old Western films on the television. It looked strong and sturdy and very cosy, and it was covered with thick fern and foliage. David Ephraim built his bivouac in a simple way, by jamming a dozen branches across two low lying trees, and covering them with bushes and shrubs.

"Well done Flight! Your bivouacs have passed my health and safety test, which is great because it saves some time, and gives you more opportunity to work on the next activity!" called Sergeant Winner, at the top of his voice.

"I shall second that, and I applaud your efforts. It's not easy working on something that is out of your comfort zone, and building a bivouac in the centre of Sherwood Forest is definitely challenging and daunting, and very much out of the comfort zone!" exclaimed Corporal Cherry.

"Now listen carefully, Flight. The next activity could have serious consequences, if you don't pay attention!" began Sergeant Winner. "What I mean by that, is this. It's imperative you concentrate on the training being provided. You shall be split up into two groups, one group shall work with Corporal Cherry, and the other will be working with me, and we will be quickly going over the rudiments of compass reading. After the briefing, you shall be let loose in the forest on a trek, that will take you into the bowels of the notorious Sherwood Forest, and you shall only have a compass to save your skins," stated Sergeant Winner.

The airmen listened with their mouths gaping open. None of them had experience of compass reading before, and neither had any of them have experience in trekking. It was all new to them, but this was the "Resources and Initiative" event, with diligence, enthusiasm, endeavour and mental agility needed to be brought to the fore, which each of them were determined to do.

"Listen in, Flight. Will these people join Sergeant Winner!" called Corporal Cherry. "Joseph Job, Mark

Lucas, Timothy Moses and David Ephraim," added the corporal.

"And will these recruits join Corporal Cherry. Joshua Peters, Daniel Thomas, Clem Harrison and Jacob Adams!" bellowed Sergeant Winner.

"Will these guys join Sergeant Winner. Ray Lord, Walt Phillips, Ken James and Denis King!" shouted Corporal Cherry.

"And will these airmen join Corporal Cherry. David Isaac, Jordan Johns, Abraham Jude and Jacob Marks!" yelled Sergeant Winner.

The airmen quickly joined their respective drill instructors, and formed two individual teams, for the compass reading training.

"Like I said before, you need to concentrate on this training, otherwise you shall be in danger of being lost in here forever, and never to be found alive again!" exclaimed Sergeant Winner dramatically.

Clem joined up along with the other seven recruits in his team, with Corporal Cherry. He listened with great intent, and watched carefully, as the corporal described the rudiments of the task ahead, and he had to admit to himself that he didn't understand a single aspect. He only hoped the other seven knew what to do, when it came to being let loose in the forest, on the trail of the mysterious trek. He glanced over to his teammates, but shrugged his shoulders in indifference, as he wasn't certain if they had fully understood the instructions either. Clem reckoned it was far too rushed, and they were not given enough opportunity to practice, under supervision.

But only time would tell if these guys got back safely to their bivouacs before dark, as it was October, and the light began to fade at four o'clock, on some days, and today was one of those days.

"Any questions, Flight?" asked Sergeant Winner.

There were no replies. The airmen were either well versed in this activity, or too frightened to admit they were clueless, and in Clem's case, it was the latter.

"Okay fine, recruits, if there's no questions, let's go!" yelled Corporal Cherry. "And, please follow your designated team leader!" he added.

The two teams separated in different directions, one taking the eastern trail, and the other taking the western. Clem was among Corporal Cherry's unit, and they marched briskly, moving eastwards.

"I shall lead you into the depths of the forest, and you will then be left to your own devices, with the aid of your compass, which you shall have at your disposal!" stated Corporal Cherry, handing a compass to each of the eight airman in the squad.

Clem looked puzzled when he glanced down at the face of the compass, and he may as well have put the implement in his pocket, for what it was worth, as he hadn't the foggiest idea on how to read it.

"Are you all comfortable with this?" asked Corporal Cherry.

The recruits nodded in the affirmative, as none of them wanted to look stupid in front of their peers. Twenty minutes later, after a steady march into the heart of the forest, Corporal Cherry stopped walking.

"Flight halt, stand at attention, and listen carefully!" ordered the corporal.

The recruits obeyed the order and waited with bated breath. Clem hoped someone in his team would understand what was going on, as he was absolutely clueless, and he feared he would be lost in the forest, along with the other seven team members, unless somebody could work out how to read a compass.

"Stand at ease, Flight!" called Corporal Cherry.

The recruits relaxed, but none of them appeared comfortable.

"When I walk away, I don't want to see anybody following me. If I catch any of you trying to cheat, you shall be placed on a charge and back-flighted two weeks! Do you understand?" shouted Corporal Cherry.

"Yes corporal!" replied the recruits, in unison.

"Give me twenty minutes, to get out of sight, before making your move, and oh, by the way, good luck!" called Corporal Cherry.

The recruits nodded in a gesture of thanks, but all of them were very unsure.

As soon as Corporal Cherry had disappeared out of view, Clem Harrison decided it was time to speak up.

"Does anyone know what the hell we are doing?" asked Clem.

"Nope, do you?" replied Joshua Peters, shaking his head in a negative manner.

"Nope, I'm clueless, to be honest. I was just hoping somebody might have been to cubs or scouts, and learnt about this, there," stated Clem.

"I'm afraid not, but surely it can't be that bad," piped up Daniel Thomas.

"Well, if you want, you can be responsible for the compass reading task, and get us out of this hole," replied Clem.

"No thanks, I'm not taking the flak, when we're supposed to be all in it together," replied Daniel Thomas.

"I think we should try and see if we can fathom this out as a team, and work through the complications as a unit. It can't be all that tough to read a compass, surely," suggested Jacob Adams.

"What about designating yourself, as the group leader?" stated Clem.

"No thanks, what about you?" replied Jacob Adams.

Clem looked around, and saw there was nobody else putting their hand up, and everyone was looking at him, with great expectation, and he nodded, smiled, and made his decision.

"Okay, I'll do it, I'll lead us through the maze of the forest. You can rely on me!" exclaimed Clem bravely, taking hold of his compass, and studying it closely. "It can't be all that difficult to understand this instrument, surely!" he added, getting his head around the problem. He spent a few minutes looking over it, and getting familiar with the dial, before smiling brightly, and moving forwards. "Come on, we can go now, Corporal Cherry's out of view, and we need to get on our way, before nightfall!" exclaimed Clem, with an upbeat positive attitude.

"Which way are we going?" asked Joshua Peters.

"This way, according to my compass," replied Clem.

"But that's not the way we came in!" shrieked Daniel Thomas.

"Never mind that, I'm sure there's plenty of trails around here, and they will all lead to our destination. So we'll be okay, and there might be a shortcut!" exclaimed Clem. "Come on let's go, and get back to base, pronto!"

The seven airmen followed Clem reluctantly, as they were certain he was jeopardising the task. But they did not complain, because after all, Clem had volunteered to be the team leader for the group, and would accept the flak for failing this mission, so the airmen had no real cause for concern.

The recruits marched for half an hour along a narrow trail, with many tall trees lined up along the edges, which gave it an eerie and spooky effect, that cast shadows along the pathway. But it didn't deter Clem, nor the other seven. They put on a brave face and carried on walking. The place was deserted, and it seemed like the airmen were being led inside a dead end, with the path becoming increasingly narrower, as they made each forward step.

"This is taking us nowhere!" complained Joshua Peters.

"And the light's failing too!" grumbled Daniel Thomas.

"Be patient, we're not far away now, I can feel it in my bones," replied Clem.

"Don't be so ridiculous!" yelled Daniel Thomas.

"Well, you can blame my compass, as it's telling me what direction to go in," replied Clem facetiously, unfazed by their complaints.

"I didn't think you could read it," piped up Jacob Adams.

"I can, but only just, as I recall being trained in the cubs many moons ago, when I was about eight years old, although it's very patchy, and it confused me then too. But I'm having a go!" replied Clem.

"Well, I think we're lost, and we should turn round and go back to where we were before, and start all over again," suggested Jacob Adams.

"That's the worst move we could possibly make. No, I insist we stay on this track, remain positive and keep moving forward," encouraged Clem, calmly and coolly.

The other seven slowly came round to Clem's way of thinking, and did as they were told. They moved through the thicket, bushes and undergrowth that had become denser, with each forward step, and it appeared to them that the trail had completely closed up.

"Keep at it, I can smell the home fires!" enthused Clem, with endless positivity pouring out from him.

"I'm sure you're suffering from delirium!" replied Daniel Thomas. "As I can smell nothing!"

"Breath in deeper, as the home fires are burning strongly! Believe me, we're not far away now!" stated Clem confidently.

The other seven airmen tutted and ridiculed his statement as rubbish. But five minutes later, the trees and bushes opened up miraculously, and there were lights, movement, noise and the smell of a burning fire, just like Clem had predicted.

"Look, we're back!" exclaimed Clem excitedly.

"Eh, how did that happen?" quizzed Daniel Thomas.

"Simple, it was all down to my trusty compass. It's brought us back from the brink!" exclaimed Clem confidently.

Chapter 26

The airmen settled back down in the confines and safety of the newly set up campsite, and were grateful to be back safe and sound. It had been an eye opener out there, and had educated them in a way that they never thought was possible. But Clem was the hero, and each of the seven recruits in the team were nagging him to explain how he managed to pull off the great escape, before darkness fell.

"Well, if you remember as we came down from the camp, we rounded a corner, which I took into consideration and used that to our advantage, and calculated that the bend we cornered could be taken cross country from the opposite direction, and save us some time. Thankfully my plan worked, and here we are!" explained Clem.

"But, was you taking a gamble in doing so?" asked Jacob Adams.

"Yes, I must admit, it was a huge risk, as there may have been a river to cross, or a stream of some kind, or other objections such as nettles, thorns and stuff like that, but we got away with it," replied Clem.

"Thanks all the same, Clem, you did a great job!" enthused Daniel Thomas, changing his tune from being a stuck up misery from earlier.

"You're welcome!" replied Clem, without hesitation.
The recruits joined the queue for their food, and discovered it was almost exactly the same as their lunch, except for the pudding, where they had a choice of chocolate or lemon sponge. Clem chose chocolate and swilled it down with a drink of cola. He didn't bother with the main course of beef, as he didn't feel all that hungry. Sergeant Winner addressed the airmen as they stood around eating and drinking their food.

"Well recruits, that's day one complete. Rest easy in your beds, and be prepared for another busy day tomorrow! You've worked hard today, building your bivouacs, and discovering about the compasses on the trails, which I must say went very well, and was extremely successful.

But tomorrow is another day and will be twice as difficult. However, don't worry about that, embrace the challenge! Good luck, and good night recruits, and sleep tight!" shouted Sergeant Winner.

Clem trooped back to his cosy bivouac. The wind had whipped up since he had returned to base and there was a slight drizzle in the air, but it did not deter Clem, he was made of stern stuff and was determined not to be disturbed by a little rainfall. But it was the breeze that was going to be the problem, as it was blowing the rain in the face of Clem's bivouac and soaking everything in sight. Fortunately for him, the extra branches he had layed had worked a treat and it provided an extra layer of damp proofing, and helped to keep the interior layers snug dry.

The wind howled against the tree tops nearby, and they screeched spookily in a manner that was loud and brash, and Clem listened to it as he tried to drift off to sleep. It helped him to relax and in next to no time, he was snoring his head off, as he lay comfortably in the deep pile of leaves, foliage and undergrowth.

Next morning, at 6 am, the campsite was awakened by the familiar sound of reveille. The airmen awoke slowly as they came to terms of where they were. Clem rubbed the sleep out of his eyes and stretched out his arms and legs to wake himself up. He had slept well during the night, and hadn't felt the chill in the air. The wind had died down and the rain had cleared up, but there was a deposit of dew on the leaves outside Clem's bivouac, which fell when shaken, and Clem made sure he didn't clatter the foliage too many times, otherwise he would be in receipt of an early shower. To stay as dry as he could, Clem shuffled through the tight hole at the front of the bivouac, and managed to squeeze himself through it. He was already fully dressed, as he had slept in his clothes, and he stepped out of the bivouac within a matter of seconds. He made his way towards the Catering HQ for breakfast, and was thankful there wasn't a bedpack to make, nor his uniform to display for inspection. Breakfast consisted of tinned meat, cola and a chocolate bar, which Clem devoured eagerly. He was starving and he could have consumed it again, without any problem. After he had eaten, Clem waited for the other airmen in his Flight to join him.

The other recruits didn't take too long to congregate around the Catering HQ for breakfast, and they tucked into their food keenly, although one or two of them turned up their noses at the choices on offer, as they were expecting toast, cereal and fruit juice. But that wasn't going to happen, slap bang in the middle of Sherwood Forest!

"How did you all sleep?" addressed Clem Harrison, in the direction of the whole Flight.

"No comment!" replied Joshua Peters, shaking his head.

"I couldn't sleep, for the damned wind!" exclaimed Daniel Thomas.

"I slept fine," answered Jacob Adams.

"Me too, I slept like a top!" replied Clem.

"What's that mean exactly?" asked Jacob Adams.

"What, sleep like a top?" replied Clem.

"Yes," stated Jacob Adams.

"I've no idea," replied Clem, with honesty.

"It means when a top is spinning quickly, it has an appearance of being so steady and quiet, and seems to be stationary and still, like it's sleeping," confirmed Daniel Thomas helpfully.

"Wow, well I never knew that! You learn something new everyday!" exclaimed Clem.

"I'm full of trivialities like this!" joked Daniel Thomas. "It must be due to all the books I've read in the library," he added.

The recruits laughed together at this revelation.

"And you learn something new about people everyday, as well!" joked Clem.

Sergeant Winner approached the recruits, with a smile on his face.

"Alright airmen, how was breakfast?" asked Sergeant Winner.

"It was fine!" replied the recruits, in unison.

"And how was your first night, under the stars?" asked the sergeant.

"Mixed!" came the recruits reply, again in unison.

"Okay, never mind. Maybe you'll all sleep better tonight, after today's exertions. There's a lot to cover," stated Sergeant Winner.

The airmen nodded in understanding, and they all appeared to be well up for it.

"So, on to today. Like I said earlier, it's going to be tough! But I will explain it to you, briefly," began Sergeant Winner. "Now yesterday, you were led on a trail, and provided with a compass each, and then asked to find your own way back, which was an overwhelming success. But today, you shall be on the trail again, and this time without a compass, and you will not be led by an NCO, but will work on your own devices, with a designated team leader from your group, in a task entitled, "Search and Detain," that will see one group go in pursuit of the other," explained Sergeant Winner, slowly and clearly.

The recruits listened intently, and were keen to get going on the task at hand. The weather was fine, there was no rain and the sun was shining brightly, even though there was a slight autumnal chill in the air.

"Are you ready troops?" asked Sergeant Winner.

"Yes sergeant!" replied the recruits, in unison.

"I shall toss a coin to decide who will be searching first," stated Sergeant Winner. "Who are the designated team leaders?"

Clem stepped forward as the leader for his team, and Mark Lucas stepped up as the other team leader.

"Okay, heads or tails?" asked Sergeant Winner, looking at the two airmen for a reply.

"Heads!" called Clem instantly.

Sergeant Winner tossed the coin, and it landed on "heads," as Clem had called.

"Clem, decides!" stated Sergeant Winner. "What do you want to do?"

"We will search first," replied Clem, without any doubt whatsoever.

"Very good, Clem, thanks. So, Mark Lucas and his team will set off and be given twenty minutes to make themselves scarce, before Clem and his team go off in search of them, and when all eight airmen are captured, the roles will be reversed, with Mark's team going off in search of Clem's group, and the winner will be the team that is the quickest in the exercise," explained Sergeant Winner. "So, if you're ready, we shall begin the proceedings. Good luck airmen!"

Clem and his team watched as the eight airmen disappeared out of view, amongst the trees, shrubs and bushes. Clem studied the way they had all stuck together, and he wondered whether they would remain like that, or disperse separately in different directions. It was food for thought for him, for later. Clem looked at his watch, and had timed his opponents, when they had departed from the base camp, and he was as eager as a beaver to get going as soon as the twenty minutes designated time allowance had been reached. He was taking this task very seriously, and wanted to win it passionately. But Clem always played to win, and whether it was a game for fun, or something that was life or death, Clem always treated it in the same way, giving it one hundred per cent, at all times. When the twenty minutes had passed, Clem looked at Sergeant Winner, and he was ready for the signal to begin the search.

"I make it time to go, sergeant!" exclaimed Clem impatiently.

"No, not yet," replied Sergeant Winner.

"But my watch says the twenty minutes is up!" pleaded Clem, in desperation.

"Maybe so, but we are going by *my watch*. So, be patient!" replied Sergeant Winner.

Clem decided to shut up, and be quiet. He knew when to argue and who to argue with, but he knew he would not get anywhere with Sergeant Winner. It was a hopeless task. So he decided to sit tight, and wait. But it made him more determined to succeed. Two minutes later, there was movement from Sergeant Winner.

"Okay Clem, you and your team can now go in search of the others. Work together in a methodical and efficient manner, and listen to each other for advice. You're all in this together, and each one of you can place valid and valuable input into the exercise. Good luck recruits!" bellowed Sergeant Winner.

"Thank you sergeant!" replied the eight airmen, in unison, as they made their way quickly forwards, in pursuit of Mark Lucas's team. Clem led the way, and the other team members followed him like sheep. Clem was in charge, and he was in the mood to lead from the front, and get a resounding result. But he knew it was going to be a massive challenge, which would require all his mental and physical strength, and acumen.

"I think it'll be a good idea to break into two groups of four, as we can do twice the work, then," stated Clem, with authority.

"How about breaking into four groups of two, then we can do even more work?" suggested Daniel Thomas.

"Yes okay, good idea!" replied Clem.

"So, what will the groups be?" asked Jacob Adams.

"I would suggest placing Joshua Peters with David Isaac, Daniel Thomas with Jordan Johns, Jacob Adams with Abraham Jude, and last but not least, me with Jacob Marks, if you're all happy with that," stated Clem, after a little thought.

"Okay, that sounds good," agreed the other seven airmen, together in unison, and nodding their approval keenly.

"Great, that's a deal then! Let's go to work and find those recruits!" exclaimed Clem.

The four pairings broke away and went in different directions, each with a definitive mindset in tracing the other eight airmen, as soon as they could.

Clem had chosen Jacob Marks to work with, for no particular reason, who was from the new Flight, that had been integrated into the original Flight.

"Hello Jacob, I'm Clem Harrison, I'm pleased to meet you," stated Clem politely, shaking hands with his new partner.

"Hello Clem, how do you do?" replied Jacob Marks, just as politely.

"I'm fine. So, what direction do you reckon we should follow?" asked Clem, getting down to the nitty gritty, without any hesitation.

"Any really, there's enough space for all four groups out here, the forest is massive!" replied Jacob Marks.

"Yes, that's true, but I was only trying to involve you in the exercise, as I have a tendency to control things," replied Clem.

"That's quite alright with me, control away! I'll go with the flow," stated Jacob confidently.

"I didn't mean it like that. I meant you need to provide some input into the exercise, to get the benefit of what we're trying to achieve," answered Clem philosophically.

"Okay," agreed Jacob, pausing for a while to think. "Oh, look over there, shall we take that track?" asked Jacob constructively.

"Yes, alright. Let's go for it!" replied Clem.

The two recruits followed a narrow path, that was lined with thistles and nettles on both sides of the trail, that were easily as tall as the trees.

The path meandered to a series of other tracks, which were wider and less populated with foliage and undergrowth, but it was clear to see, the thistles and nettles were just as high.

"Which way now?" asked Jacob, scratching his head.

"This way, along the narrow trail, as it'll give us enough cover to stop us from being spotted, and then we can craftily catch them, unawares," advised Clem.

"Have you done *this kind of thing before*?" asked Jacob.

"Nope, but it's common sense really, isn't it?" replied Clem.

"Yes, I suppose it is," agreed Jacob.

"The wider trails will be far more populated by ramblers, hikers and also our opponents, so let's stick to this narrower, unkempt pathway," reiterated Clem.

"I've got it!" snapped Jacob impatiently.

The two airmen continued on the walk along the winding trail, and there was nobody in sight. Then suddenly a group of people, who appeared to be hikers, came from nowhere and were standing in front of them, and for some strange reason, Jacob made his way towards them, to chat.

"Where are *you* going?" asked Clem.

"Hang on, I'm asking for directions," replied Jacob.

"No, we're supposed to do this on our own, not with the help of other people," called Clem.

"I won't be a minute! It's only a little information I need to find out, come over and join me," answered Jacob.

"No, stop! Come back here!" shouted Clem angrily.

But Jacob wouldn't have any of it, and he ignored Clem's pleading to return. He stopped the group of four walkers and got into a conversation with them. Clem watched in horror when he spotted Jacob moving in the opposite direction to him, along with the group of four, leaving Clem behind, and on his own.

"Hey, where do you think *you're going*?" shouted Clem.

But Jacob did not reply and Clem was livid. He couldn't believe what he was seeing. It didn't add up. What on earth was Jacob thinking of? It was desertion of duty, and a form of AWOL, reckoned Clem, and he wondered what was going to become of AC Jacob Marks.

Chapter 27

Clem was in a quandary, and he wondered deeply on what to do next. He was caught between the devil and the deep blue sea, and he pondered on what was the best action. Did he follow Jacob and reckon everything was hunky-dory, or did he go his own way and search for the opposing airmen, like he was supposed to do? After a few seconds careful consideration, Clem decided to fight his demons and decided to trundle on in search of Mark Lucas and his team of eight recruits, like he was supposed to, and he let Jacob go his own way and face the consequences later on. He hadn't a guilty conscience about this, as he had done all he could to stop Jacob's stupidity, but alas, to no avail.

As Clem made his way forward in the dense undergrowth and foliage, he thought he had spotted two of the opposing recruits, hiding behind a clump of bushes, and he instantly made his way quietly through the thistles, nettles and long grass, to hopefully claim his first two detainees. It was a result he hadn't expected, and he was over the moon to have captured Joseph Job and Mark Lucas.

"Gotcha!" yelled Clem, in the direction of Joseph and Mark. "Two down and six to go!" he added smugly.

"Eh, what's going on? How come you've split up into single players?" asked Mark Lucas.

"Forget it, it's a long story, but it'll have its repercussions later, so watch this space. But besides that, you're nicked. So, come on, let's be having you!" joked Clem jovially.

"Okay, okay, we're on our way," replied Joseph Job, with his hands up, in surrender.

Clem laughed out loud, and was in a far better mood than he was a few minutes ago.

"What happens now?" asked Mark Lucas.

"I don't know, to be honest, but you're out of the game, and I've got six more to find and catch, along with my colleagues. So, if I were you, I'd start walking back to the base camp, and prepare for your turn," suggested Clem.

"Yep, I think you're right," agreed Mark Lucas.

Clem continued with his duties, and stayed in the same area, as he could smell more detainees nearby. He worked hard for another half an hour, but didn't manage to make any inroads into finding any more of Mark Lucas's team. He gathered that they must have split up and were in another part of the forest, so he trudged off to a different area, and hit the wider trail to take him there.

There was no sign of any of the opposing team, nor for that matter, any of his own team, and Clem began to wonder what was happening. It crossed his mind that the search was over, and that everyone had returned to base, but it was a gamble to go back, so Clem decided against that plan, to make extra sure that there were no stragglers left.

Clem spent another half an hour rummaging around the trees and shrubs and came to a complete blank, and he decided there and then to make tracks back to the base camp. On the way there, Clem accidentally bumped into two more opposing team members, Timothy Moses and David Ephraim, and he gleefully punched the air in delight. They were found hiding up a tree, and he sent them packing back to base camp.

"Four down, and four to go," muttered Clem, in the direction of Timothy and David. "And that's just me, on my own. Goodness knows what the others have done," he added.

"Really? Well done, that's very impressive! But how come you're working by yourself?" asked Timothy Moses.

"Don't ask, it's a long story!" replied Clem. "But all will be revealed later, I expect."

"Okay, that sounds very intriguing," declared David Ephraim.

"It is, trust me. But don't worry, it'll all come out in the wash!" replied Clem.

"That's cool, I can hardly wait!" exclaimed David facetiously.

"You'd better get yourself back to base camp, and prepare for *your search,* as it's not a bed of roses, you know!" stated Clem.

"Yep, we are, see you later," replied Timothy Moses.

Clem nodded, and then continued on his quest to find the other four opposing airmen. He didn't have much luck, and it seemed his fortunes had deserted him. But capturing four was not a bad return, and he just hoped the other four had been caught by his colleagues in his team.

Clem hit the trail, and headed for the base camp. He was pleased to be back, half an hour later, and was eager for a drink. He helped himself to a can of cola and swigged it down heartily. He hadn't enjoyed a drink as much as this, in his life. It was much appreciated by Clem.

"Welcome back, Clem. How did you do?" asked Sergeant Winner.

"I managed to claim four," replied Clem proudly.

"Excellent work, but where are the other four, in your team?" asked Sergeant Winner.

"I've got no idea! I was expecting them to be back here, as it's so quiet out there. But there's no sign of my team, or the opposing side anywhere," explained Clem.

"You'd better get back out there and rally round them, as you're running out of time!" exclaimed Sergeant Winner.

"What do you mean, running out of time?" asked Clem.

"I forgot to tell you, this is time based, and you have half an hour left!" stated Sergeant Winner.

"Okay, fine, I'm on my way," replied Clem despondently. As he turned to go back out in the forest, he felt a splash of water hitting his head from above him, and he looked up to find the seven colleagues in his team, twenty feet up in a tree, with an empty bucket, and he felt his head and hoped and prayed it was water, and not urine.

"What are you doing up there?" shouted Clem.

"We're looking for conkers!" replied Daniel Thomas, with tongue in cheek.

"Conkers? You're bonkers!" joked Clem, jovially.

The airmen jumped down from the tree and joined Clem, their team leader.

"How did it go?" asked Joshua Peters.

"Not bad, I got four!" replied Clem. "What about you lot?"

"We got one," stated Joshua.

"We got two," revealed Jacob Adams.

"We got one," said Daniel Thomas.

Sergeant Winner appeared again.

"Ah Clem, I see we've got a result for your team. You've captured all eight. Well done to you too Clem, in finding four, on your own. You're currently leading the race as the "top searcher." As for your buddy, Jacob Marks, he was a "plant" placed by me and Corporal Cherry, to hinder your progress in the search, but you did well to overcome that challenge, and carry on!" praised Sergeant Winner.

"A "plant?" Wow, that's weird. I didn't expect that, sergeant," replied Clem.

"Don't take anyone, or anything for granted. All is not what it seems. Follow your gut instincts at all times, and I'm pleased to see, that you did exactly that!" exclaimed Sergeant Winner.

Clem gasped in shock, and was relieved he had continued to follow the rules, and not go off with Jacob Marks and the four hikers, as he was sure it would have been detrimental to his RAF career, if he had done so.

"Okay airmen, you've got a result and did it with half an hour to spare, but can you beat the others? Only time will tell!" stated Sergeant Winner.

Mark Lucas and his team lined up in front of Clem Harrison's team, and wore determined expressions on their faces, in a bid to throw down the gauntlet to their rivals, and it was now the turn of Clem and his team to make themselves scarce, as Mark Lucas's group were keen and eager to get searching, and try to beat the time that was set by Clem and his mob.

"Are you ready, Team Harrison?" yelled Sergeant Winner.

"Yes sergeant!" replied Team Harrison loudly.

"Off you go then, and you've twenty minutes to disappear into thin air!" bellowed Sergeant Winner.

Clem Harrison and his team made their way quickly through the long grass and shrubs, and disappeared quickly out of view. But they did not stay as a unit. They split into eight individuals, to give themselves more chance of winning the task, which was the brainchild of Daniel Thomas, who was full of useful ideas. It must have been all the books he had read, that he was bristling with brainwaves. When the twenty minutes had ticked slowly by, Corporal Cherry stepped forward.

"Time to go and do your duty, Team Lucas! Listen to each other, take on board what is advised by your colleagues, and don't underestimate the smallest grain of advice, as Rome wasn't built in a day!" shouted Corporal Cherry. "Now move it! And good luck and good searching!" he added.

Team Lucas were chomping at the bit, and they showed a similar eagerness to Team Harrison in getting a fast start and they made progress quickly, following the exact course that Clem and his team had taken.

The weather took a turn for the worse, however, the wind and rain whipped up from nowhere, giving both the teams uncomfortable conditions. It was easier for Clem's team, as they could find a spot to stay and hide in, and not worry about being out in the elements, but Mark Lucas's team had it all to do, outside. They were taking it on the chin however, and soldiered on bravely, in awful inclement conditions, that was worsening, as the day wore on.

Clem was on his own, which was just as he liked it, and he found a dry patch of grass, under a large oak tree, that was suitable to hang around in, whilst the weather was as bad as this. There was no call for him being outside. The onus was on Team Lucas to do their work and find him, and he was quite happy sitting tight, until someone discovered his hideaway.

An hour passed, and the weather had not improved. The rain was still pelting down, and the wind was blowing a gale force ten. Clem was pleased he wasn't out in the open. It was just a waiting game now, and as each minute passed, he was sixty seconds nearer to winning the assignment, so

Clem hoped he could see out the rest of the designated time that was earmarked for his team, and win the challenge.

Half an hour later, just as Clem was thinking of moving on, he was disturbed by the rustling of grass nearby. He dare not move, and stayed as still as he could.

"Let's hang around under here, and dry off a bit," suggested a voice that sounded similar to that of Mark Lucas.

Clem cringed when he discovered who it was, and his heartbeat increased, ten fold. He was scared and nervous, and did not want to be caught, at this late stage of the proceedings.

"Okay, I'm shattered to tell you the truth, and could do with a rest," agreed Joseph Job, who was working in tandem with Mark Lucas.

"Me too, if I've got to be honest. It's pretty rough out there!" replied Mark Lucas.

The two airmen moved further into the small enclosure, but failed to spot Clem, who was hiding in the shade of the corner, and was trembling like a leaf.

"We can dry off in here for ten minutes, then get back on to it," stated Joseph Job.

"Yep, it's a pity there isn't a drinks machine around here, I could murder a cup of coffee!" exclaimed Mark Lucas.

"So could I, I'm gagging for a drink!" agreed Joseph Job.

Clem remained silent and still, but he didn't know for how long, as he was beginning to get cramp in his legs. He needed to stretch them, but knew if he did, his cover would be blown, so he put up with the pain for the cause. But, without knowing, he accidentally scuffed a tree with his boot.

"Did you hear that?" asked Mark, in the direction of Joseph Job.

"Nope, I didn't hear a thing. What was it?" replied Joseph.

"It sounded like someone trying to climb a tree, back there," stated Mark Lucas.

"Really? Let me take a look, then," said Joseph, moving quickly towards the back of the enclosure.

Clem crouched down behind a clump of grass, but it barely covered his frame.

"What do we have here, then?" asked Joseph Job facetiously.

"Why, what's up?" asked Mark, laying lazily across the dry undergrowth on the ground, and relishing the respite from the rain.

"A pair of feet, two legs and a shape looking distinctly like an airman from RAF Swinderby!" joked Joseph.

"Okay! Okay! You've got me, I'm done. Congrats!" exclaimed Clem Harrison.

"Hey Clem, gotcha!" shouted Joseph excitedly. "Let's be having you!"

An hour later, and the game was over. Sixteen tired airmen slumped wearily on the ground, back at the base camp and they were exhausted. The weather had cleared up, and the rain clouds had been replaced by white fluffy ones, blue sky and sunshine, although the wind was still keen and blowing hard through the branches of the trees.

Clem had no idea who had won, and at that precise moment, he didn't care. He was shattered, both mentally and physically.

"Listen in, recruits, I have the result, and it's a close one!" called Sergeant Winner.

The airmen sat up and listened keenly, and were all interested to find out who was victorious, even though they were dog-tired.

"And the winner is," called Sergeant Winner, keeping the recruits in suspense. "Team Lucas and Team Harrison, in a dead heat!" he added.

The airmen gasped with shock, and couldn't believe what they were hearing.

"Yep indeed. The clock doesn't lie, and both teams recorded exactly the same time, to the very last second," explained Sergeant Winner.

"Is there a prize?" called Clem Harrison.

"Nope, there isn't. But it shall be recorded on your personnel notes, and carried forward to your trade training, and then on to your permanent posting," replied Sergeant Winner. "And by the way Clem, you were successful in claiming the greatest amount of detainees, with four, as nobody came anywhere near that!" added the sergeant.

"Cheers, that's great to know, thanks sergeant!" exclaimed Clem.

The recruits took on board what was being said, and nodded in acknowledgement, and they were pleased there were no losers. Mark Lucas's team deserved their success, for working in the pouring rain, whilst Clem Harrison's mob were worthy joint winners, after Clem had been duped by one of his own teammates, and was tested to the limit. It was a fair result and nobody could complain, although it crossed Clem's mind that the result was slightly doctored by Sergeant Winner, to keep everyone sweet.

"Have something to eat now, recruits, and take the weight off your feet. You've earnt it!" shouted Sergeant Winner.

The airmen shuffled off to the Catering HQ, and queued up for their lunch, and for what it was worth, it hadn't changed, and was the same as yesterday's food.

"How did the exercise go for you lot, did you find good hideaways?" asked Clem, as he munched on the same old dry beef from a tin.

"No, I was caught by David Ephraim, just about immediately. I think it was because I was having a sneezing fit at the time, so that didn't help," replied Joshua Peters.

"Oh dear, that spoiled your chances of going undetected. But never mind, these things happen," stated Clem with empathy.

"I was caught as I tried to climb a tree, but the rain made it slippery and I fell from it, right in the path of Timothy Moses," revealed Jacob Adams.

"A similar thing happened to me, but instead of falling in the path of a searcher, I needed help to get down, as I got my foot stuck in a branch, and instead of risking breaking my leg, I had to bawl and shout for help, and guess who turned up?" asked Daniel Thomas.

"Who?" replied the airmen, with intrigue.

"Timothy Moses!" revealed Daniel Thomas. "Again!" he added.

"Ha ha, that means he nabbed two of you, stuck up a tree!" joked Clem.

"Yep, he must have thought it was his birthday and Christmas Day, rolled into one!" replied Daniel Thomas, with tongue in cheek.

"Another two, and he would have equalled my score of four!" stated Clem. "And that would have been better than his birthday, and Christmas Day!" he added.

"Yep, that's true enough," agreed Daniel Thomas. "And for doing, absolutely nothing!"

"How was you caught?" asked Jacob Adams, directing his question at Clem Harrison.

"I was hiding under a large oak tree to keep dry, and thought I was safe and sound, but unfortunately, Mark Lucas and Joseph Job turned up, and stopped there for a few minutes. I was okay hiding at the back, but when I got cramp in my leg and moved my foot by accident, my boot scraped a tree and made a hell of a noise, and that was it for me. It roused the two airmens attention, and I was caught like a sitting duck," explained Clem.

"That's unlucky, really. If you hadn't have got cramp, they may not have known you were there, and we might have claimed an outright win!" exclaimed Jacob Adams.

"Yes, true, but that's the way the cookie crumbles!" replied Clem, with a sigh of disappointment. "Anyway, what about you guys, *how were you caught?"* asked Clem, looking at the airmen from the other Flight, that had merged with them.

"I was caught by Ray Lord, when I was rustling about in some bushes, looking for a dry spot, but I was dithering around too much, and was nabbed for being too slow," revealed David Isaac, with honesty.

"Unlucky! If it hadn't have been raining, you may still be hiding now," expressed Clem positively.

"Yep," agreed David Isaac. "As I would have dived into a dry den, without dithering around, that's for sure!" he added.

"I was caught by Walt Phillips, even before I found a den to hide in. I don't know how he had caught me so quickly, I'm sure he'd jumped the gun and set off before the twenty minutes waiting time was up," stated Jordan Johns.

"No, I don't think Sergeant Winner would let them go early. Walt Phillips must have got lucky, or you were very unlucky!" replied Clem.

"Perhaps. But it seemed odd that I hadn't got into some shelter. But I suppose that's the way it goes," answered Jordan Johns.

"I was nabbed when I got my feet caught in some undergrowth," began Abraham Jude. "I couldn't move and needed someone to cut away the twine, reeds and thorny bushes, as I was really caught up in it, badly," he added dramatically.

"And what happened?" asked Clem.

"Ken James rolled up, freed me, and then nabbed me, so that was that!" exclaimed Abraham Jude.

"At least you got cut from the thorns," joked Clem.

"Yes, I suppose that was a consolation," agreed Abraham.

"*I was caught in a similar fashion to you, Clem.* I was hiding behind a large clump of bushes, which were as dry as gunpowder, but when Denis King appeared, I had to crouch down, and in doing so, both my knee joints cracked, which of course alerted Denis's attention, and that was my chances gone!" explained Jacob Marks.

"More bad luck there then, I see! But you will have to get your dodgy knees checked out at the doctor's, just in case!" said Clem facetiously, with tongue in cheek. "Well, as far as I'm concerned, I think we can count ourselves very unlucky today. We were so close to winning this challenge, I think. But life goes on, and I'm sure that what we've learned today and yesterday, will go a long way in helping us in our RAF careers, providing us all with an abundance of coolness, calmness and collectiveness, that can only be for our benefit!" exclaimed Clem.

After lunch, the airmen loitered around the campsite, waiting for the next assignment. Each of them had to admit that the food was not as good as the RAF Swinderby grub, and they couldn't wait to get back there, even if it was just for the tea and bromide and the shower facilities, as there had been nowhere to wash and shave out here.

"Has everyone eaten?" shouted Sergeant Winner.

"Yes sergeant!" bellowed the airmen, in reply.

"Good," replied Sergeant Winner. "It's time to pack up the stuff, tidy away the bivouacs and load the bus, as we're off back to RAF Swinderby, as our job is done here!" he added, with a smile.

"Yes sergeant!" called out the recruits in unison, with relief in their tones.

They packed up the equipment and food, and loaded the bus with the cases of drink, tables, grub and cutlery, and tidied up any mess that had accrued from the eating, and left the place in an immaculate condition, before getting on the bus, for the journey back to RAF Swinderby.

Chapter 28

The journey to RAF Swinderby seemed to fly-by, but Clem fell asleep almost immediately his torso hit the seat of the bus, and he missed the majority of the trip back, as he was more than just ultra-shattered, in both body and mind, he was comatised almost. However, when he awoke, just as the bus arrived at the main gates of the RAF Swinderby station, he felt a great deal better for the power nap.

The two days away in Sherwood Forest had been refreshingly positive, thought Clem, but he had to admit to himself that the work had been as tough as anything he had ever witnessed in his entire life. It didn't seem bad at the time, but the stress and fatigue had suddenly hit him on the bus journey taking him back to the training camp.

"Wakey, wakey, rise and shine!" shouted Sergeant Winner. "We are home, troops!"

The bus full of bleary eyed, dreamy recruits, looked out of the window, and slowly but surely, they realised where they were, and they stretched and yawned, to help them come to terms with being part of the land of the living, once again.

"Queue in single file, and slowly disembark from the bus, once it has stopped. We need the food, drink and equipment unloading from the back, so don't disappear into thin air!" yelled Sergeant Winner.

The airmen mooched off the bus, and slouched to the boot, at the rear of the vehicle, to help with the gear, and they lugged the boxes and tables off, towards the Airmen's Mess.

"Okay Flight, thank you for that. Now, as you've worked so hard, you've got the rest of the day off. It's three o'clock, and as food in the Airmen's Mess isn't served until four, you've got an hour to shower, shave and do whatever else you want to do, in that time, before you can eat. Enjoy your afternoon, and evening, and both Corporal Cherry and myself shall see you bright eyed and bushy tailed tomorrow morning, at seven forty five!" stated Sergeant Winner clearly.

"Yes sergeant, thank you!" replied the recruits, in unison. The other merged Flight of airmen returned to their billet, and Clem and his colleagues headed to the ablutions for a freshen up, with Clem making sure he was one of the first in the queue, as he was stinking like a bear in the woods, and needed to shower and shave desperately.

After showering and shaving, Clem headed back to his bed, and changed into civvy clothes. His stomach rumbled like thunder, and he couldn't wait to tuck into a lovely greasy fry-up of egg, beans, chips, bacon and burger, and he knew there and then, it would be well received. His belly thought his throat had been cut. The food did not disappoint. It was even tastier than he had expected. He particularly enjoyed the tomato sauce that he smeared all over, and of course, the tea and bromide, was just as bad as it normally was. After tea, Clem bought a newspaper from the vending stand, and caught up with the latest gossip, as well as everything connected to his two football teams, Tottenham Hotspur and Aston Villa.

Lights went out at 10 pm, as the airmen were dog-tired. The food in the Airmen's Mess had filled them all to the brim, and with the exertions of Sherwood Forest taking its toll. None of the airmen fancied a night out in the NAAFI Club, and they all turned in early.

Reveille sounded next morning at the normal time of 6.15 am, and the recruits struggled to wake up. Clem was okay, just like he usually was, and he was first in the ablutions for a shower and shave, again. He didn't think he had got all the dirt and grime off him, from the filthy grounds of Sherwood Forest, and reckoned it would take half a dozen showers to fully cleanse him.

After his hot, refreshing shower, he made his bed pack, and had to think hard on how it was made, after being excused for a day or two, whilst serving in the Sherwood Forest. After a dozen attempts, which frustrated him, he eventually attained to the standards that he was used to, and was satisfied that it would not be sent flying across the floor, or out of the window.

Breakfast was on the horizon. Clem waited for the other airmen to shower and shave and make their bedpacks and they all strolled to the Airmen's Mess together, as a team.

After breakfast, Clem and the rest of the airmen in the Flight, put the finishing touches to their uniform display, shoes and bedpacks, with a view to hopefully putting their drill instructors in a good mood. They did not want to start off on a bad footing, after having such a successful time on tour at Sherwood Forest.

At 7.45 am, on the dot, Sergeant Winner and Corporal Cherry appeared, looking determined and steely eyed, and wearing a stern, studious expression in an attempt to weed out any poor efforts, for a bedpack. They were pleasantly surprised with everyone's display of both the bedpacks and uniform, and hadn't any complaints. The early night for the recruits had helped them immensely, and there was not one that deserved being sent across the room, in the "Flight of Shame."

"Well done recruits, nice work, all round! Usually after a couple of days away in the fresh air of Sherwood Forest, the standard for bedpacks and uniform display drops, but not today, and not for you lot, so once again, well done Flight!" enthused Sergeant Winner.

The airmen looked pleased with themselves, and were relieved to see the floor had not been littered with bed linen, uniforms and boots. It appeared that both Sergeant

Winner and Corporal Cherry were in a good mood, this morning.

"Now, airmen! We have a lot to do on the parade square, to make you come up to scratch, for your "Passing Out" parade, and this will be our priority for the next few days. It will be drill, drill and more drill, as you've got to nail this "Presenting Arms" skill, like your life depended on it!" stressed Sergeant Winner, keenly.

"Excuse me, Sergeant Winner. Before we start the drill, I have more mail to hand out!" piped up Corporal Cherry. "As before, when I call out your name, come and collect your post," he added.

The recruits waited with bated breath, and Clem wondered if he would get a letter from Ellie.

"Clem Harrison," shouted Corporal Cherry, handing over a letter.

Clem approached the corporal, and wondered who it was from.

"Thank you corporal," said Clem, taking the mail with gratitude.

He looked at the front of the envelope and tried to work out whose handwriting it was, as he did not recognise it at all. He opened it keenly, and discovered it wasn't from Ellie, but from his dad. The letter read as follows;

"Dear Clem,

I hope you're enjoying your RAF basic training, although I expect it's been tough and physical. But nothing you can't handle.

I remember when I did my National Service in the 1950's, and how demanding it could be, but it made a man of me, and I'm sure it'll make a man of you too, and help you mature quickly.

Your friends from school, Toby and Grant have asked about your progress, and I've told them you're doing fine, and are enjoying yourself.

I have been busy at work, during the day with my handicraft instructor's job at the unit for the educationally subnormal, and of course I've been drumming in the evenings, every weekend, at the Lawns Club in Sutton, so life for me is very busy, like yours, I suppose.

That's all for now,

Take care,

Love from dad."

Clem read it with interest, and was surprised, as he had not expected a letter from his dad. He hardly ever wrote anything, except for the song words he needed to learn for the Lawns Club, which he wrote on the back of the spare cardboard that he had retrieved from a new shirt packet, after purchasing from a shop, which was not very often. But Clem had to admit to himself he was saddened by the lack of post from Ellie.

"That's the lot for you today, but I'm sure there'll be more tomorrow," stated Corporal Cherry, after handing out the letters to the eight airmen, who each received at least one each.

"That's the correspondence dealt with, so let's get back to the serious business now, and smash this task!" snarled Sergeant Winner, with determination in his tone.

The airmen waited for the next order, and it didn't take long.

"Airmen, stand at attention! Right turn, quick march, left, right, left, right, left, right!" bellowed Sergeant Winner.

The recruits marched outside, and continued all the way to the parade square.

The next half an hour, was a complete disaster for everybody connected to Sergeant Winner's Flight, as it seemed like everything they had been taught on the parade square, prior to the break at Sherwood Forest, had been forgotten. The recruits were an embarrassment to themselves, and couldn't get anything right. They stumbled, staggered, hesitated, and there were more contertinas' in that half an hour, than for the whole of their three weeks of training, put together.

"Flight halt! What on earth has come over you lot?" screamed Sergeant Winner, after watching and squirming, for the last thirty minutes.

There was no response from the recruits. They remained silent, and could not give any explanation, whatsoever. They were like strangers, that had not marched together before.

"Well, I'm waiting for an answer?" quizzed Sergeant Winner.

"We need more practice, sergeant!" replied Mark Lucas, bravely.

"That's an understatement!" yelled Sergeant Winner angrily.

"If you don't pull your socks up in the next hour or so, you shall all be back-flighted two weeks!" screamed Corporal Cherry, with venom evident in his tone and expression, showing that he meant every word.

"Shall we try again?" asked Sergeant Winner, calmly.

"Yes sergeant!" replied the recruits, quietly, and in unison.

"But first, I think it will be best for you all to have a coffee break, to relax, re-gather your thoughts, and to think long and hard on where you're going wrong," suggested Sergeant Winner, coolly. "Flight dismiss!"

The recruits headed to the vending machine, and nothing was spoken by any of them, as they concentrated on finding a way of correcting their mistakes, in their own minds, and alone, as they knew they had let themselves down, as well as Sergeant Winner, and Corporal Cherry.

They formed a queue at the drinks machine, with their heads down, and they didn't make any eye contact with anyone. Clem was annoyed with himself, as he knew he had not concentrated hard enough, but it was not just down to him, but everyone in the Flight was to blame, and they were all in the same boat.

"*What's going wrong?*" asked Mark Lucas, directing his question to the other fifteen airmen, present at the tea and coffee machine.

"Don't ask me!" replied Joseph Job, with an edge to his tone.

"And I've no idea, either!" exclaimed David Ephraim, equally as sharp and cutting, in his attitude.

"Okay, okay, don't bite my head off, I'm only asking!" stated Mark Lucas, in a defensive manner.

"Steady on, lads. Let's not fall out over this. Let's keep a level head. *It's all of our faults,* because we haven't concentrated well enough, and have forgotten to look down the line, at the next man to us. If we keep an eye on our neighbour, we can't go far wrong. That's what we did before, so let's get back on the horse, and try again, even if it takes us until midnight! Because I'm prepared to work, till I drop!" exclaimed Clem Harrison, with a fervent passion.

"Here, here, well said, Clem! That's the correct attitude to have!" enthused Mark Lucas. "Let's put into practice what Clem has just pointed out. Watch the lines, and keep in step with your next door neighbour, to maintain the teamwork! Let's do it!"

The airmen drank up their coffee, and were in a very determined mood. The pep talks from Mark Lucas and Clem Harrison seemed to have re-ignited their desire, and it woke them up. They knew it was going to be rough and tough, but with a focused attitude, and a will-to-win, they realised that if they put into practice the tips given to them from Mark and Clem, they had an opportunity to right all the wrongs.

"Okay Flight, are we ready to continue?" asked Corporal Cherry, amicably, as he approached the recruits at the vending machine.

"Yes, corporal!" yelled the recruits together, in unison.

"Have you had a heart-to-heart with each other, on what went wrong earlier?" asked Corporal Cherry.

"Yes corporal!" replied the airmen loudly, and again in unison.

"Good, let's go for it, then! Flight, right wheel, left, right, left, right, left, right!" screamed Corporal Cherry.

The recruits set off and marched impeccably around the parade square, like the Coldstream Guards, and the instant transformation amazed both Sergeant Winner and Corporal Cherry, alike. They were both very impressed with the recruits attitude, and work rate.

Chapter 29

Things were on the up and up, for the sixteen recruits in the recently formed Flight. The marching was impeccable, the lines were perfect, and the energy and passion to make a success of the drill, on the parade ground, was faultless. The acid test was yet to come, however, when the airmen were to collect a rifle each, from the Armoury, and perform a "Present Arms" routine. They had mastered it before, prior to going to Sherwood Forest, and they were certain they could replicate their previous success, with a rifle in their hands, and nail the job, with flying colours. It was all about attitude, positive thinking, and working hard as a team. They knew what to do, and they were all very determined to carry this off, in a spectacular manner.

"Okay Flight, it's time to collect your rifles, from the Armoury and prepare for your big chance to impress! Both Corporal Cherry and myself know you can do it, after performing so admirably in the basic drill skills. So fill your boots, grasp the nettle and give it your best shot! Flight, forward march, left, right, left, right, left, right!" bawled Sergeant Winner.

The airmen arrived at the Armoury building, and their hearts skipped a beat, as they knew what was coming. It was the moment of truth. Did the recruits have the knowledge to make a success of "Presenting Arms?" Did they have the bottle to work as a team, and smash this task out of the parade square? It was a tall order, but each and every one of the airmen were primed for success, and they concentrated on what Mark Lucas and Clem Harrison had stated earlier, and they were ready to give it all they had.

After queuing up at the door, the recruits moved single file into the Armoury, and collected a rifle each, before quickly moving back outside, and preparing to march towards the parade square. The nerves twitched, the adrenalin zoomed, and the anticipation filled their heads. But the recruits focused on what had to be done, and they were ready, willing and able to do themselves justice, and give themselves something to be proud of.

"Forward march, to the parade square, left, right, left, right, left, right!" bellowed Sergeant Winner.

The airmen duly obliged, and marched majestically to their destination, as ordered. They did not show any weaknesses in the line, nor was there any signs of a concertina, anywhere to be seen. It was a pleasure to watch, and Corporal Cherry shared a beaming smile of pride with Sergeant Winner, as the subordinates had come to the party, with a massive bang.

"Continue around the parade square, left, right, left, right, left, right!" yelled Sergeant Winner.

The recruits stride did not waver. They ambled coolly and effortlessly around the square, and when it came to the first tricky corner, they mastered it with perfection.

It was close to the moment of truth, however, and each recruit braced themselves for the order of "Present Arms," and when that order was bellowed out by Sergeant Winner, the airmen executed the motion, with first class results, and nailed it, without any shadow of a doubt. It was poetry in motion, as the airmen threw the rifles high into the air, and "Presented Arms," perfectly.

The result was just what Sergeant Winner and Corporal Cherry required. They had not fancied going back to basics with this Flight, and they were praying they smashed it first time, and they were not disappointed.

"Well done, recruits! Flight halt!" screamed Sergeant Winner.

The airmen came to a shuddering stop.

"Stand at ease! I'm extremely pleased with your efforts. You've done very well. But I shall not labour the point, and I will not work you into the ground, as you've surpassed all my expectations. Now go and take yourselves off to the vending machine, for a coffee," ordered Sergeant Winner.

The airmen disappeared quickly, and queued up for a drink. It was a time for celebrating, although without any alcohol in sight. They had to make do with a hot cup of coffee, to warm their hands. The alcohol would come later, there was no doubt about that. After a series of back-slapping, handshakes and high fives, the recruits were ready to return, to find out what was next on the agenda. When the airmen went back to their places on the parade square, they were greeted by a smiling Sergeant Winner.

"Welcome back, recruits. Now, you all need to let your family, friends and loved ones know about your "Passing Out" parade, that will be taking place in a couple of weeks time. Please hand out the invites that you shall be provided with, at lunchtime, to your guests, as nobody will be allowed into the station grounds without an official invite. I hope you can generate enough interest among your friends and family, and make this event as successful as possible. There will be a fly-past by an aircraft from the Royal Air Force, on the day, following the "Passing Out" parade, although as yet, I'm not sure what aircraft it will be. That'll be our little secret, and a big surprise for everyone. Now, let's get back to it, and execute another "Presenting Arms," just as good as the last one. Flight attention! Quick march, left, right, left, right, left, right!" screamed Sergeant Winner.

The airmen went around the parade square again, and dealt with the corners, lines, concertinas and "Presenting Arms," with great aplomb.

When Clem got back to the billet at 5pm, after a long, busy day of drill practice, where it had been "Presenting Arms" all day long, the first thing he did was soak his aching feet in the bath. He had never known such an arduous task in his life. It was "Present Arms," "Present Arms," "Present Arms," for the entire day, and it was nearly driving him mad. He hoped he succeeded on the "Passing Out" parade day, as he was not sure he could cope with a back-flight, and face more "Presenting Arms." It was almost finishing him off. If this was the reason to pull the troops together and make this "Passing Out" parade a success, then Clem was going to work his socks off, to ensure everybody in the Flight pulled their weight, and make it a massive accomplishment.

He bought a box of plasters from the NAAFI shop on the way back to the billet after his tea, and he carefully stuck a plaster on each of the dozen or so blisters, on both of his feet, and it helped to ease the pain.

"Who's off to the NAAFI club, for a game of snooker?" asked Mark Lucas.

David Ephraim raised his arm.

"I'm up for it," replied David.

"Anyone else interested?" asked Mark Lucas.

"Yep, me! Why not?" replied Joseph Job.

"Is that the lot, just the three of us? Come on guys, let's let our hair down. We've earnt it, after a day like today!" exclaimed Mark Lucas.

"Go on, then, I'll make the effort. You've twisted my arm!" stated Clem Harrison. "It might make me forget the painful blisters on my feet!"

The airmen laughed, and then all four headed out to the snooker table in the NAAFI club, and were looking forward to some leisure time, for a change.

David Ephraim was drawn to play against Mark Lucas, and Joseph Job was taking on Clem Harrison, with the winners playing each other to find the Champion of Champions, whilst the losers would play one another to discover the 3rd and 4th places. It was a close call in the first round of matches, with David beating Mark 100-78, whilst Clem beat Joseph 98-80, to clinch a final place.

The deciding matches were ready to begin, with Clem Harrison v David Ephraim in the Champion of Champions final, and Mark Lucas v Joseph Job in the 3rd and 4th place play-off, with that particular loser ending up with the wooden spoon. The tension was building, but Clem tried to counteract the drama by cracking jokes and making fun of the blisters on his feet, saying they were playing him up.

"I can hardly walk around this table!" stated Clem facetiously.

"Is that an excuse for a cop out? Are you forfeiting the match?" quizzed David Ephraim cheekily.

"Nope, not on your Nelly!" exclaimed Clem, loudly.

"Come on then, let's toss a coin to find who breaks first. Heads or tails?" asked David Ephraim, as he hurled a silver ten pence piece high into the air.

"I'll call heads!" shouted Clem.

The coin landed on the snooker table.

"It's heads!" bellowed David. "Are you breaking first, or offering that honour to me?" he added.

"I'll break first, thank you very much!" replied Clem, with tongue in cheek.

"Let the final commence!" howled David Ephraim excitedly.

Clem proceeded to break, and when he did, he wished he had lost the toss, as the white ball skimmed a red ball in the pack, and hurtled across the green baize table into the corner pocket, which meant he started the game in the worst possible fashion, by forfeiting four points, and giving his opponent a free shot.

David Ephraim did not waste the big opportunity to fill his boots, and he potted a red, followed by the black, and then another red, before sinking another black, to build up a 20 point advantage, which had been handed to him on a plate.

Clem battled back and when David missed an easy red, Clem stepped up to the mark and graciously sunk the red, and followed it up by sinking a pink, a red, a blue, a red and a black, to take his total to 21 points, and go into the lead by a single point.

David returned to the table and could not make any score, although he was very close when the red rattled the pocket, in the centre.

Clem picked up the pieces and potted the red, sunk a blue, another red and then he rattled the pocket as well, when attempting to sink another blue, but it increased Clem's lead to eight points, with the score standing at 28 points to 20.

This spurred on David Ephraim to make a decent break of 40, which put the cat among the pigeons, and placed the pressure on Clem Harrison, as he trailed 60-28.

Clem tried to make a long shot pot, that bounced in and out of the pocket, but did not count. David took advantage and potted the red, to place more pressure on Clem. David needed a black to crank up the pressure on Clem, but failed by a millimetre.

Clem grasped his chance. He potted a red, a blue, a red, a yellow and another red, to give him a tidy break of 12 points, and bring him back into the game at 61-40, with only 21 points in it.

David returned to the table and made a nervous break of 8, to edge closer to victory, meaning Clem needed a match-winning break, as the balls were dispersed all over the table. He started well, potted the red, followed by a black, another red, a pink, a red, a black, and a red, followed by a black to move ahead of David by 71 points to 69.

David went back to the table and scored 10 points, but slipped up and missed a sitter, with the pocket at his mercy. Was the pressure getting to him? 79-71 to David.

Clem knew if he cleaned up, he would win, and he duly pocketed all the colours, except the blue, pink and black, to make the score 80-79, in Clem's favour, and it provided David with a chance to pip Clem, with 18 points still available. A steady nerve was required, and David potted the blue to go 84-80 ahead, and he needed the pink to wrap up the match. But he flopped with the shot, and the pink rattled the pocket, leaving Clem with an opportunity to secure the win, and when he potted the pink, it put him 86-84 ahead. Clem had the black to sink, to confirm the win and become Champion of Champions, and he did not make any mistake, duly sinking the black ball to win the gripping match 93-84.

"Well done, Clem. That was a close game, but you took your chances very well," stated David, shaking Clem by the hand.

"Cheers, and well played to you too! It was touch and go at the end, but hard luck," replied Clem.

Mark Lucas finished third, when he trounced Joseph Job 100-50, in the wooden spoon match.

Chapter 30

Clem picked up the invites for his "Passing Out" parade at lunch time, and couldn't wait to hand them out. He wondered who would attend. Would it be Ellie? His mum? His dad? His two brothers? His two friends from school? He wasn't sure if any of them could get the time off from work, as it was at the end of the working week, but he did not worry about it. He decided on inviting all those aforementioned people anyway, and picked up seven invite cards and envelopes.

The day continued and was a series of drill, cross country, more drill, weight training, even more drill, RAF education, an extra exercise of drill and then further drill, just in case. It was tiring, but Clem got through it, and slept like a top.

The rest of the week was on similar lines, with drill taking centre stage alongside the contrast of football, rifle range and weapon cleaning duties, in-between the drill. The "Present Arms" was now near to perfect, as the "Passing Out" parade got nearer.

Clem and the others in the Flight just hoped they had not peaked too early, as they would have hated to have made a fool of themselves in front of their friends and family, at the incredibly prestigious "Passing Out" parade.

When Clem went home on a Weekend Pass on the Friday night, he hoped to see Ellie, but could not get through to her on the telephone. He called her half a dozen times, but got no joy. He decided it was one of those things, but didn't fret over it.

Clem was a home bird all weekend long, and put his blistered and aching feet up. He tried calling Ellie on the Saturday morning, afternoon and evening, but alas to no avail. It did not prove fruitful. He gathered she was away.

Clem wrote the weekend off as regards to seeing Ellie, but still delivered the invite to her house on the Sunday morning, and popped it through the letter box, and also delivered invites to his two friends from school, as well as handing over an invite to his two brothers, and to his mam and dad.

Clem travelled back to RAF Swinderby earlier than normal, on the Sunday evening, and caught the 5.07 pm train. He arrived back at the billet room at 7.30 pm, ready to hit the NAAFI club for a drink, grab a bite to eat, and have a relaxing winding down session. Clem put the thought of Ellie out of his head. He knew that if he stewed over her, he would not get anything done, so he merely put it down to experience, and left the ball in her court. If she came to the "Passing Out" parade to see him, then he knew the romance was back on.

The week was long, hard and drawn out, with further drill practice, including "Presenting Arms" and circuit training in the gym, and Clem was thrilled that the "Passing Out" parade was only a few days away.

After the Thursday morning inspection, Corporal Cherry issued more mail to the recruits, but Clem did not receive any, not from Ellie, nor his dad. The correspondence had completely dried up. But he did not worry about it. Like his mam once told him when he was younger, "Whatever will be, will be," and that saying had stuck with Clem for many years. And it was true.

The preparation was completed. The drill was over. The recruits were primed, and there was no turning back. Tomorrow was "Passing Out" parade day. Clem was nervous, but excited. He knew that he had done everything he could, to make this a success, and everyone in the Flight had given 100 per cent. There was no better equipped airmen in the RAF Swinderby grounds, at that moment in time.

"Bring it on!" exclaimed Clem, as the airmen enjoyed a little light relief in the NAAFI club, on the eve of the "Passing Out" parade. Nobody was drinking alcohol however, as they wanted clear heads in the morning, because at 11 am, the "Passing Out" parade would begin. Even the heavy drinkers were tea-total tonight. A game of darts, a game of pool, a game of snooker, a laugh, a joke, and some banter among the recruits, was the order of the evening, on this, their final night at RAF Swinderby, before they all went their separate ways, in different directions, for their trade training. Clem was to be posted to RAF Hereford, for his trade training, after a week's leave.

Next day, Clem got dressed into his Number One uniform, that he had pressed at 5 am. He bulled his Number One shoes up to a gleaming shine, and he felt like a million dollars. The pressing of his uniform was so precise, it was dangerous to walk around in, as the creases could be deemed as a lethal weapon, as they were as sharp as needles.

The nerves fluttered in the pit of Clem's stomach, as the adrenaline rushed around his body. He had no idea who was turning up to watch him, but he knew there was going to be an audience of some kind there, even if it was just the Royal Air Force top brass from the Ministry of Defence, and the drill instructors. So Clem knew he had to be at the top of his game, at his best, and with no shirking, or slacking.

Although Clem felt the butterflies fluttering like a pack of wolves in his stomach, he managed to eat breakfast, make a bedpack, and prepare his other working uniform for the morning inspection, and it helped to take his mind off the "Passing Out" parade. Clem was hoping he didn't have his bedpack hurled across the billet room, on his last day at RAF Swinderby, as it would not go down well with him, before the parade. So he made extra sure his bedpack was immaculately built. Clem need not have worried, as everyone's bedpack was hailed a success by Sergeant Winner and Corporal Cherry, and it put every recruit on the front foot, for the big day.

The weather was kind to them too, as the sun shined keenly in the sky, and there wasn't a cloud to be seen. It was not a bad day for mid November. The clear weather was a God send, as it was deemed to be fine enough for the RAF aircraft fly-past, although the identity of the plane was still not revealed. It would be a surprise until the very last moment.

With half an hour to go before the parade, the airmen congregated in the billet, and let off some last minute nerves, to get to grips with what was going to be a memorable occasion.

The other recruits that had merged with the original Flight arrived, and looked nervous and sheepish, but they soon found their self-confidence, after mixing with Clem and his mates, for a short while.

"Recruits! Stand at attention!" bellowed Sergeant Winner, dressed in a smart Number One uniform, that had sharper creases than Clem's, and shoes that gleamed even shinier than the sun. "It's your moment of truth! You've all done very well to reach this stage, now go and smash it on the parade square, in front of your family and friends! Put into action what you've practiced for these last six weeks! Good luck, and there'll be no mention of the 0-0 draw between Lincoln City and Rotherham United, the other day!" joked Sergeant Winner, with tongue in cheek.

The airmen had a chuckle amongst themselves, then stood tall and proud, and waited for the next order.

"Recruits, forward march, and proceed to the parade square. Left, right, left, right, left, right!" barked Sergeant Winner.

The recruits moved like gazelles in the wild, with grace, panache and style. They marched impeccably from the billet, to the awaiting crowd on the familiar parade ground, and each airmen kept in time with one another. The spectacle was truly sensational. The lines were fantastic, and there was not a concertina in sight. The airmen marched a full circuit of the parade square, and came around to where the stands were holding the audience.

"Flight, halt!" yelled Sergeant Winner. "Flight, "Present Arms!"

The recruits threw the rifles around in such an amazing manner, that it drew gasps from the enthralled crowd. It was breathtaking to watch, and the relatives and friends of the recruits could not believe it was their son, nephew, cousin, boyfriend, mate, husband, or brother, as it seemed surreal, and like they were watching professionals.

More gasps were heard, when the airmen continued with the "Present Arms" routine, and it was their greatest one yet. They had saved the best until last. It was a remarkable result for the sixteen airmen, and two drill instructors.

"Flight attention, right wheel, forward march, left, right, left, right, left, right," ordered Sergeant Winner, and the recruits were off again, marching around the square. They marched a full circle, and as they entered the home straight for the final time, the sound of a thundering engine in the sky beckoned the guests to look up, and watch a supersonic Royal Air Force English Electric Lightning aircraft zooming by, in the official fly-past, to rubber stamp the "Passing Out" parade, and it put the finishing touches to the grand and prestigious show.

It had been nerve wracking, but exciting for the airmen to take part in, and Clem was as proud as punch, when he noticed his mother, his eldest brother, and his brother's girlfriend, were watching from the stands. But there was no sign of Ellie anywhere to be seen. But Clem did not mind, it was her loss, and he shrugged his shoulders, and joined his guests to celebrate a massive achievement in his life, before looking forward to the Supply Training, commencing at RAF Hereford, in seven days time.

The End

Printed in Great Britain
by Amazon